PAST & PRESENT

DOWNTOWN OKLAHOMA CITY

OPPOSITE: On Independence Day 1907, Oklahoma City was just four short months from gaining statehood. Eighteen years after its establishment, the population of Oklahoma City had grown to over 32,000 people. This view of a parade on Broadway Avenue looks north from Sheridan Avenue, which was known as Grand Avenue at the time. On the right is the Huckins Hotel, where the business of the state capitol was temporarily conducted. (Courtesy of the Oklahoma Historical Society.)

PAST & PRESENT

DOWNTOWN OKLAHOMA CITY

Rachel E. Mosman and Steve Lackmeyer

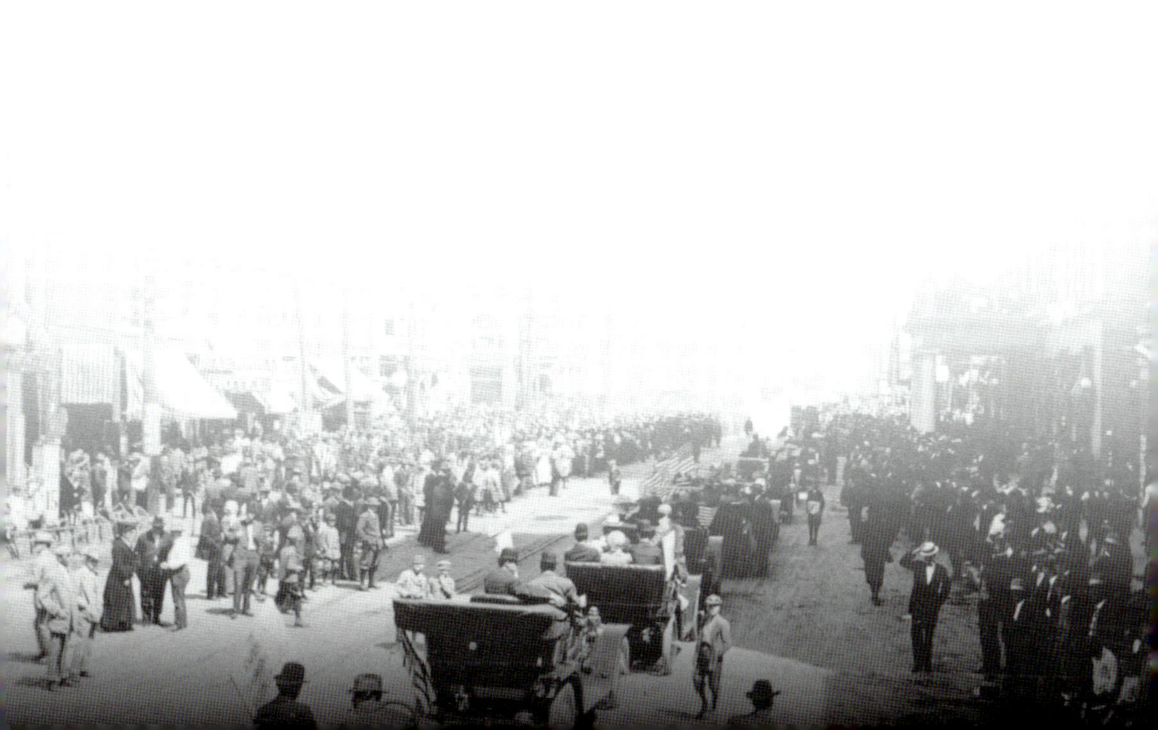

ISBN 978-1-4671-0890-4

Library of Congress Control Number: 2022945229

Published by Arcadia Publishing
Charleston, South Carolina

Printed in the United States of America

For all general information, please contact Arcadia Publishing:
Telephone 843-853-2070
Fax 843-853-0044
E-mail sales@arcadiapublishing.com
For customer service and orders:
Toll-Free 1-888-313-2665

Visit us on the Internet at www.arcadiapublishing.com

FRONT COVER: Automobile Alley, which stretches from Northwest Fourth Street to Northwest Thirteenth Street on Broadway Avenue, housed most of the city's car dealerships between 1907 and 1930. After decades of blight, and damage from the Alfred P. Murrah Building bombing, the area began focusing on revitalization in 1996. (Past, courtesy of the Oklahoma Historical Society; present, photograph by the authors.)

BACK COVER: In May 1980, Fidelity Bank's 'Falling Waters" fountain was an oasis for children searching for relief from that summer's heat wave. The moving sculpture was created by internationally renowned artist Lin Emery, whose abstract design was inspired by the Scissortailed-flycatcher. (Courtesy of the *Oklahoman*.)

Contents

ACKNOWLEDGMENTS

It is a common perception among Oklahoma City residents who lived through the urban renewal era of the 1970s that the entirety of the downtown they fondly remember was destroyed with very little left to remind people of the past.

The city did tear down hundreds of buildings, but the demise of our history is greatly exaggerated. It is with this in mind that we joined up to document surviving pieces of our history and to match them up with their appearance in 2022.

We are grateful for the assistance of Robert Wehrle and Hannah Mosman provided driving Rachel as she took photographs matching images taken decades earlier. Jim Meeks provided help with photograph selection. Lee Allan Smith generously shared his archives.

We thank the historians who wrote nominations for many of the surviving structures to be placed in the National Register of Historic Places. Many were written by Bob Blackburn, the state's premier historian for over a half century starting in the late 1970s.

Historic building preservation requires a mix of creativity, vision, and a willingness to accept structures dictate budgets, timelines, and complications. Some of the developers were ahead of their time. Those names include Neal Horton, who saved the Colcord Building and much of Bricktown, and Thurman Magbee, who saved and preserved Union Station.

Marva Ellard took a gutted Sieber Hotel and saved it from collapse. Her award-winning restoration included salvaging the mosaic tile in the building's lobby. Her latest effort is the restoration of the Villa Teresa school into a boutique hotel.

The Skirvin was a test of the city's resolve to save its history after the destruction of so many landmarks in the 1960s and 1970s (in one nomination for a historic register application, Blackburn referred to the clearance as a holocaust).

In many of the more recent building rescues, success required a successful partnership between private developers and city hall.

Kirk Humphreys, a suburban developer elected mayor in 1998, brought an array of interests together to formulate a plan on how to save the Skirvin and then recruited a team, led by the late John Weeman, to restore it and open it as a Hilton hotel.

Gary Brooks, meanwhile, took on the task of bringing First National back to yet another era of glory as a hotel and apartments. We thank all of these visionaries for providing us the stories to make this book possible.

Introduction

Oklahoma City is and may always be the only city to emerge from nothing in one day. Settlers participating in the Land Run of 1889 rushed into an area surrounding a pre-existing Santa Fe depot, Oklahoma Station, and staked out lots and fired a few shots when disputes turned ugly. Historians estimate 10,000 called Oklahoma City home on that first day of April 22, 1889.

The first Oklahoma City consisted of tents and wood-frame buildings, a temporary and disposable attempt at town building that a dozen years later would shift to more permanent, architecturally significant structures. It is this second wave of which a few, but not many, buildings survive. The skyline began to emerge in 1910 when voters of the new state chose Oklahoma City as their capital.

Some of the landmarks added to the skyline in the post-statehood era are still standing and include the Colcord (converted in 2006 from offices to a hotel), Central High School (purchased by Oklahoma City University [OCU] in 2012 and converted into the OCU School of Law), Hotel Marion (rebuilt into apartments), the Skirvin Hotel (extensively renovated after being closed a dozen years), the former home of the *Oklahoman*, and an array of buildings in Midtown, Bricktown, and Film Row.

A drive down Broadway Avenue between Northwest Fourth Street and Northwest Thirteenth Street, Automobile Alley, is to see the history of how car dealerships evolved in the early 1900s. A well-preserved 1916 Ford Model T was converted into the 21c Museum Hotel, which includes a curated art gallery open to the public at all hours and throughout the year.

The discovery of oil and the growing popularity of traveling by automobile triggered yet another step forward with the emergence of gas stations and car dealerships. Monumental train stations were built by railways with the belief that rail would always be the mode of choice for traveling across the country. Fortunes boosted by the oil industry also spurred the construction of even taller buildings at a time when much of the country's economy was stalling due to the Great Depression.

The Great Depression did little to slow the momentum. The skyline grew higher and higher; First National Bank and Walter Ramsey drew excited spectators as the two rich and powerful interests competed to see who could finish building a tower in less time. Ramsey won the race, but First National won the title for tallest building.

At the corner of Grand Avenue (now named Sheridan Avenue) and Robinson Avenue, the 33-story, 619-room Biltmore Hotel expanded the skyline and brought new competition for the Skirvin Hotel and the Huckins Hotel, both of which had dominated the hospitality side of downtown for more than 20 years.

Good fortune would not last forever. The oil boom delayed but did not stop the Depression from hitting Oklahoma City in the mid-1930s. Hotelier W.B. Skirvin started construction of the Skirvin Tower, an envisioned annex for his hotel. The 26-story addition would add 700 rooms to Skirvin's operation. Construction started in 1931 but halted a year later when Skirvin ran out of money.

Construction did not resume until 1934, and when it was wrapped up, the tower was capped off at 14 stories. Some floors went unfinished for years.

World War II brought some relief, but when the crowds dispersed on Victory in Europe Day, they soon discovered they could go elsewhere for their shopping, dining, and recreation. Downtown stagnated during the ensuing suburban migration.

An urban renewal program started in the 1960s triggered a rebuilding of the urban core that included the destruction of hundreds of older buildings. The Criterion, Warner, and other movie palaces were leveled, leaving Centre Theater as the only surviving cinema. The Art Deco facade was stripped off of Skirvin Tower, the interior was gutted, and the building was reskinned with glass and concrete.

When the Biltmore Hotel was taken down with 900 explosives in 1977, it was televised across the country. Dean A. McGee, one of the most powerful business leaders in town, led the charge to clear four city blocks to create the Myriad Gardens. A glass encased botanical tube was built bridging over a small lake. The tube would provide visitors with a contained environment featuring both desert and tropical environments.

A new skyline emerged. Kerr McGee built a 29-story headquarters, Liberty Bank built a 36-story tower, and Fidelity Bank built a 17-story tower. Speculative office space included the 31-story Oklahoma Tower, 22-story Leadership Square, 19-story Mid-America Tower (Continental Resources headquarters in 2022), and the 14-story Corporate Tower.

The economy came crashing down when Penn Square Bank, heavily involved in energy lending, was declared insolvent. A wave of bank failures followed, the real estate market collapsed, and the city's best and brightest were moving elsewhere. Downtown had been torn up by an aggressive urban renewal program but not totally rebuilt.

The city's urban core was a ghost of the vibrant destination remembered by old-timers. "Downtown is dead," the late councilman I.G. Purser stated back in 1988. "And we helped kill it."

The comeback started with voters approving the Metropolitan Area Projects initiative, a five-year, 1¢ sales tax to bring life back to downtown that would include a riverwalk through an emerging Bricktown entertainment district, a modernization of Civic Center Music Hall, a downtown ballpark, expansion of the convention center, a downtown library, and an arena that would ultimately draw an National Basketball Association (NBA) team to the city.

The latest evolution of the city's urban core includes hundreds of apartments and condos, retail, theaters, museums, hotels, and restaurants. The skyline again expanded with a 50-story Devon Energy headquarters, a 27-story BOK Park Plaza, and a 17-story Omni Hotel.

Once forgotten buildings in downtown neighborhoods were brought back to life as the urban transformation grew to include Midtown, Bricktown, Deep Deuce, Film Row, and the century-old former dealership showrooms on Broadway Avenue along Automobile Alley.

Old landmarks got a new lease on life. The Skirvin Hotel, closed since 1988, was fully renovated and reopened in 2016. First National, in distress since the bank failed in 1987, was renovated into a hotel, apartments, and retail in 2021.

Two surviving train stations almost lost to time and neglect were preserved as well, with the Santa Fe station renovated and reopened for restored Amtrak passenger service. The Union station, meanwhile, is set to be renovated as a jewel of the recently opened Scissortail Park.

As of 2022, less than a handful of historic downtown buildings have yet to be restored and brought back to life, including the Gothic Telephone Building at 405 North Broadway Avenue.

More than $2 billion has been spent in the past quarter century rebuilding the heart of downtown Oklahoma City, and while much changed, a glimpse of the past dreams and ambitions can still be found in the grandest spaces where bankers and oil wildcatters did deals and where mechanics and hotel porters kept business going.

CHAPTER 1

A Capital City

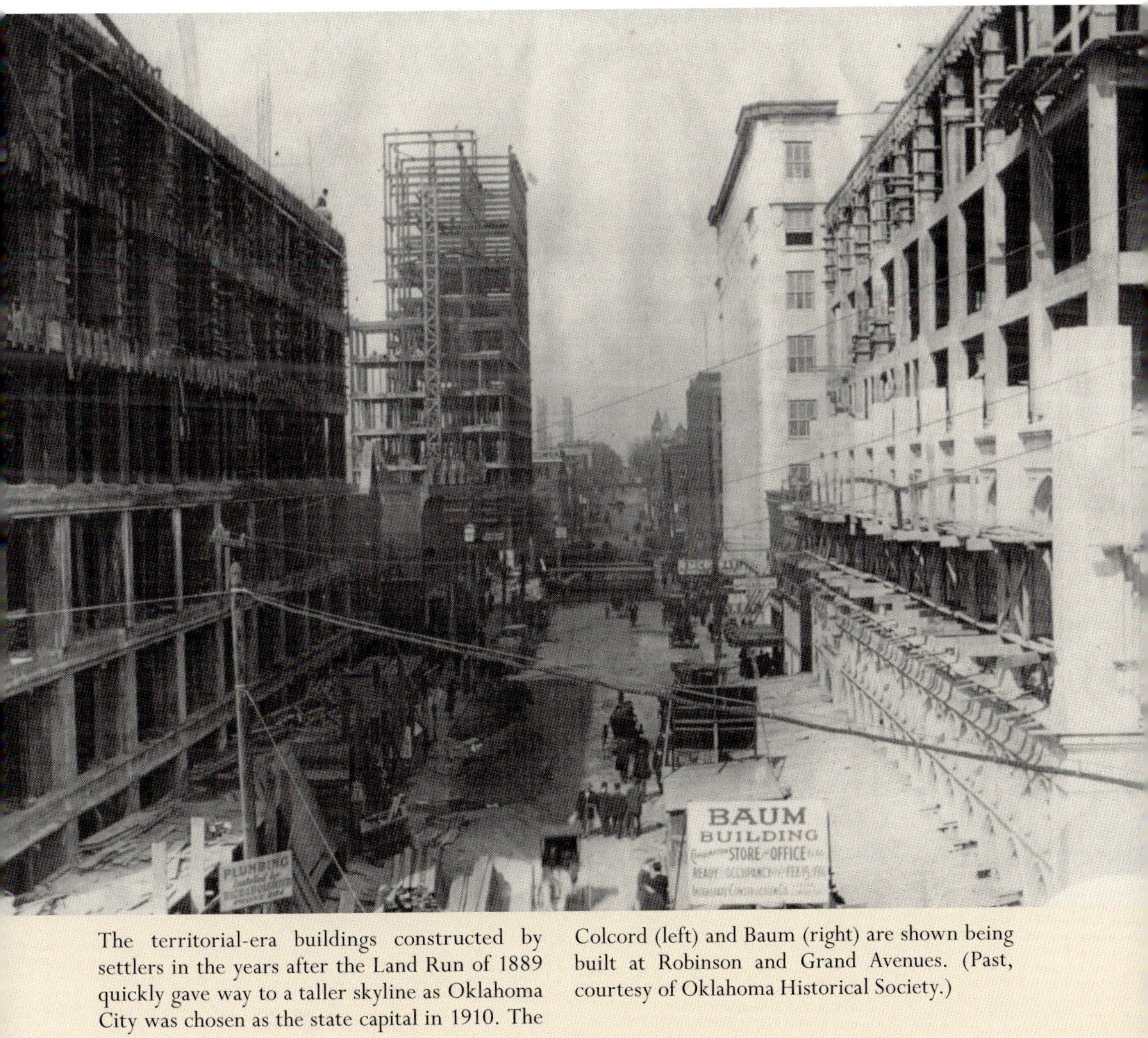

The territorial-era buildings constructed by settlers in the years after the Land Run of 1889 quickly gave way to a taller skyline as Oklahoma City was chosen as the state capital in 1910. The Colcord (left) and Baum (right) are shown being built at Robinson and Grand Avenues. (Past, courtesy of Oklahoma Historical Society.)

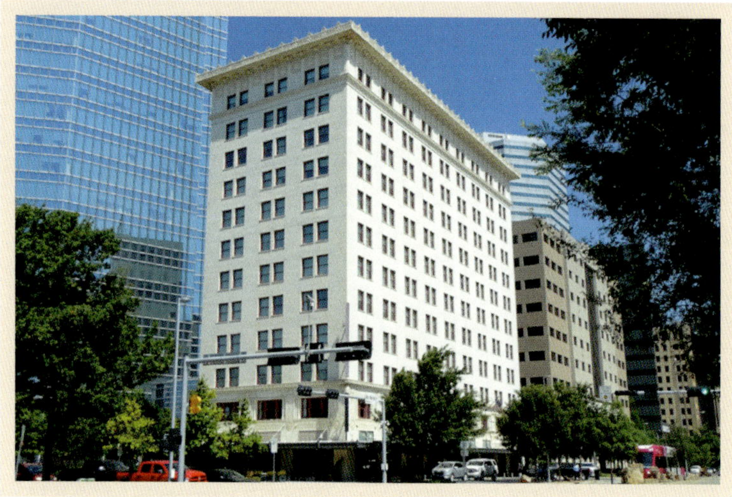

Construction started on the Baum and Colcord Buildings at Sheridan and Robinson Avenues in 1909. The Baum design was inspired by Doges Palace in Venice. Oilman Charles Colcord built the 12-story Colcord, considered to be the city's first skyscraper. On the left is Great Western Bank, one of the oldest structures from downtown's early settlement. The Baum was torn down in 1973. The Colcord was renovated into a hotel in 2006. (Past, courtesy of the Oklahoma Historical Society.)

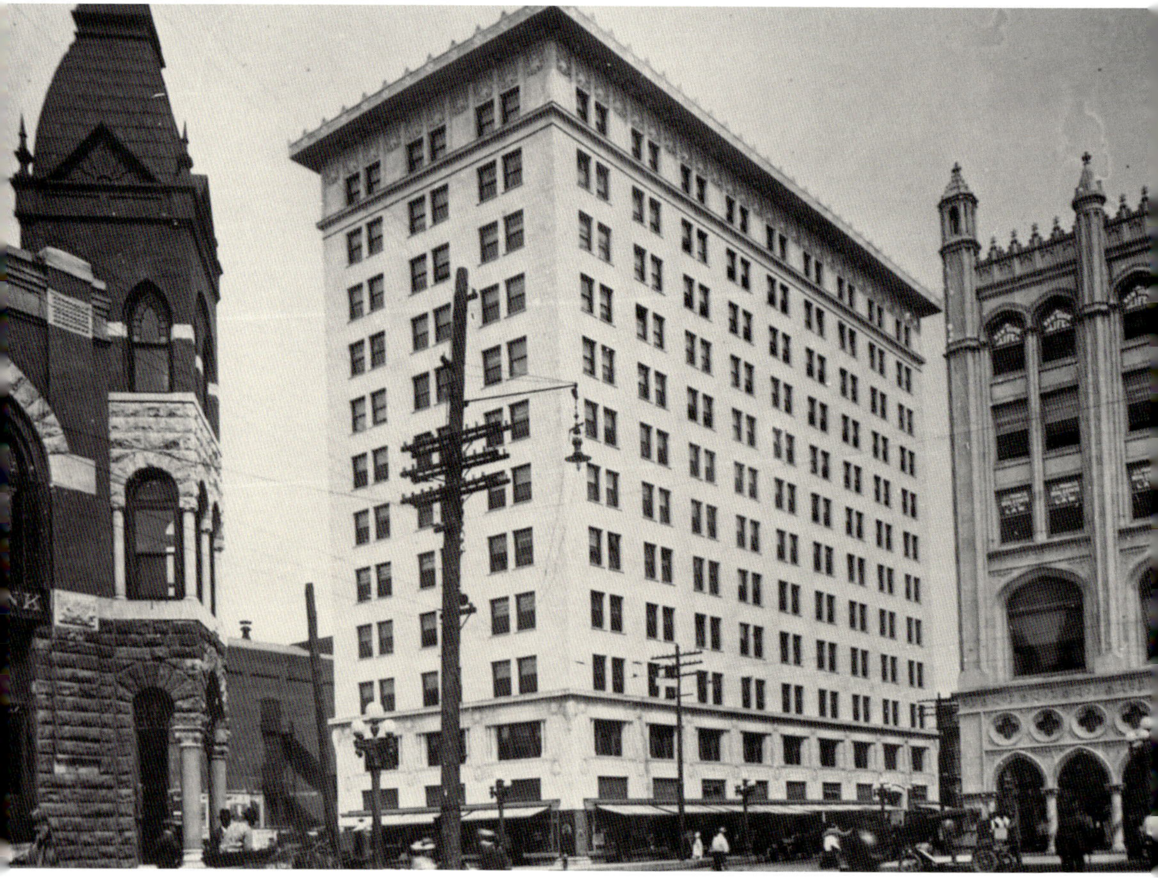

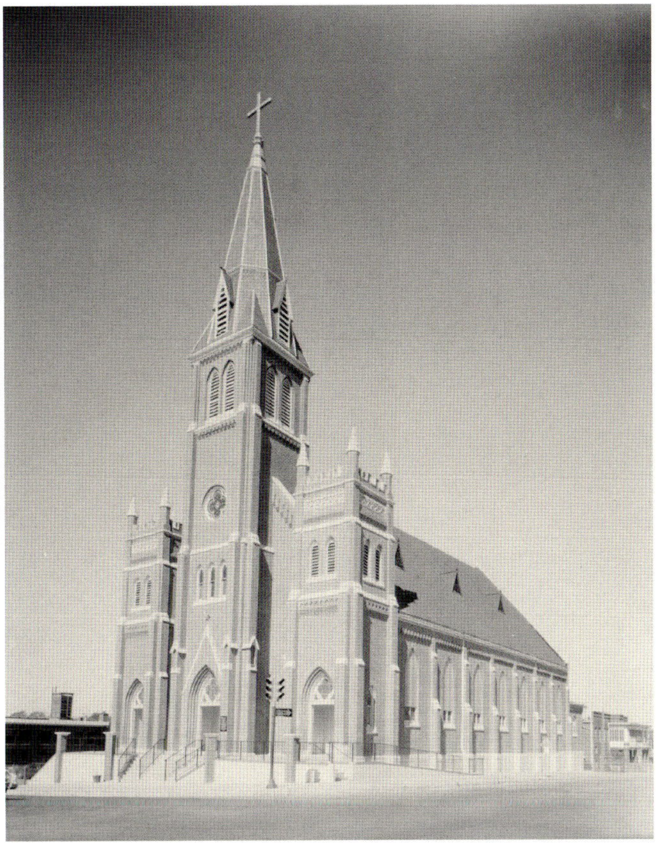

St. Joseph's Old Cathedral got its start with a service held by Nicolas F. Scallon, the first priest to arrive, on April 22, 1889. The current building, the oldest church in the city, was built in 1902, and that year, a cornerstone was placed proclaiming that it was "founded by the '89ers.'" The church sustained damage from the 1995 bombing of the Murrah Federal Building but was fully repaired and remains an active parish. (Past, courtesy of Oklahoma Historical Society.)

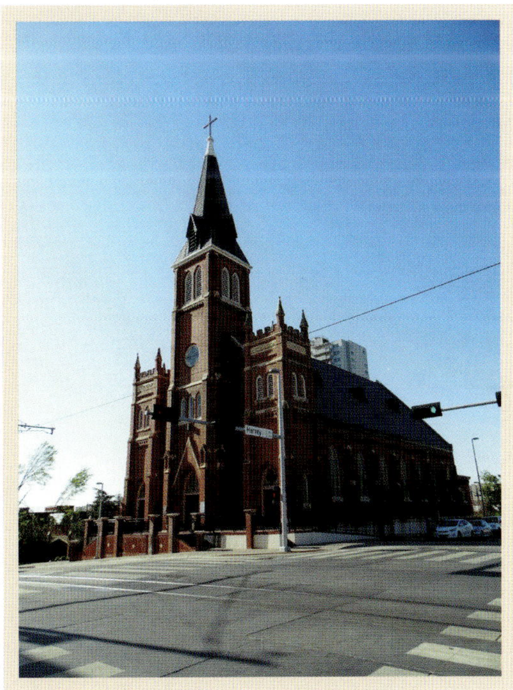

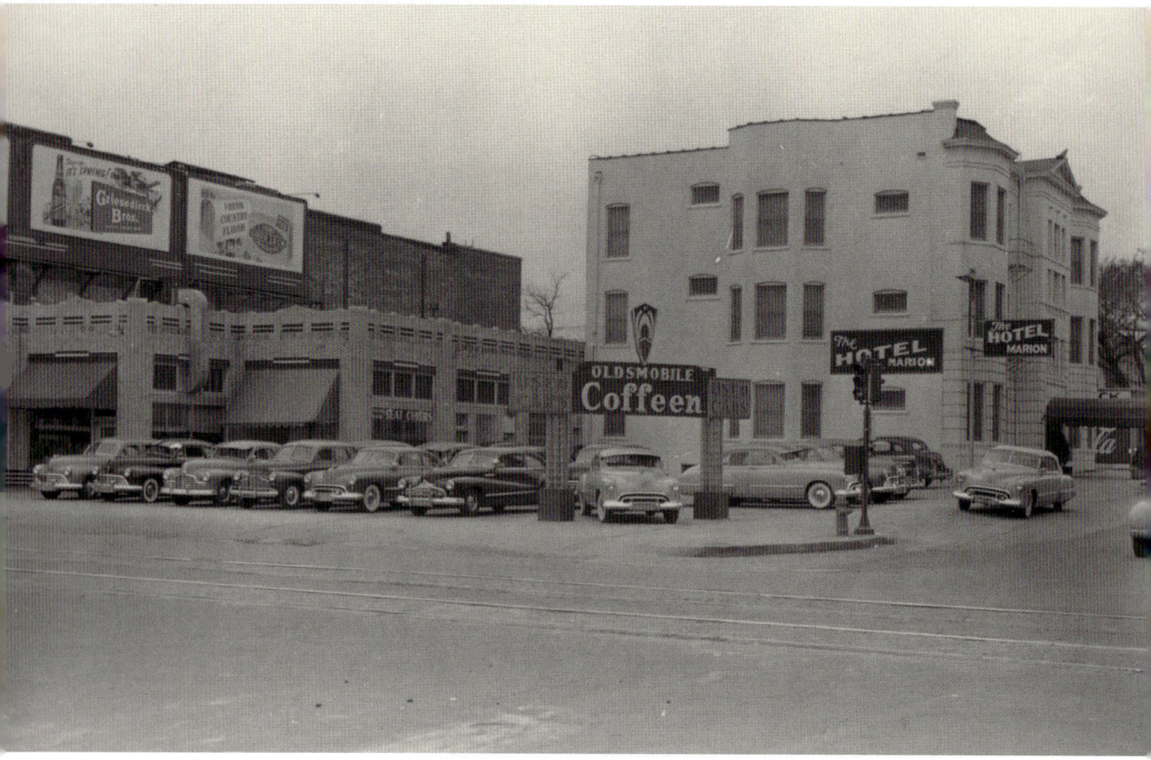

The Hotel Marion, 110 Northwest Tenth Street, was built in 1904 and was converted into apartments a few years after opening. The Marion closed in the mid-1980s when downtown was hit by an oil bust. It was in danger of collapse when Midtown Renaissance bought the building in 2006. The building was gutted, but the facade was restored for conversion into upscale apartments. (Past, courtesy of Oklahoma Historical Society.)

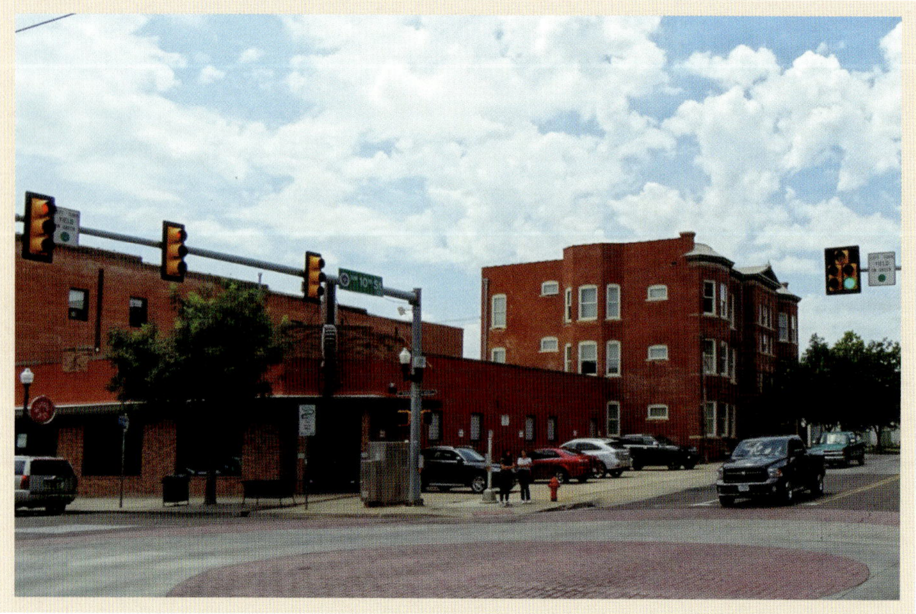

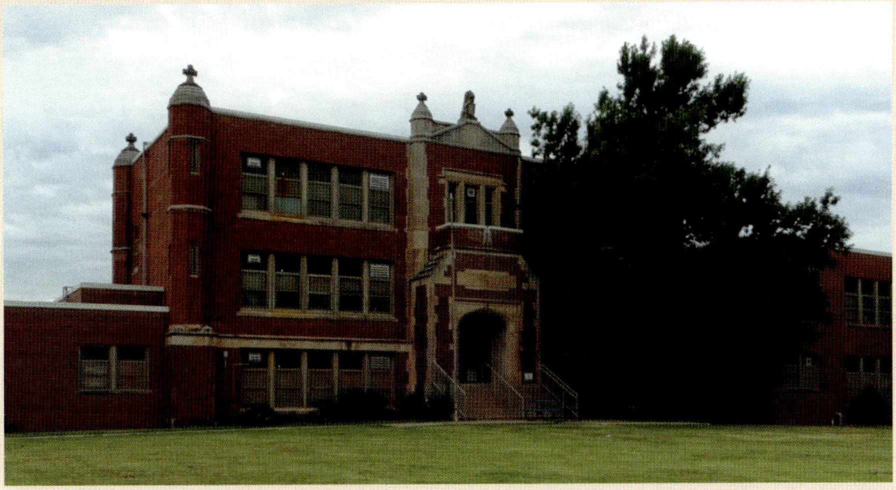

Emerson School was first built in 1895 at one of the highest points in the territorial city at 715 North Walker Avenue. The first building burned in 1907 and was rebuilt in New Collegiate Gothic style with a stone lion and rings featured as gargoyles. The school expanded several times over the decades. Emerson was being used as an alternative school in 2022. (Past, courtesy of Oklahoma Historical Society.)

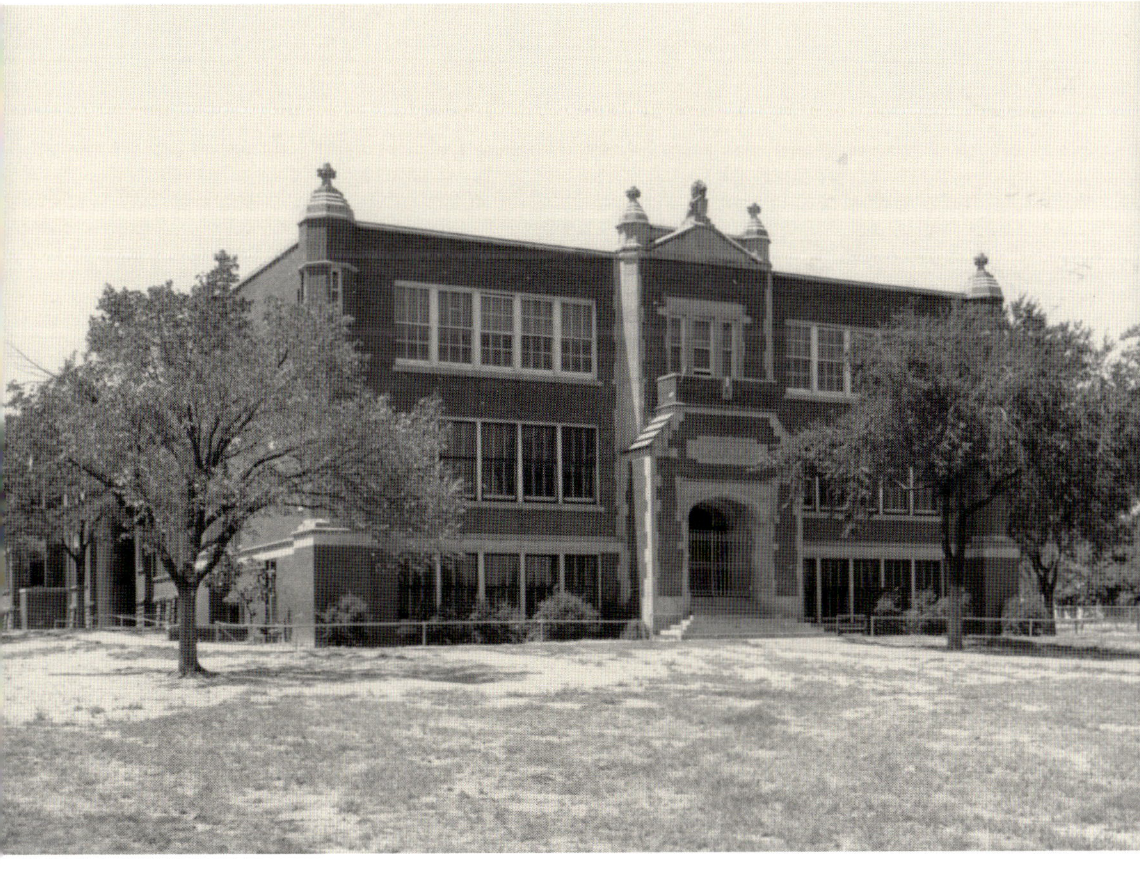

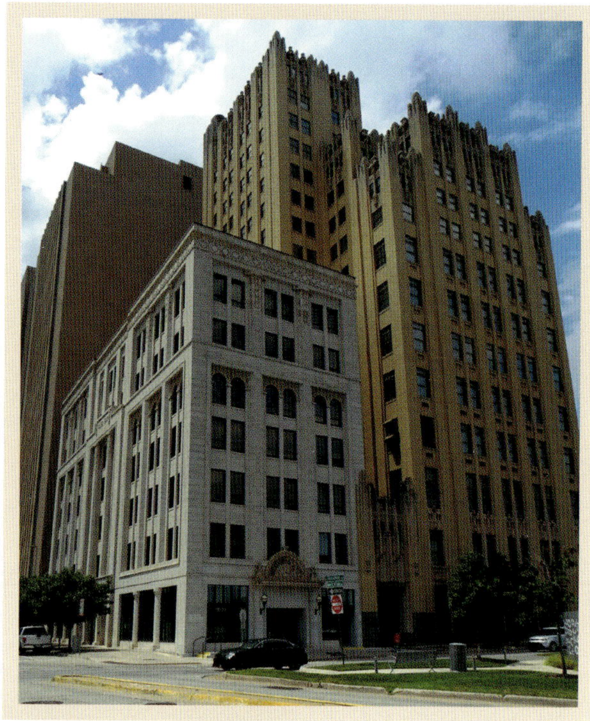

Pioneer Telephone Company was the first to secure telephone service for all of Oklahoma City when it built a new seven-story, gray limestone building as its headquarters in 1907. In later years, the company and building were acquired by AT&T, which ultimately sealed the ground floor windows with marble. The building was purchased and restored in 2016 by developers Mark Beffort and Andy Burnett. (Past, courtesy of Oklahoma Historical Society.)

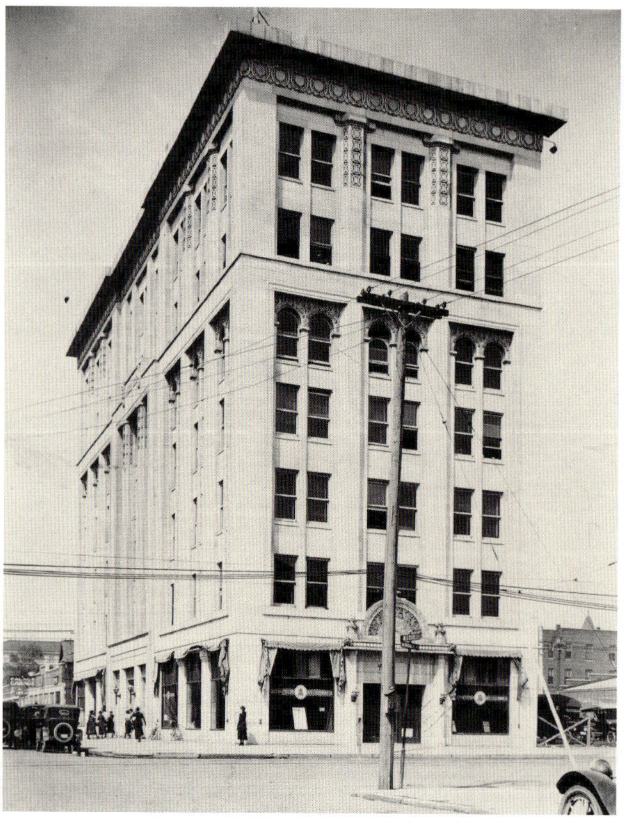

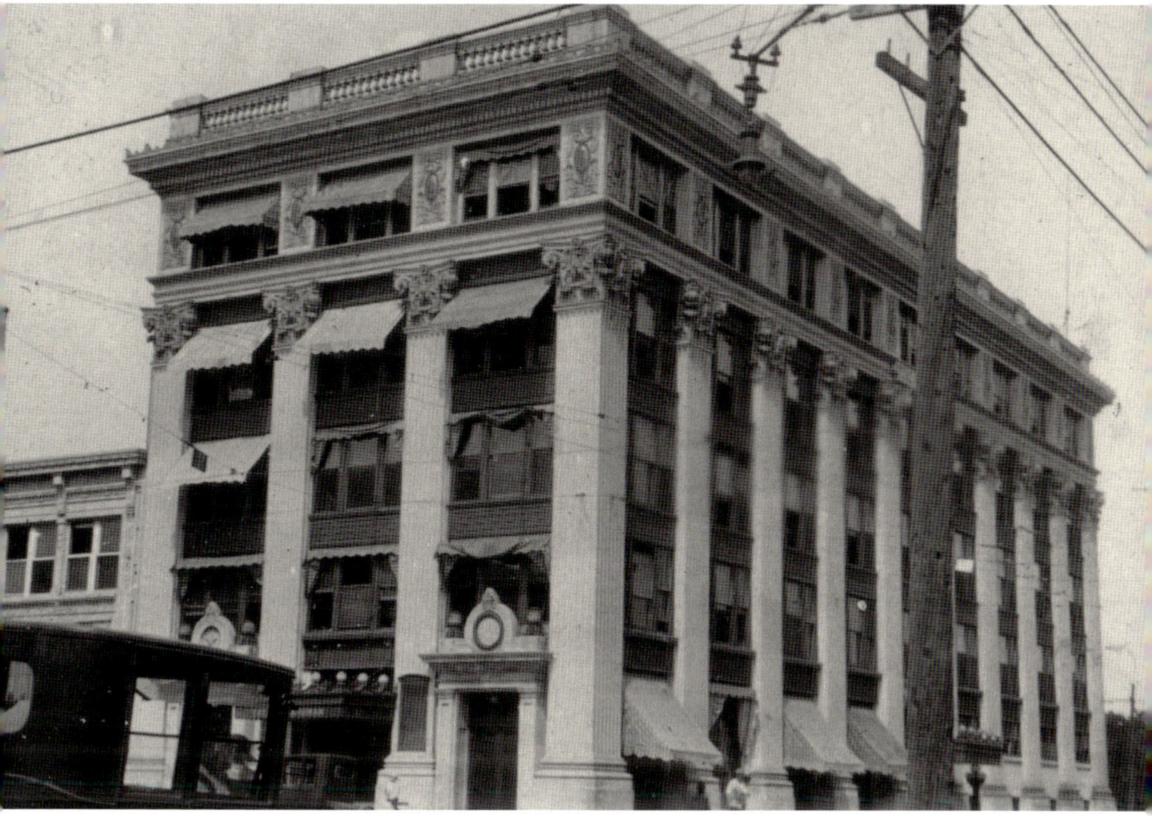

The *Daily Oklahoman* was emerging as Oklahoma City's leading newspaper when, under the leadership of E.K. Gaylord, a new five-story building was erected in 1909 for the growing operation. Designed by architect Solomon Andrew Layton, the classical building features columns topped with federal eagles. The *Oklahoman* moved out of the building in 1992, and the structure was later donated to the YMCA of Central Oklahoma. (Past, courtesy of Oklahoma Historical Society.)

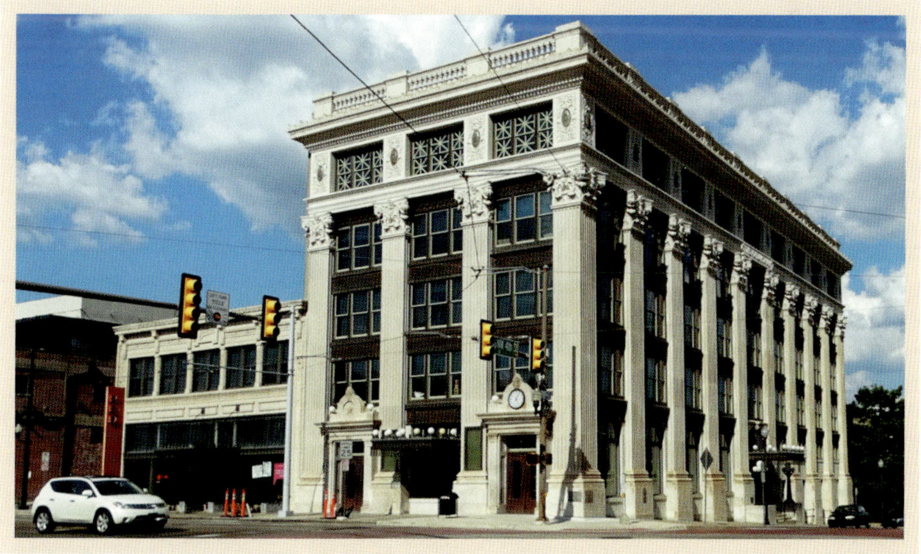

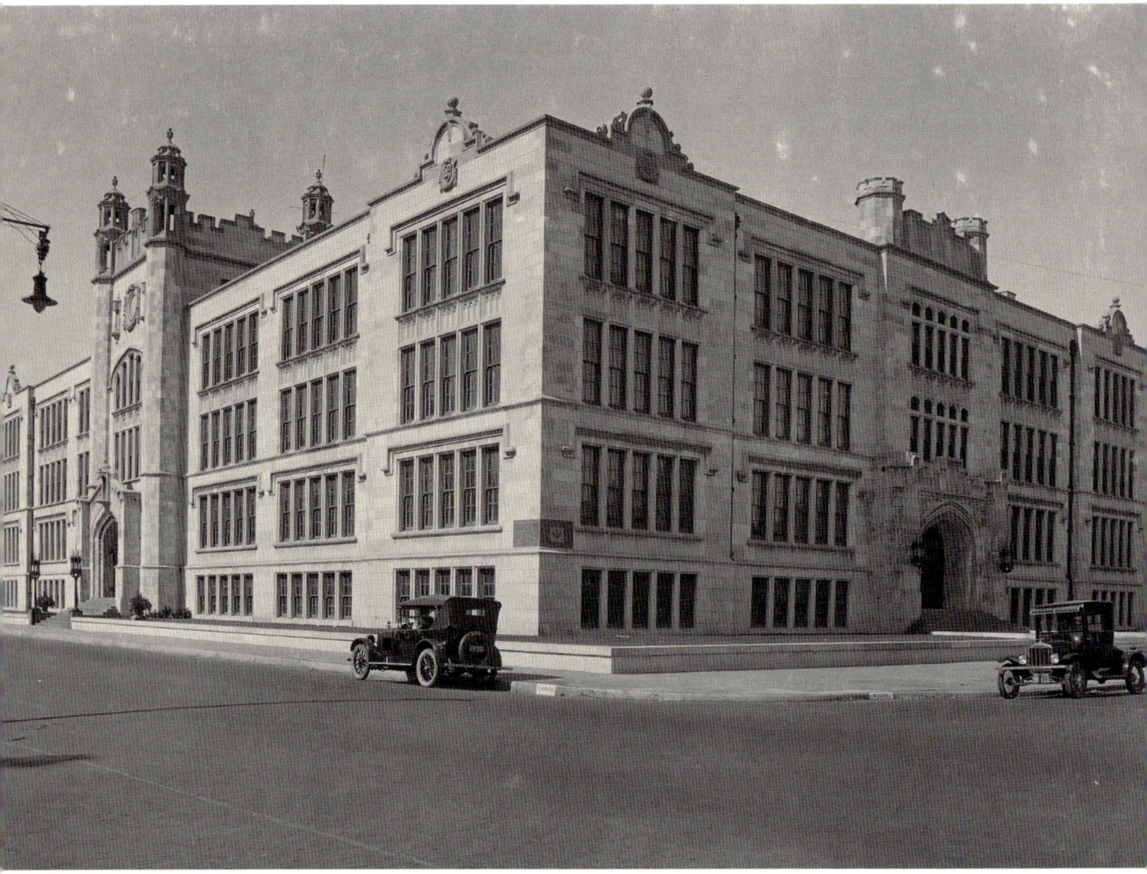

Central High School, 801 North Robinson Avenue, was designed by architect Andrew Solomon Layton and built in 1910 to accommodate a growing student population. The school closed in 1968 and was in disrepair when it was bought and restored by Southwestern Bell. The landmark was bought by OCU in 2013 and converted into a new home for its law school. (Past, courtesy of the Oklahoma Historical Society.)

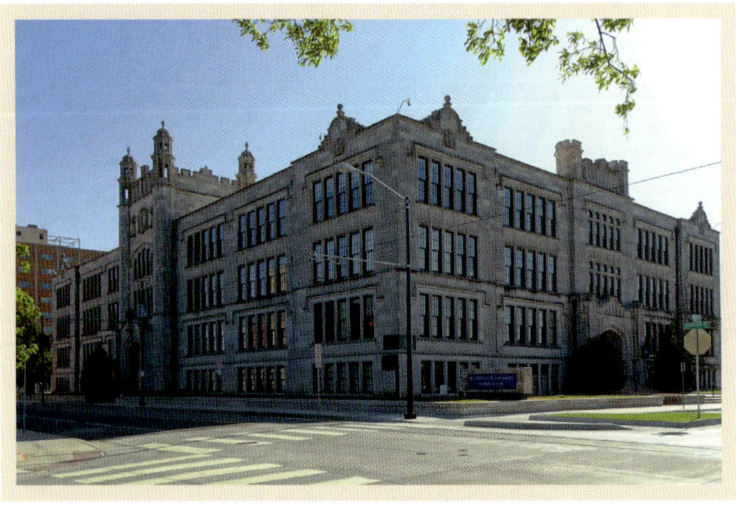

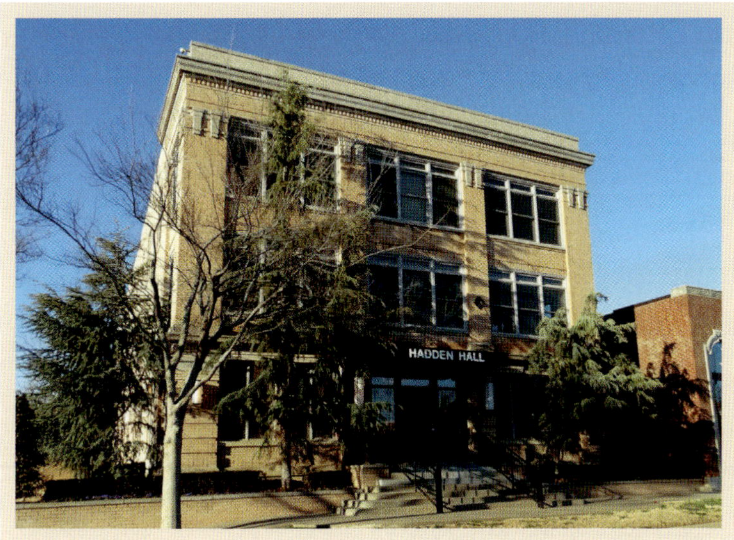

The three-story Hadden Hall, 215 Northwest Tenth Street, was built around 1910 and was promoted as a place for visitors to stay when they wanted something homier than a hotel. The building was operating as low-end housing until developers Bob Howard, Mickey Clagg, and Chris Fleming bought, renovated, and placed it in the National Register of Historic Places in 2011. (Past, courtesy of Oklahoma Historical Society.)

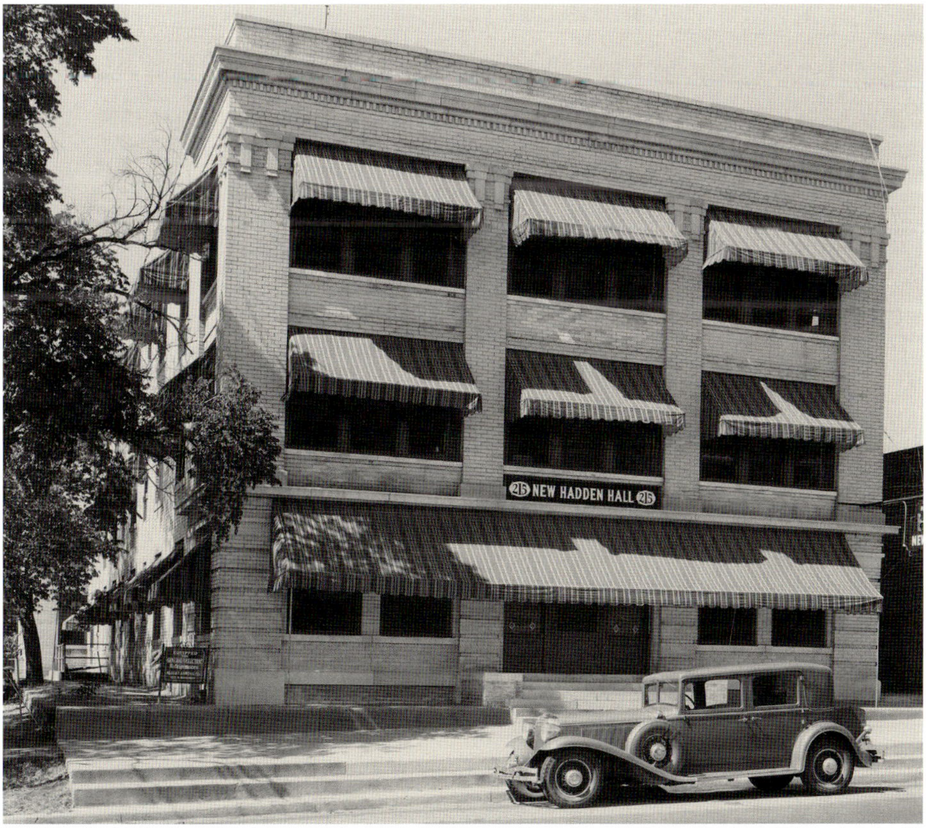

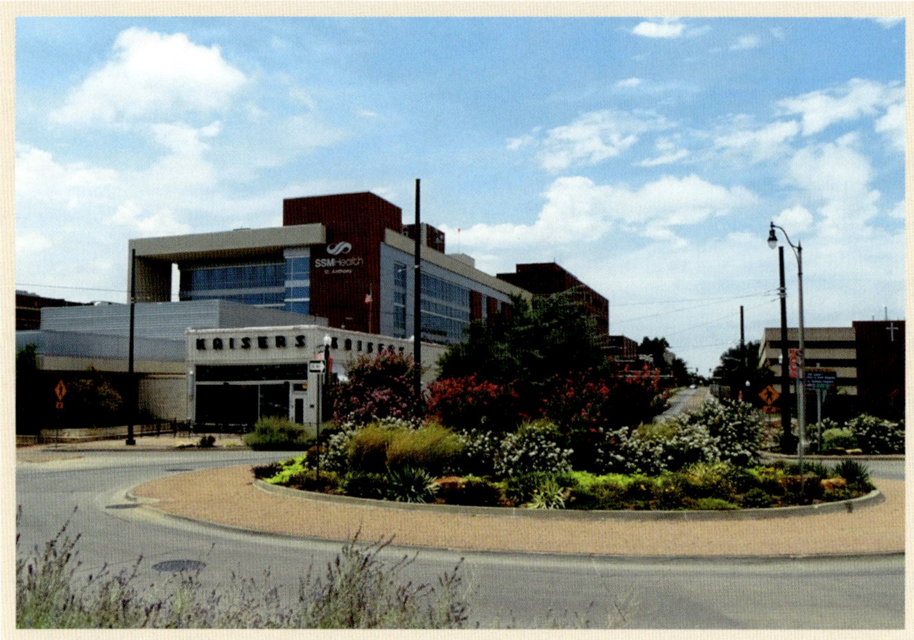

Kaiser's Ice Cream was founded in 1917 by Swiss immigrant Anthony J. Kaiser, who started out selling family-recipe homemade ice cream out of a three-court freezer. He opened at 1039 North Walker Avenue in 1921. The Kaiser family sold the business in the 1970s. Kaiser's Grateful Bean Café remains in business, operated by Pete Schaffer, an attorney who preserved the building and kept it open when the Midtown neighborhood was in decline. (Past, courtesy of Oklahoma Historical Society.)

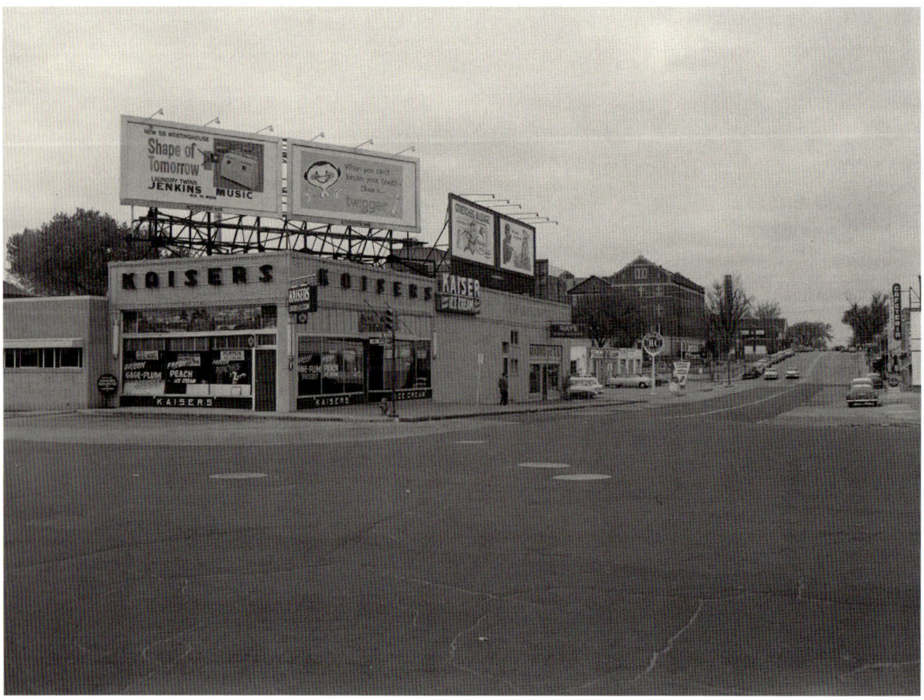

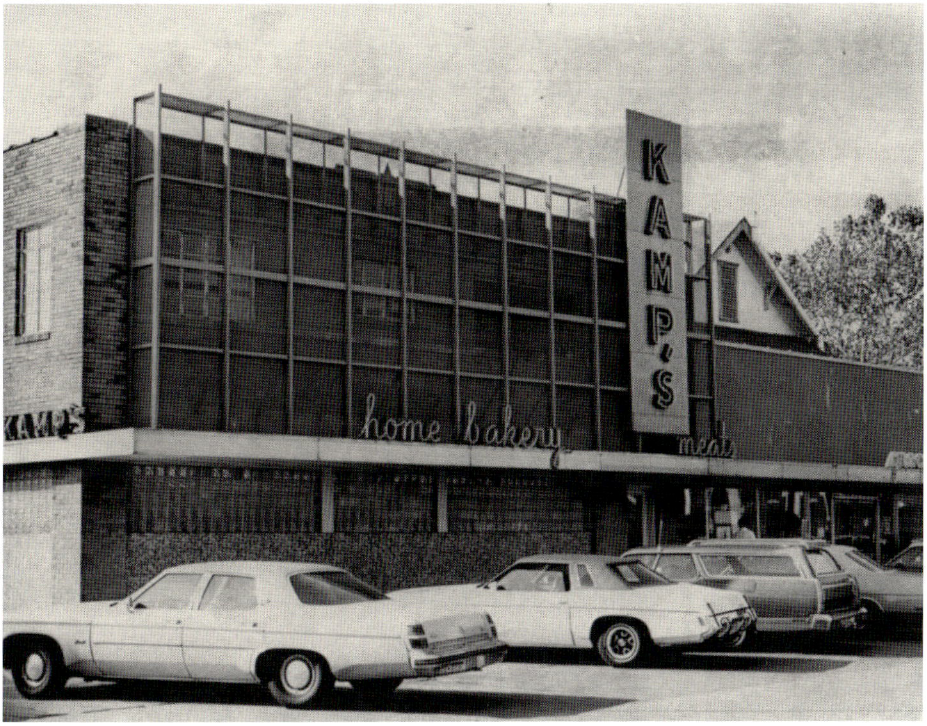

Henry Kamp, a German immigrant, was on a cross-country train ride west to the Pacific Northwest in 1910 when he stopped in Oklahoma City and convinced his brothers William and Alfred to join him in opening a market. Their store at 1310 Northwest Twenty-fifth Street passed through multiple generations before selling it in 2005. The store was shut down and reopened in 2013 as a restaurant and nightclub. (Past, courtesy of Oklahoma Historical Society.)

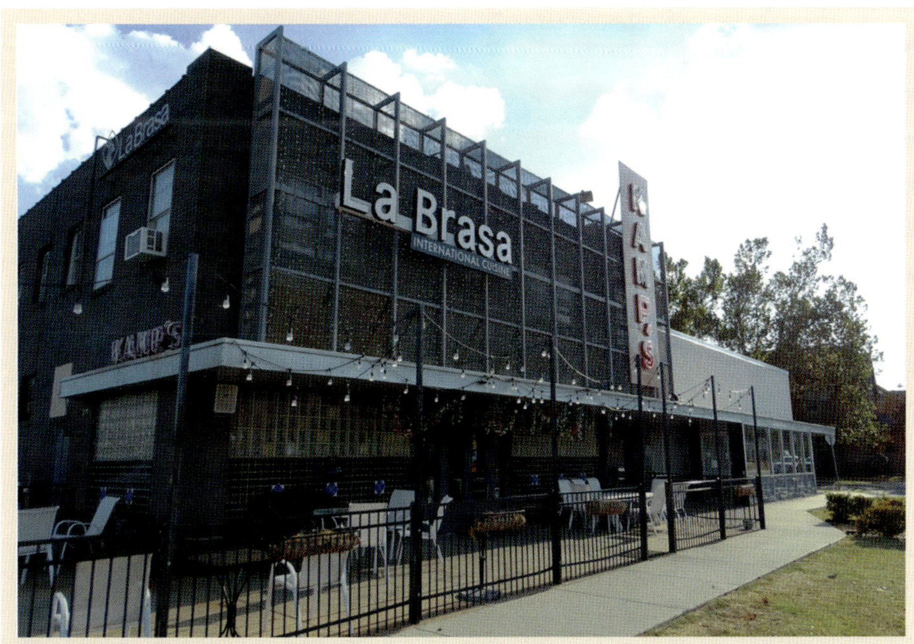

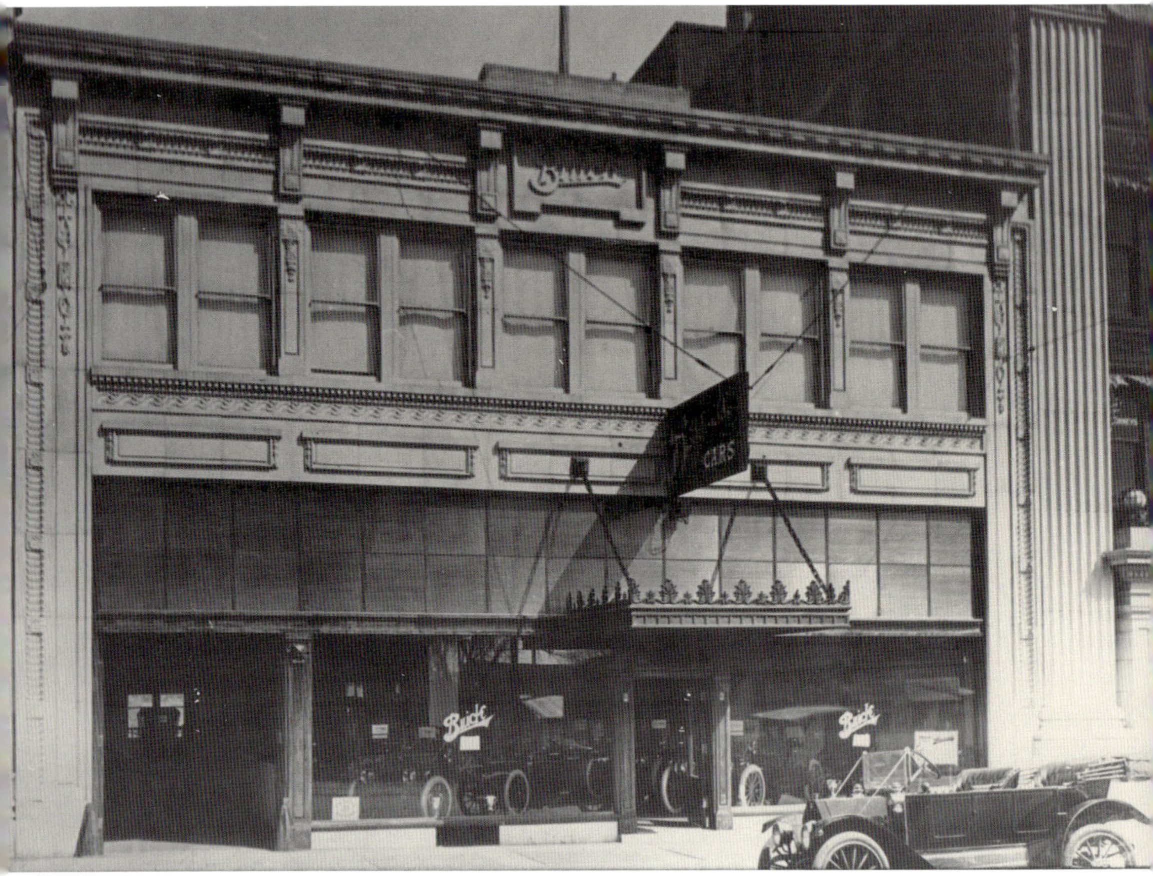

One of the earliest dealerships along Automobile Alley is also the oldest-surviving examples of when showrooms existed to help customers order a vehicle to be delivered at a later time. The Buick building at 504 North Broadway opened in 1911 when less than seven cars were registered for every 100,000 people. Rand and Jeanette Elliott purchased the building in 1999 and restored the facade. The building was home to Red Prime Steakhouse in 2022. (Past, courtesy of Oklahoma Historical Society.)

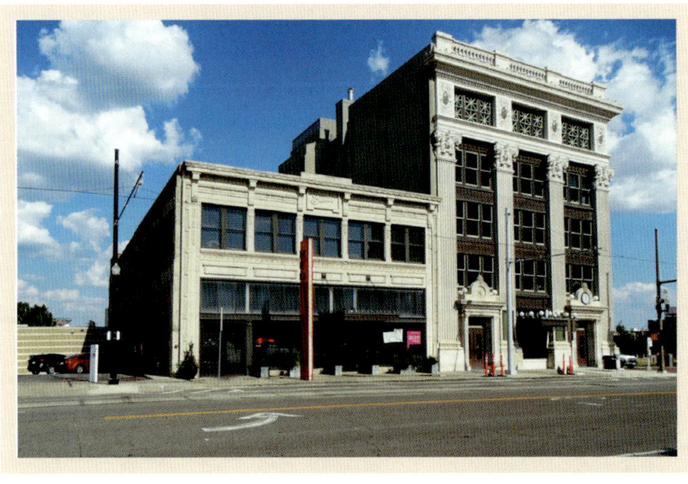

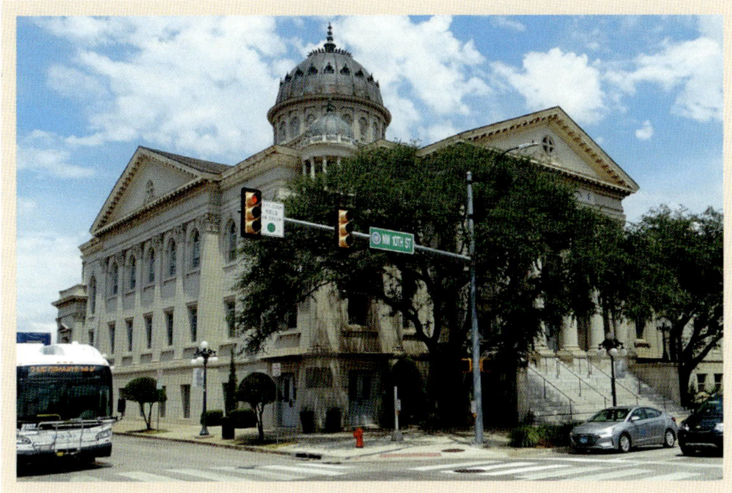

Robinson Avenue was emerging as church row when First Christian Church opened in 1911. The Neoclassical Revival church at 1104 North Robinson Avenue hosted its first church service on December 3, 1911. The congregation moved to a new location a half-century later. The building remained in use, on and off, for years as its condition declined until it was purchased in 2011 by Frontline Church and underwent a complete renovation. (Past, courtesy of Oklahoma Historical Society.)

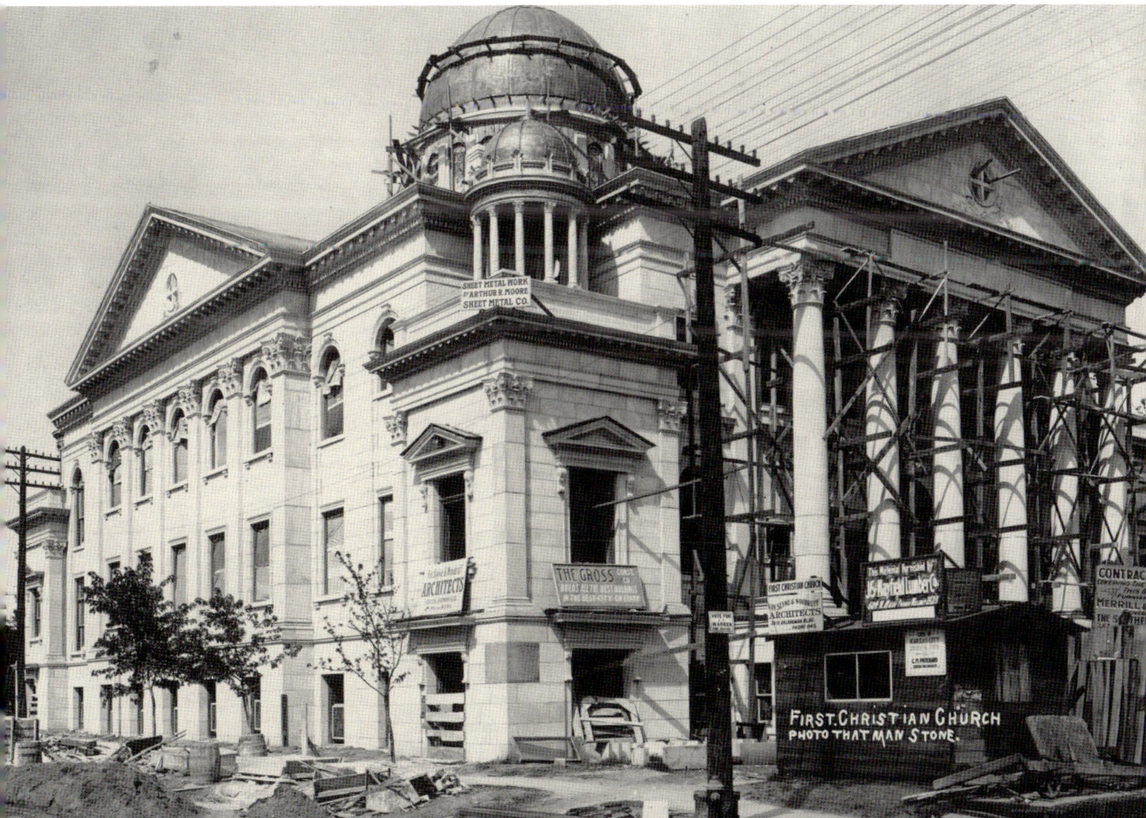

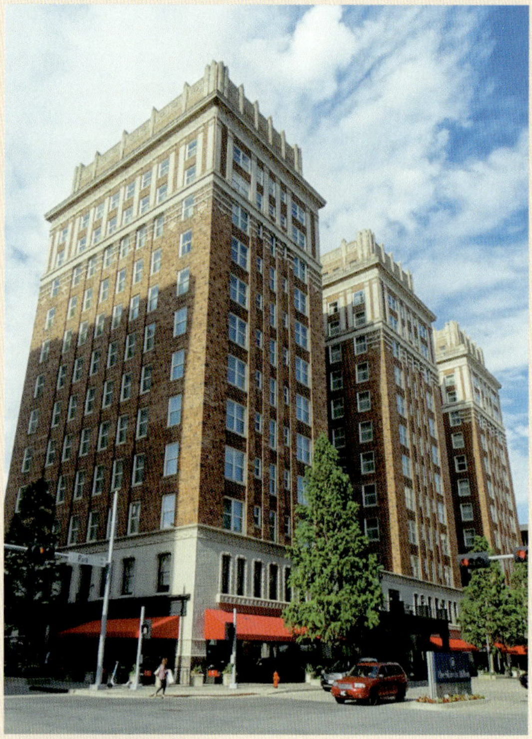

The Skirvin Hotel, 1 Park Avenue, was built in 1911 by oilman W.B. Skirvin and hosted presidents, Hollywood royalty, and corporate titans on the next half century. It fell into decline in the 1970s, closed in 1988, and was fully renovated and restored for a reopening in 2006. The hotel is once again one of the city's top destinations. (Past, courtesy of Oklahoma Historical Society.)

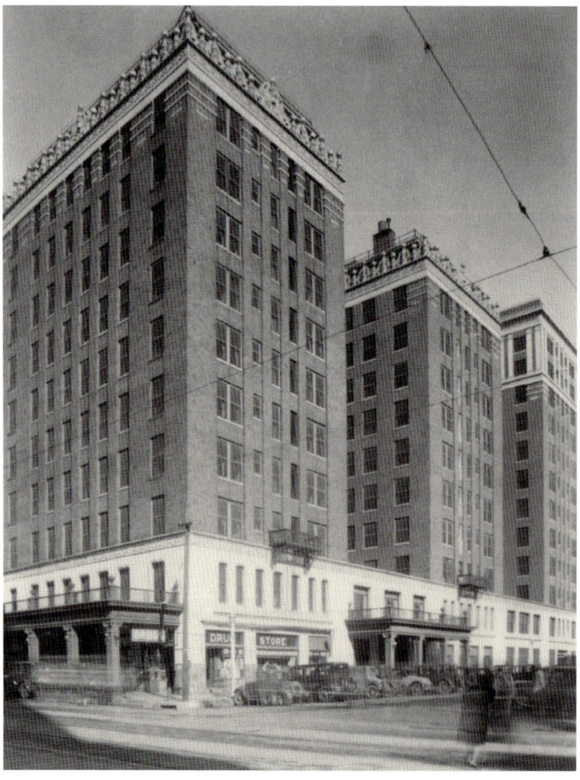

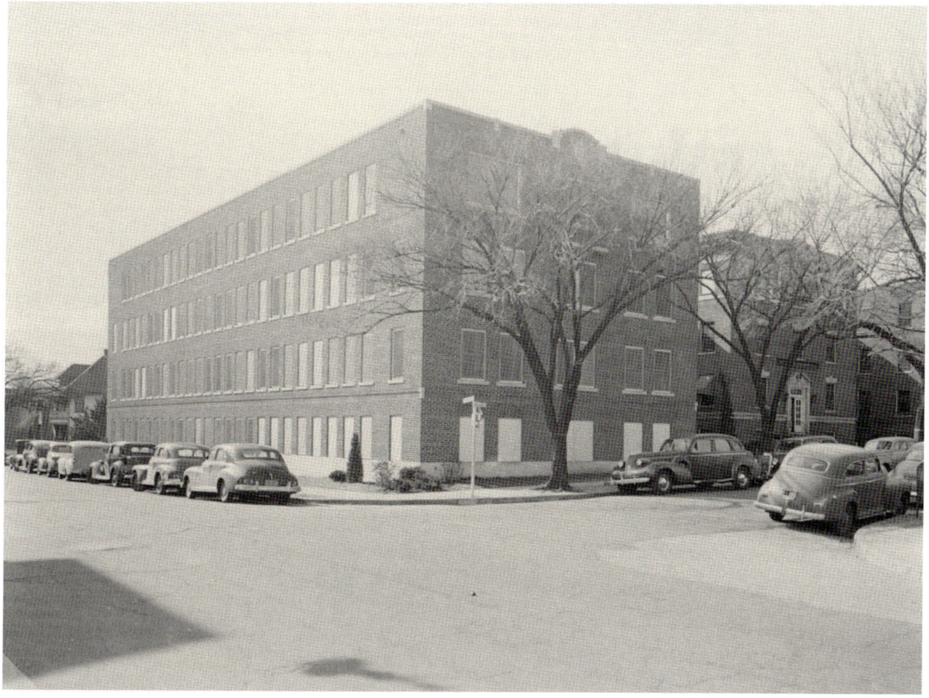

Wesley Hospital was started in 1910 and moved into its home at 300 Northwest Twelfth Street in 1911. Over the next half century, it was expanded and rebuilt several times and was one of the city's biggest hospitals until it was unable to grow any further and closed in 1964. The north building was converted into senior apartments while the south building was vacant for years until 2005, when it was converted into condominiums. (Past, courtesy of Oklahoma Historical Society.)

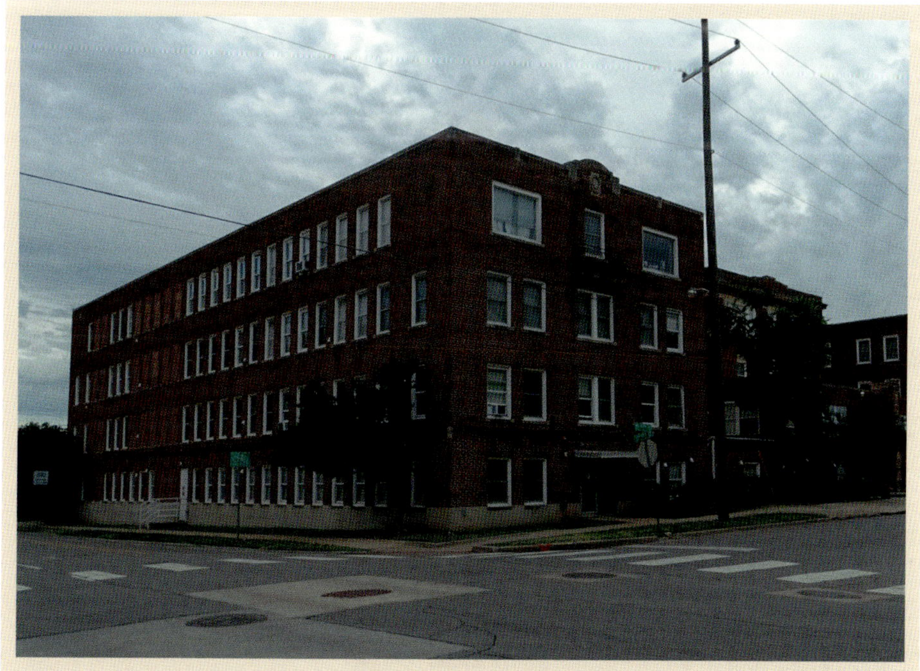

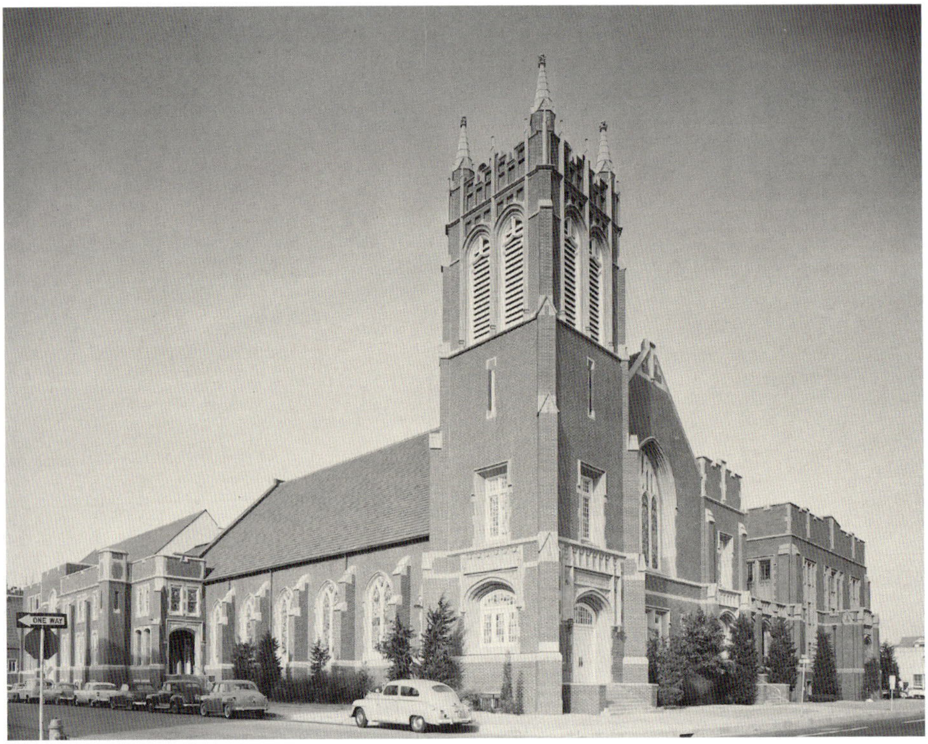

First Baptist Church of Oklahoma City was organized in 1889 and built the Gothic-style sanctuary in 1912. The congregation grew into one of the city's largest, and a 1952 educational building was one of the first to feature a full gymnasium that doubled as a roller-skating rink. Visitors included John F. Kennedy and Lyndon B. Johnson. The educational wing in 2022 was home to the Academy of Classical Christian Studies. (Past, courtesy of Oklahoma Historical Society.)

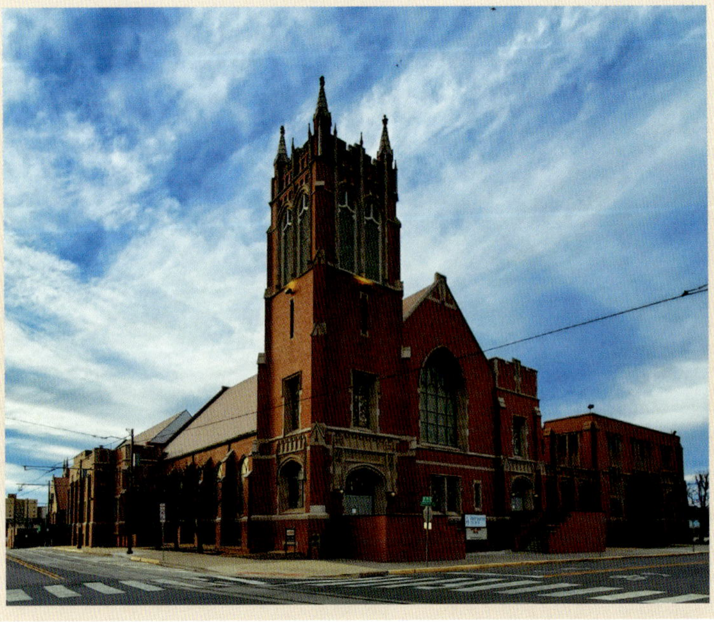

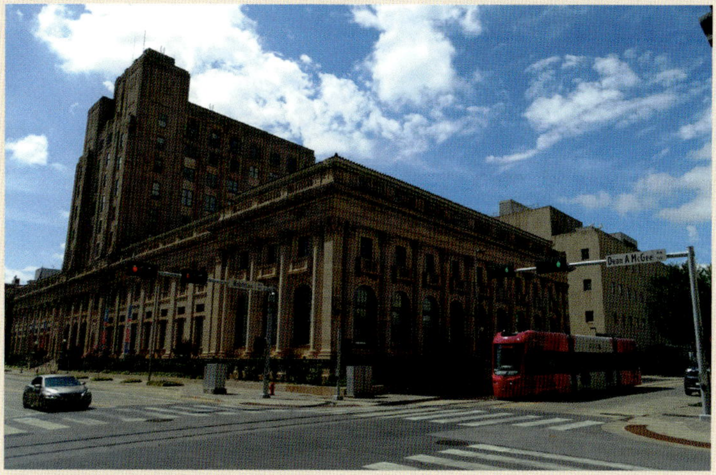

The Federal Courthouse and US Post Office Building was built in three phases starting in 1912 with additions completed in 1919 and 1932. The light gray limestone structure features a nine-story tower with three-story annexes on each side. Those tried in the courthouse included George "Machine Gun" Kelly, found guilty of kidnapping an Oklahoma City oilman. The post office relocated in 1966, leaving the complex for growth of federal courts in Oklahoma City. (Past, courtesy of Oklahoma Historical Society.)

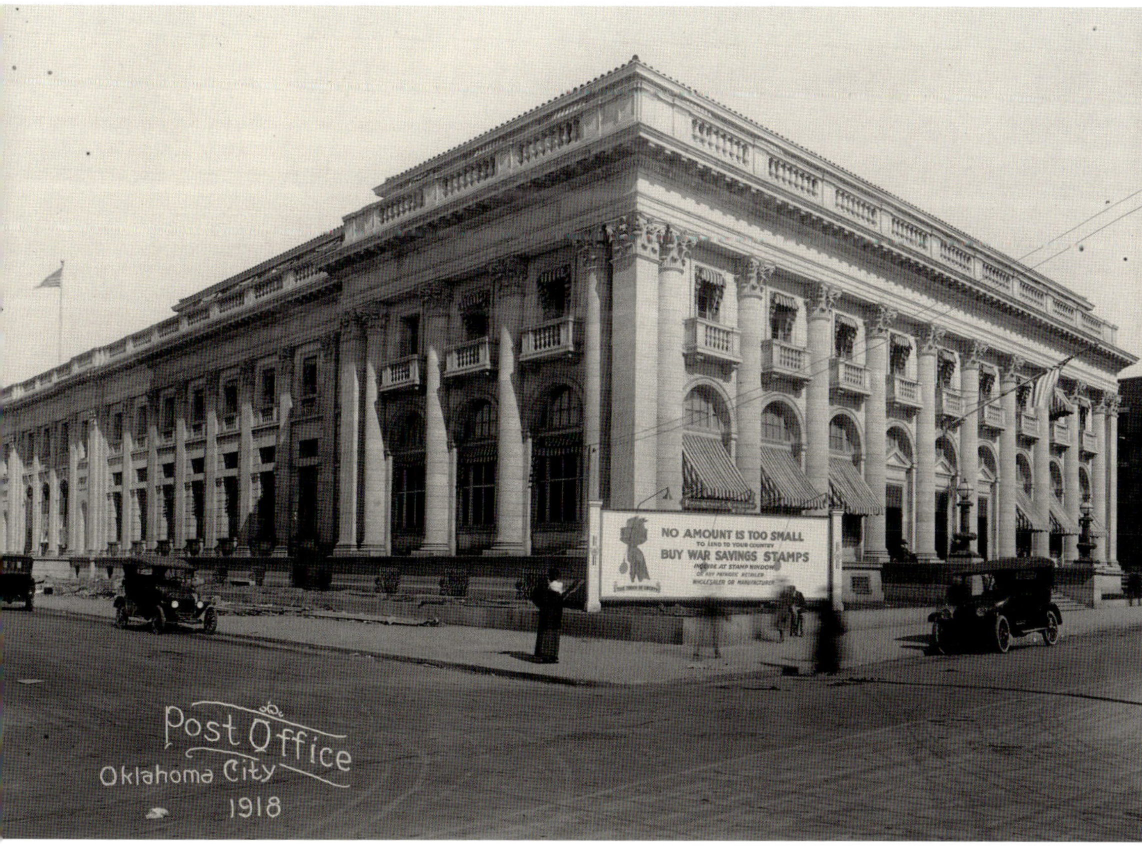

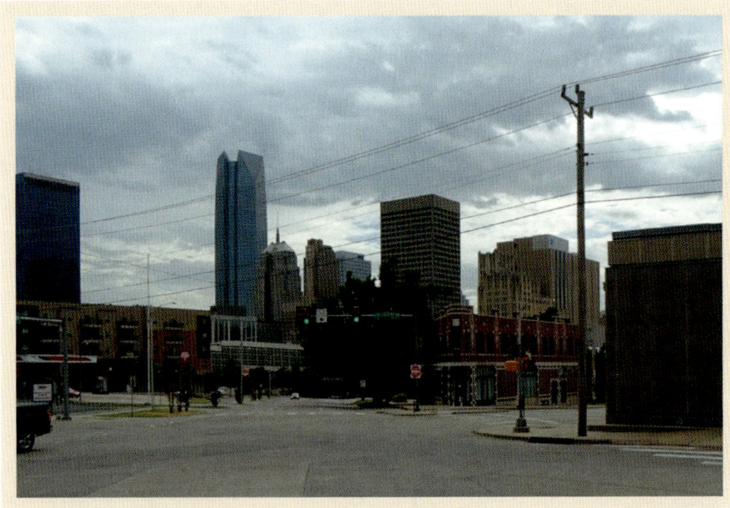

Brothers August and Fred Heierding were German immigrants, born to a family of meat-cutters, when they moved to Oklahoma City and built a triangular-shaped two-story building at 1111 Harrison Avenue in 1914. The family closed the market in 1960 but continued to lease storage lockers for another nine years. It remained empty until architect Rand Elliott purchased the building and restored it for his offices in 1995. (Past, courtesy of Oklahoma Historical Society.)

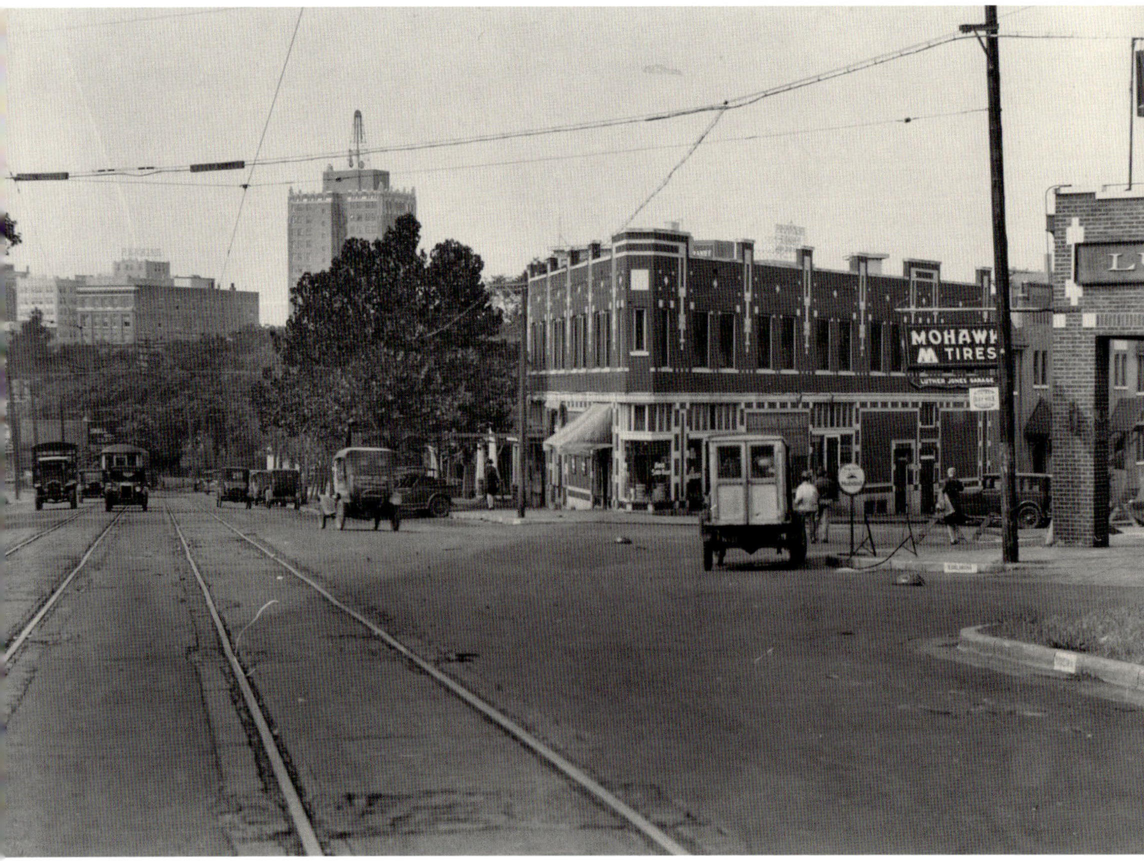

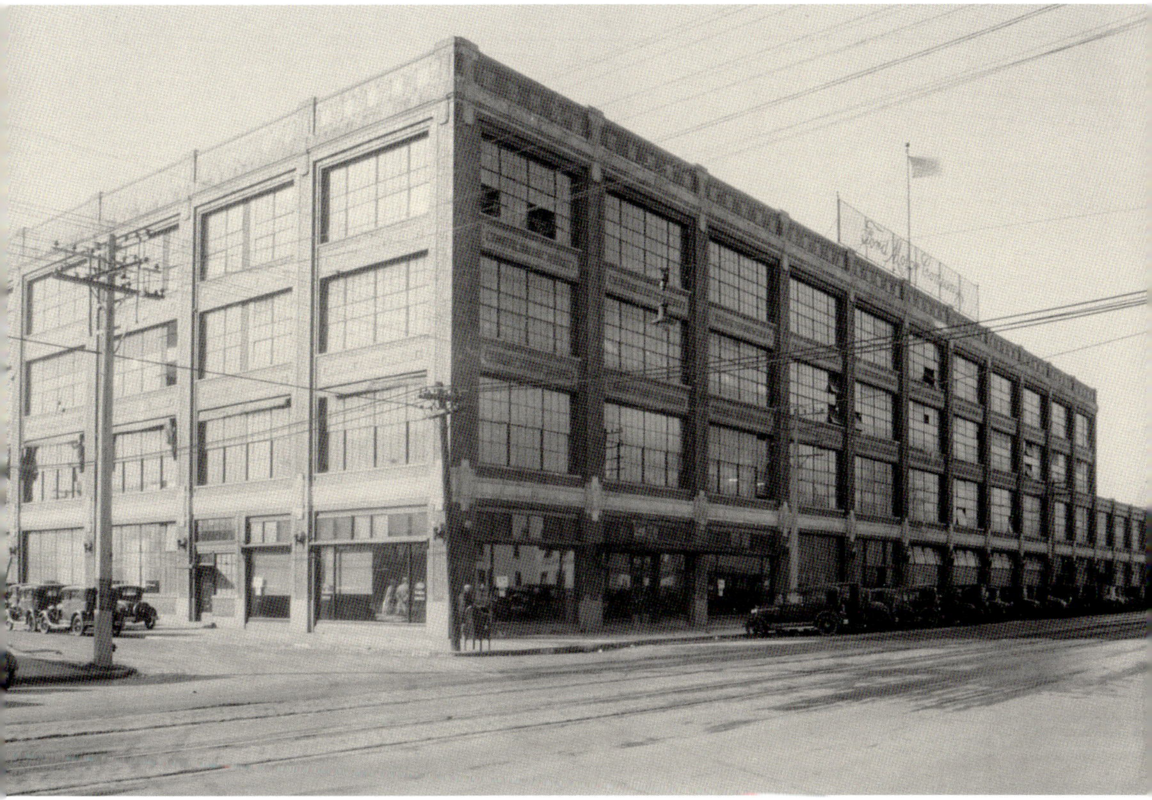

Sales of Henry Ford's Model T more than doubled to 501,462 in just three years when, in 1915, he built regional assembly plants that could quickly construct the cars from premade kits. Famed industrial architect Albert Kahn oversaw the design of the Oklahoma City plant, built in 1916. At its peak, it employed several hundred workers who could produce 200 cars a day. The plant was converted into a 21c Museum Hotel in 2018. (Past, courtesy of Oklahoma Historical Society.)

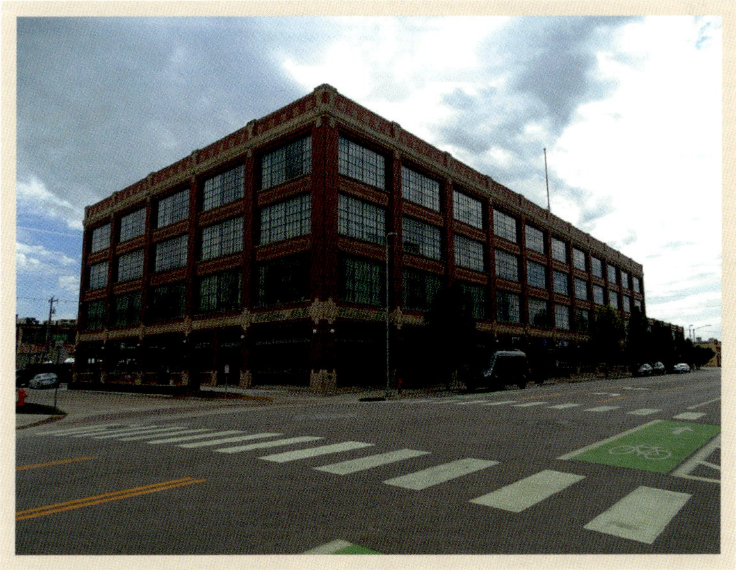

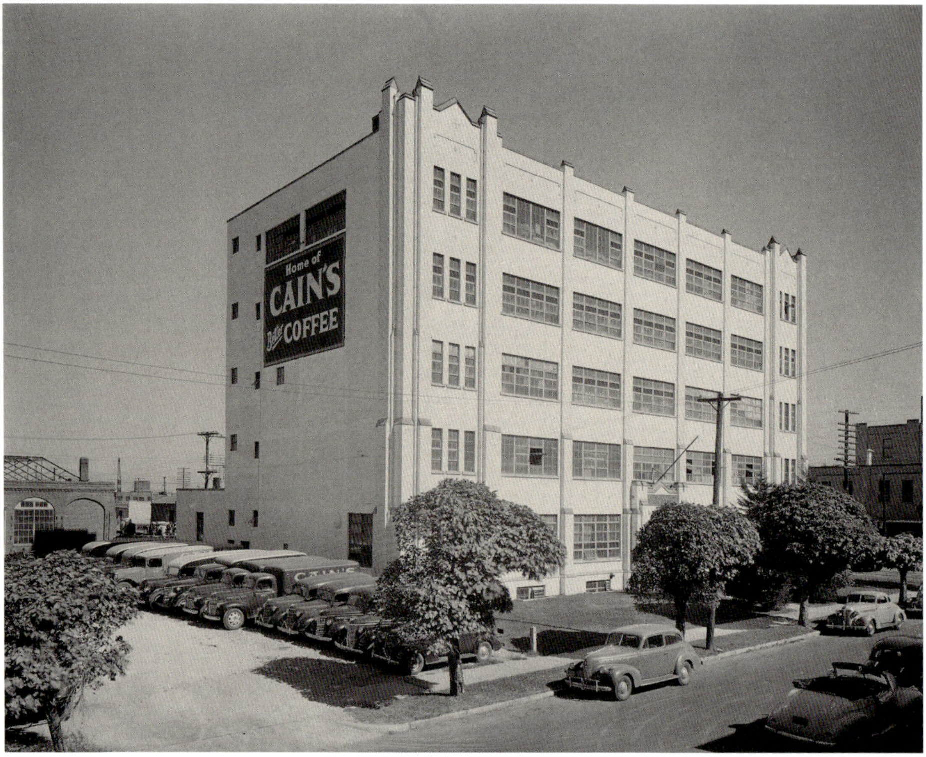

The Cain's Coffee building at 1 Northwest Twelfth Street was built in 1919 as the home of Sifers Candy Co.; later, it was home to a brewery and mattress company before it was taken over by Cain's Coffee in 1941. In 1961, Cain's left for a new plant. The building was being renovated into offices in 2022. The building's facade consists of a glossy white brick, a rarity in Oklahoma City. (Past, courtesy of Oklahoma Historical Society.)

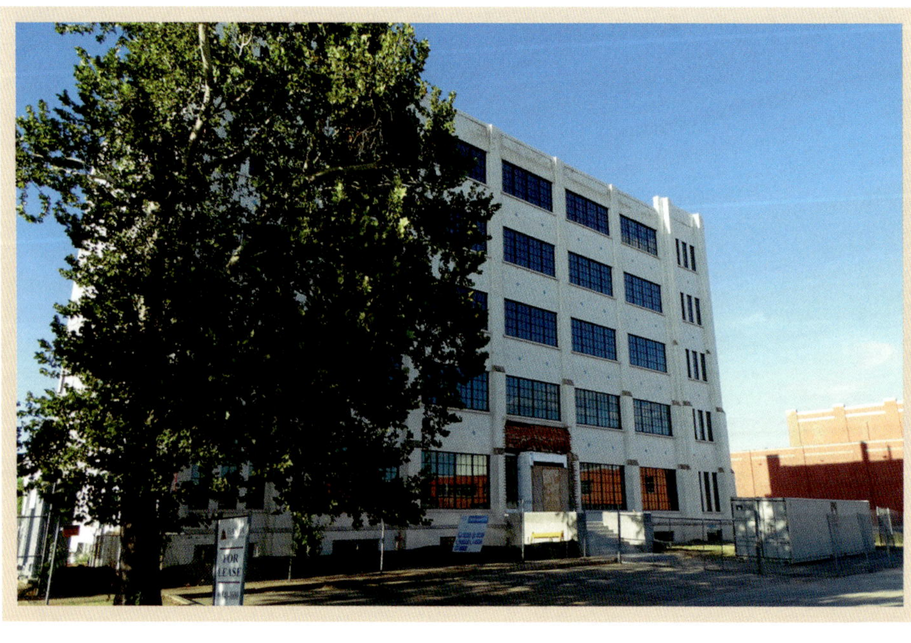

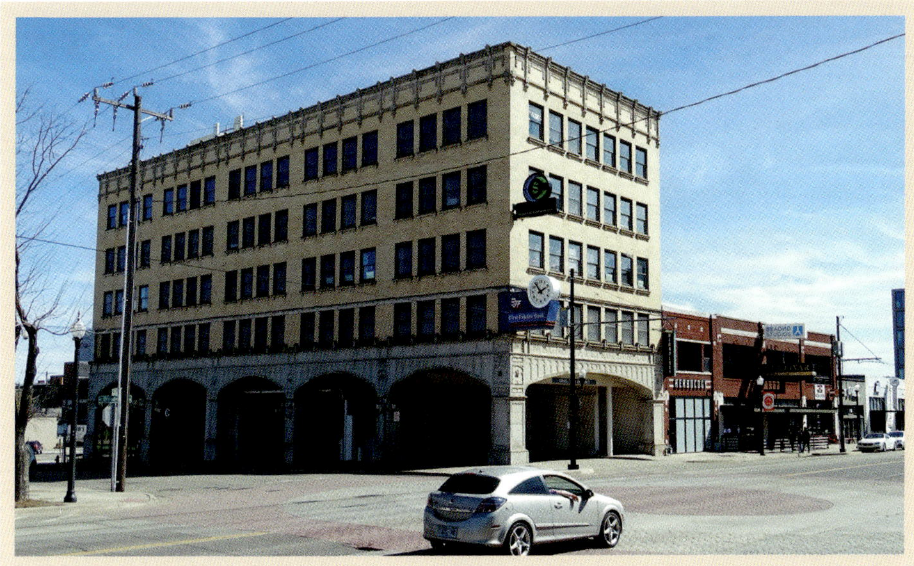

Magnolia Petroleum erected the five-story building at 722 North Broadway Avenue in 1919 with a distinctive arched opening on the first floor for a gas station that remained in operation until 1960. The filling station space was later enclosed as office space until it was reopened in 1996 by owner Chris Salyer for it to be used as a bank drive through for BancFirst. The drive-through was later taken over by First Fidelity Bank. (Past, courtesy of Oklahoma Historical Society.)

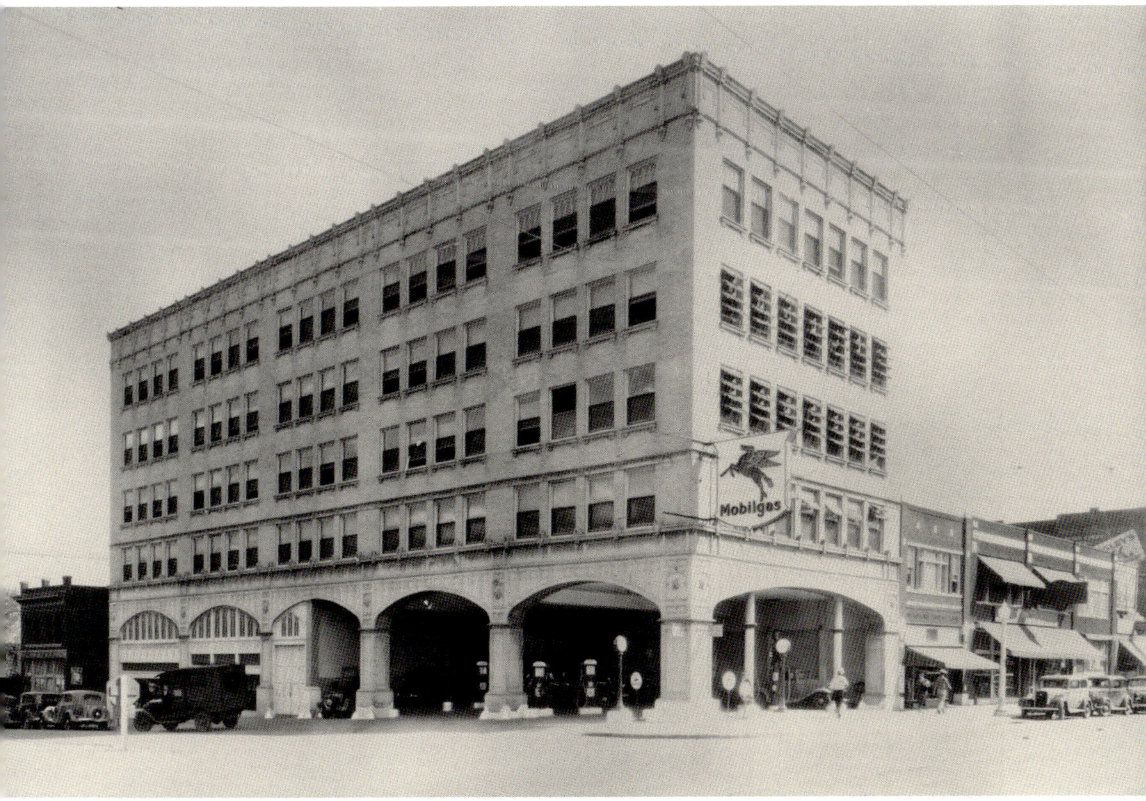

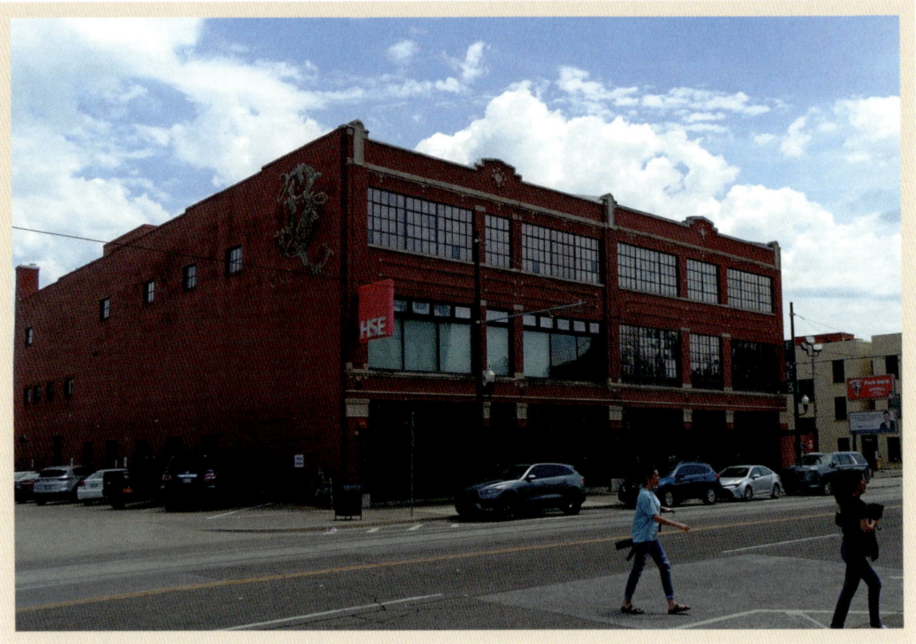

Greenlease Cadillac was one of the city's leading luxury car dealers when it commissioned architect Solomon Andrew Layton to design a three-story showroom at 914 North Broadway Avenue. A second, almost identical building was added in 1923 to the first one, which was built in 1920. The building was later home to Kings Moving and Storage until 1978, when it went bankrupt. The building was restored into offices in 2006. (Past, courtesy of Oklahoma Historical Society.)

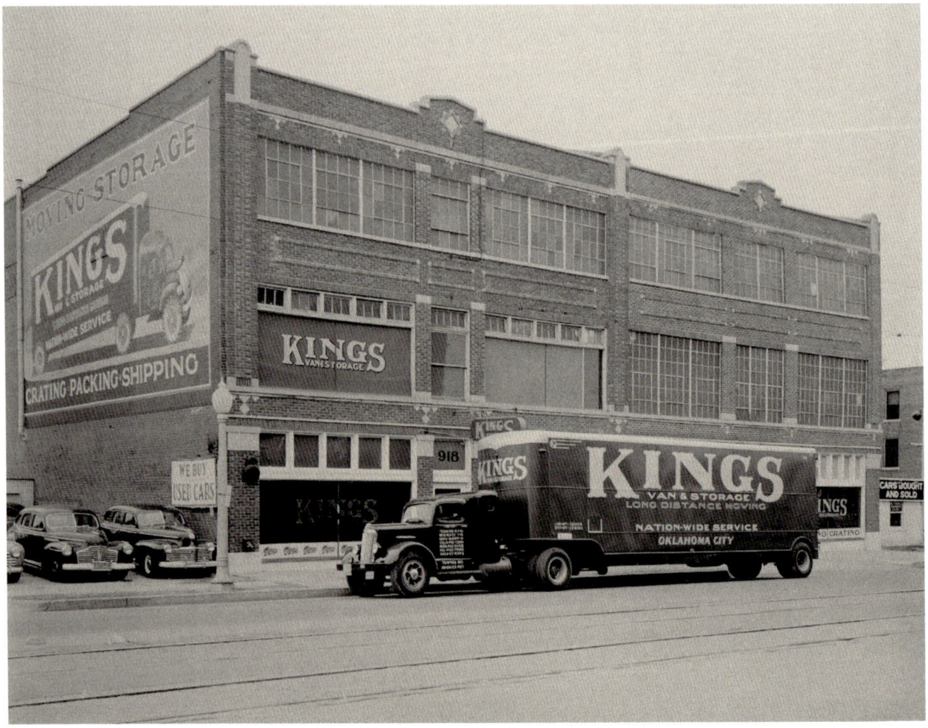

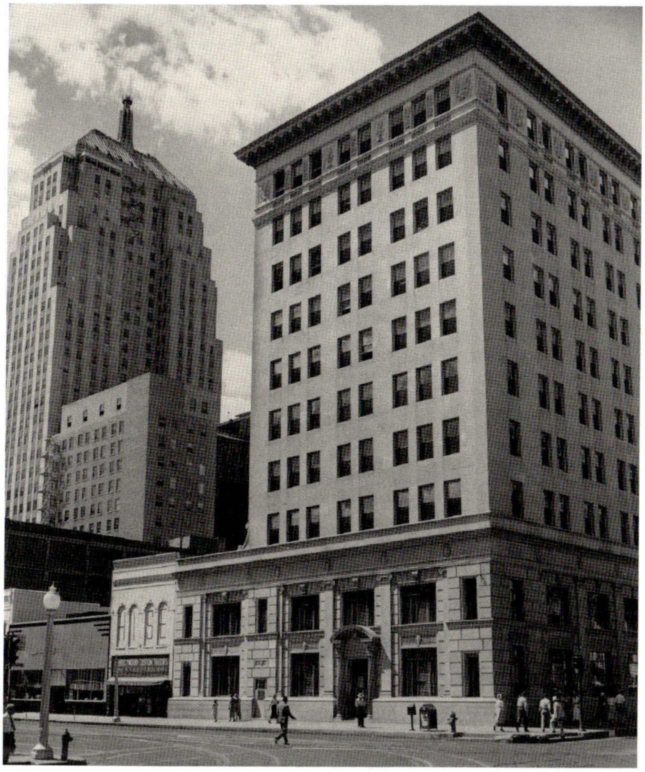

Tradesman's National Bank got its start in 1909 and was rapidly expanding when it built a 10-story building at 100 North Broadway Avenue. The bank merged with First National in 1949 and City National Bank took over as the anchor tenant through 1971. It was replaced by Frontier Federal Savings and Loan and then BancFirst, which, in 2021, moved across the street. (Past, courtesy of Oklahoma Historical Society.)

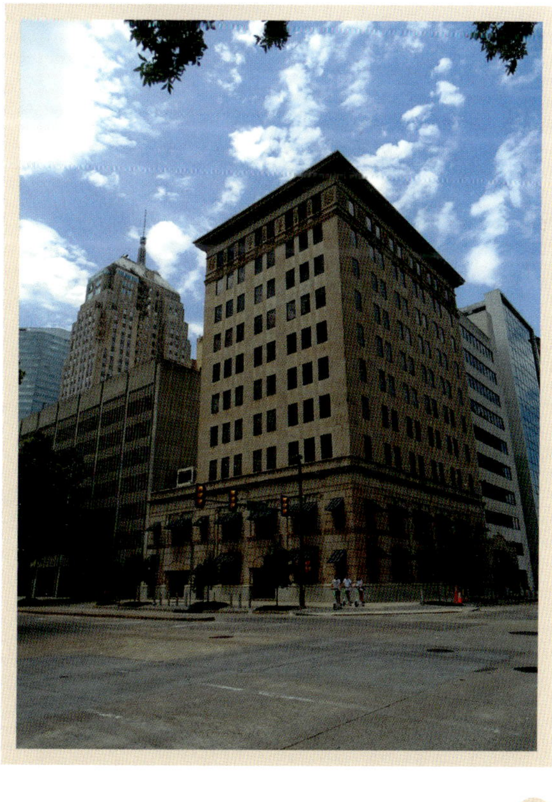

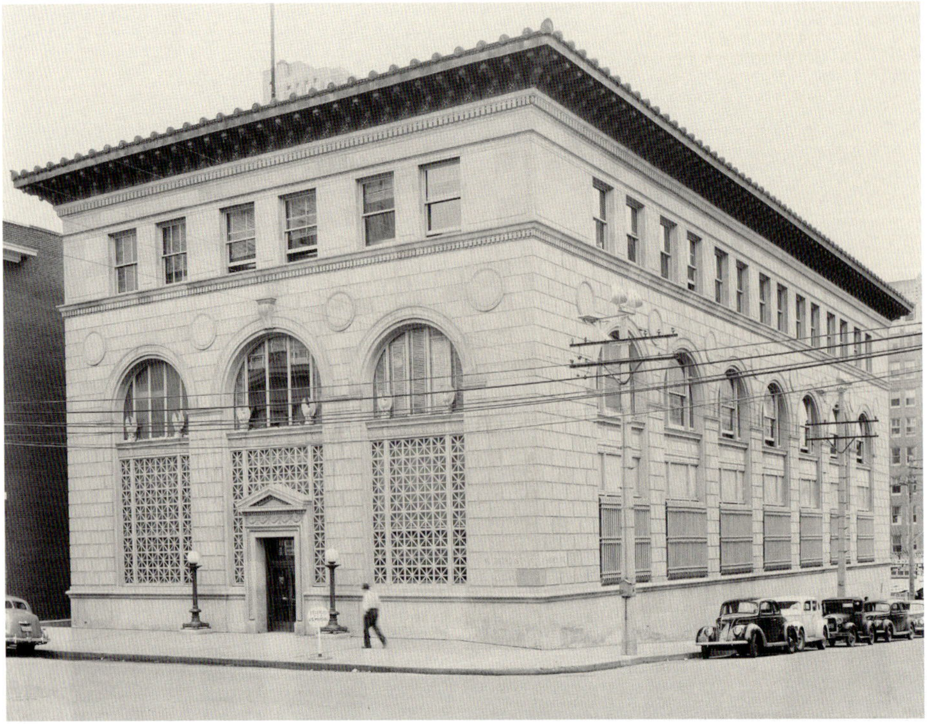

Oklahoma City was experiencing rapid growth when the Federal Reserve built a new home at 226 Dean A. McGee Avenue in 1922. The federal bank branch was built to withstand attacks by robbers and featured a 100,000-pound vault door. The building was expanded in 1958 and renovated in the 1990. Check use dropped, and the building was sold to investors in 2007. The reserve continued to lease the third floor. (Past, courtesy of Oklahoma Historical Society.)

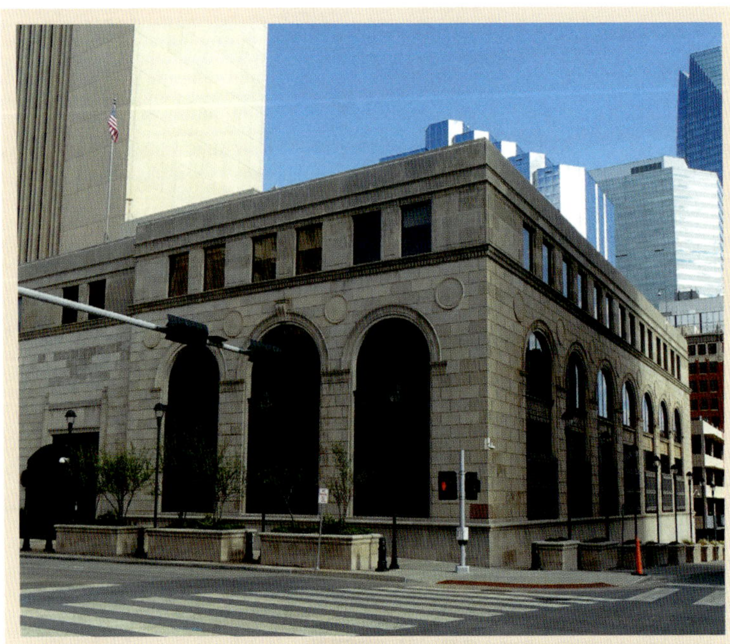

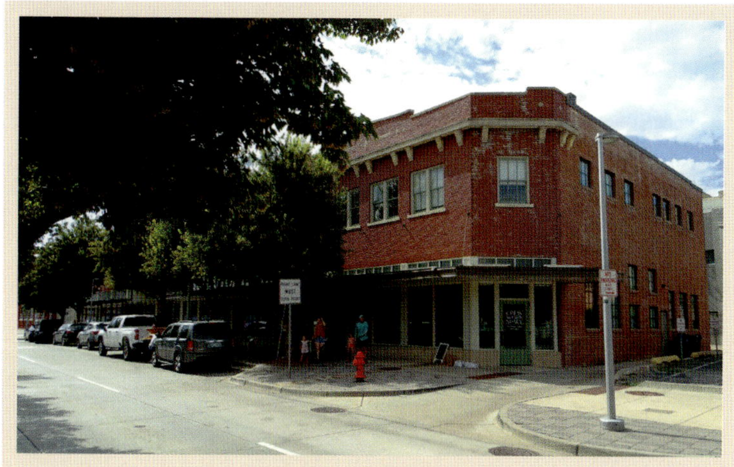

The Main Street Arcade, located at 629 West Main Street, was built in 1922 and was home to Hill's Business College until 1968. The two-story building was designed for a mix of uses but ended up as home to the Downtown Baptist Church where a soup kitchen provided relief to the homeless. The building was purchased by Pivot Project in 2014 and restored to its historic use and appearance. (Past, courtesy of Oklahoma Historical Society.)

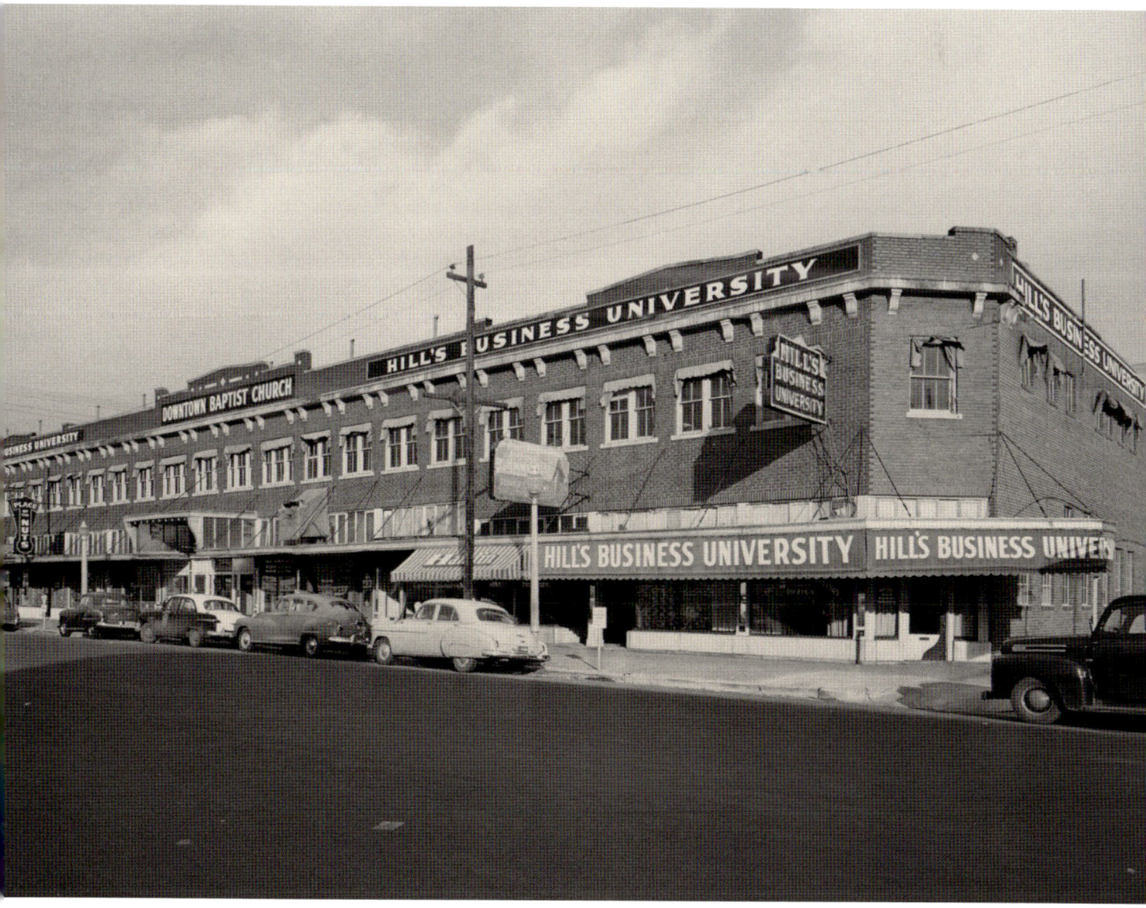

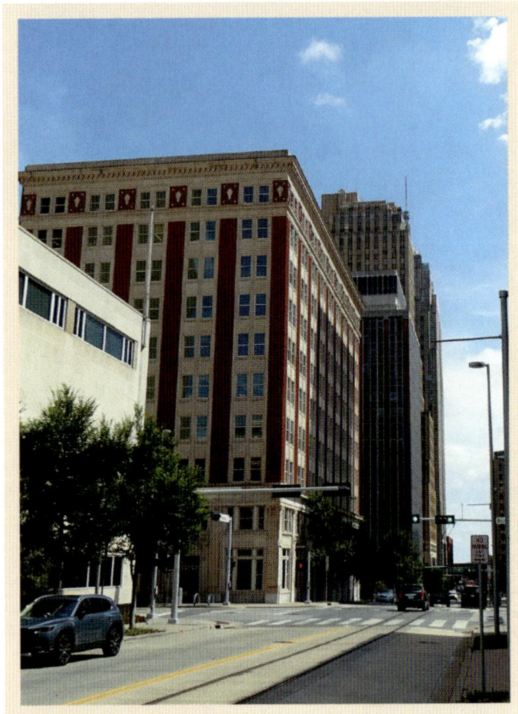

Thomas Braniff built the 10-story Braniff Building at 324 North Robinson Avenue in 1923 as a headquarters for his insurance company, and later, it was home to Braniff Airways. The airline moved operations to Dallas in the early 1940s, and the building was sold to Kerr-McGee, which painted it a gray color. SandRidge Energy restored the building's deep-red color of brick and added a modern glass facade on the former alley side. (Past, courtesy of Oklahoma Historical Society.)

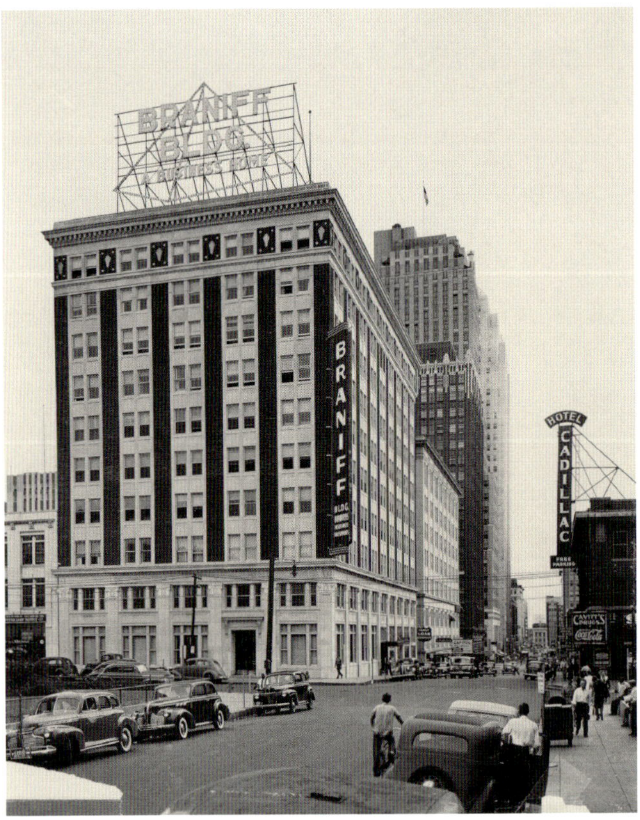

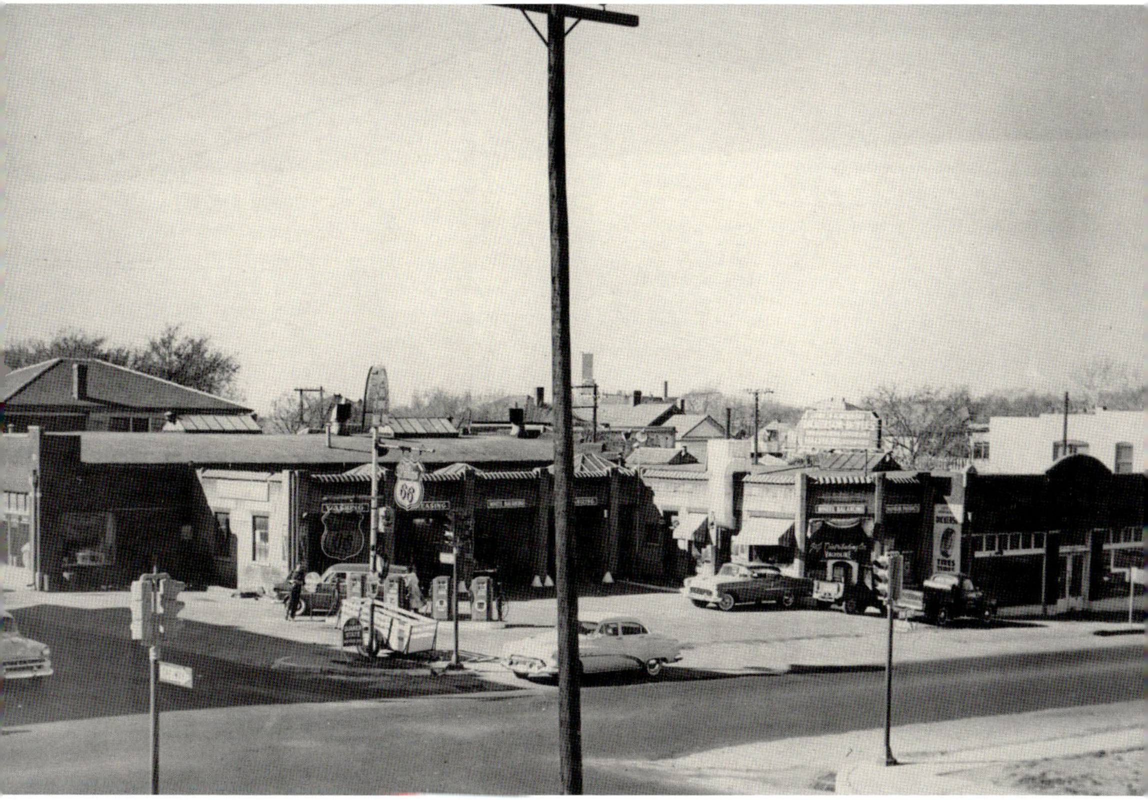

Before being turned into a Phillips 66 service station, the one-story building built in 1923 at 308 Northwest Tenth Street was home to a Harley-Davidson motorcycle dealership. The building also was used as an upholstering shop and air conditioning installation garage. The building was later boarded up, neglected, and filled with junk for decades until 2016, when it was bought by Northline Development and turned into the Collective, a mix of restaurants and bars. (Past, courtesy of Lee Allan Smith).

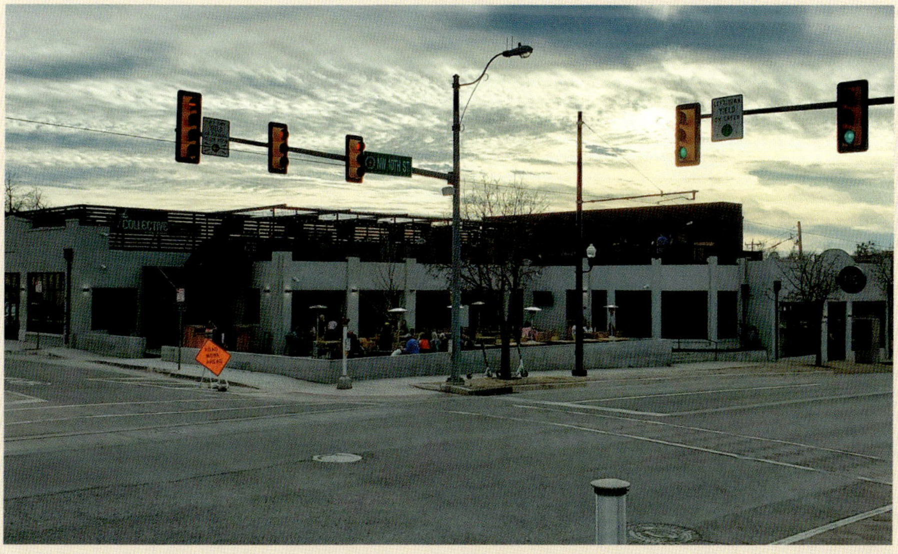

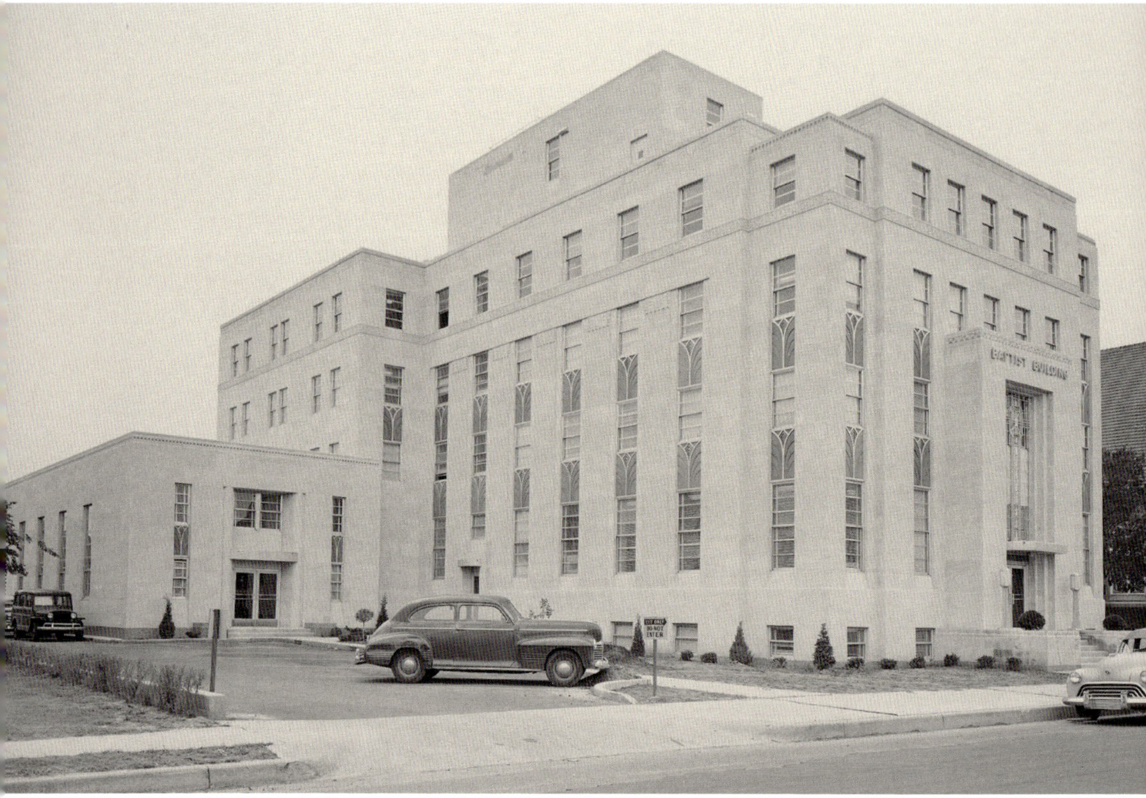

The Masonic Temple was built in 621 North Robinson Avenue with an auditorium to host 3,000 people. The temple fell behind on payments during the Great Depression, and the building was bought by Home State Life and then the Journal Record. The 1995 federal building bombing damaged the former temple, but it was repaired and made the home of the Oklahoma City National Memorial and other tenants. (Past, courtesy of Oklahoma Historical Society.)

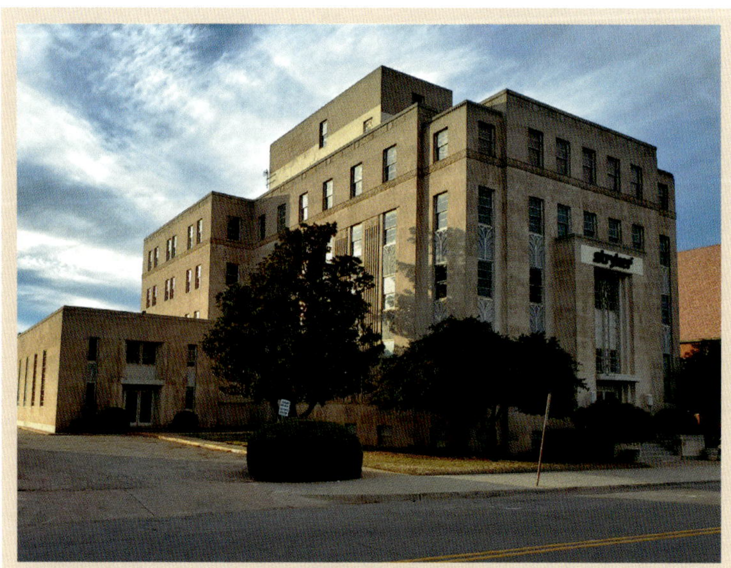

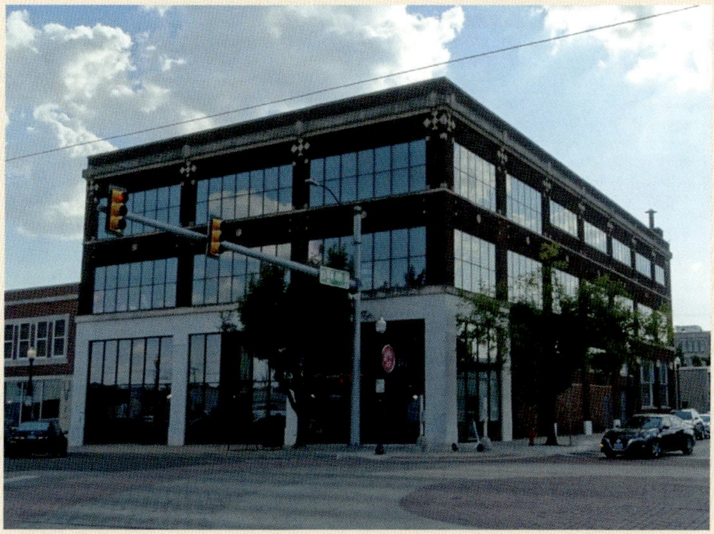

McClelland Gentry Auto built a Packard dealership at 825 North Broadway Avenue as the corridor emerged as Oklahoma City's Automobile Alley in the 1920s. The building was next home to a Hudson-Essex dealership before turning into an Army recruiting station and offices for the discount retailer TG&Y. Nick Preftakes bought the building in 1998 and restored it as office space with a glowing Hudson sign lighting up the first-floor garage. (Past, courtesy of Oklahoma Historical Society.)

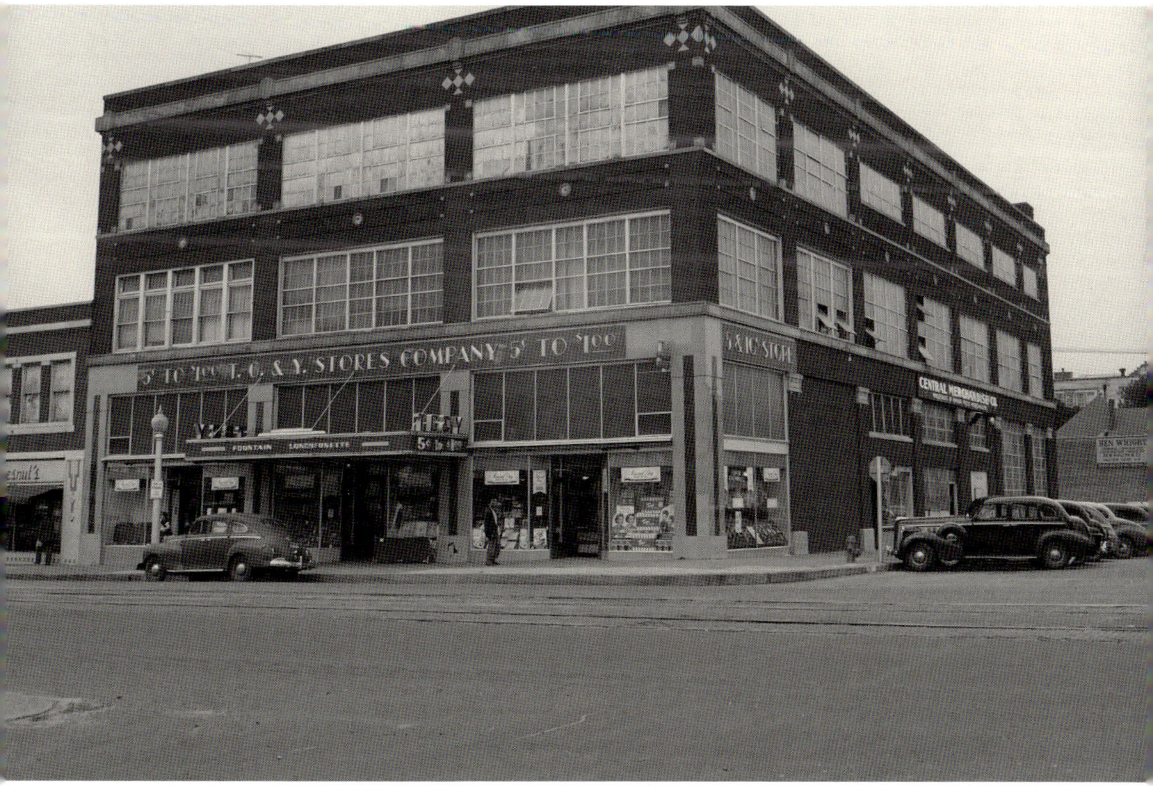

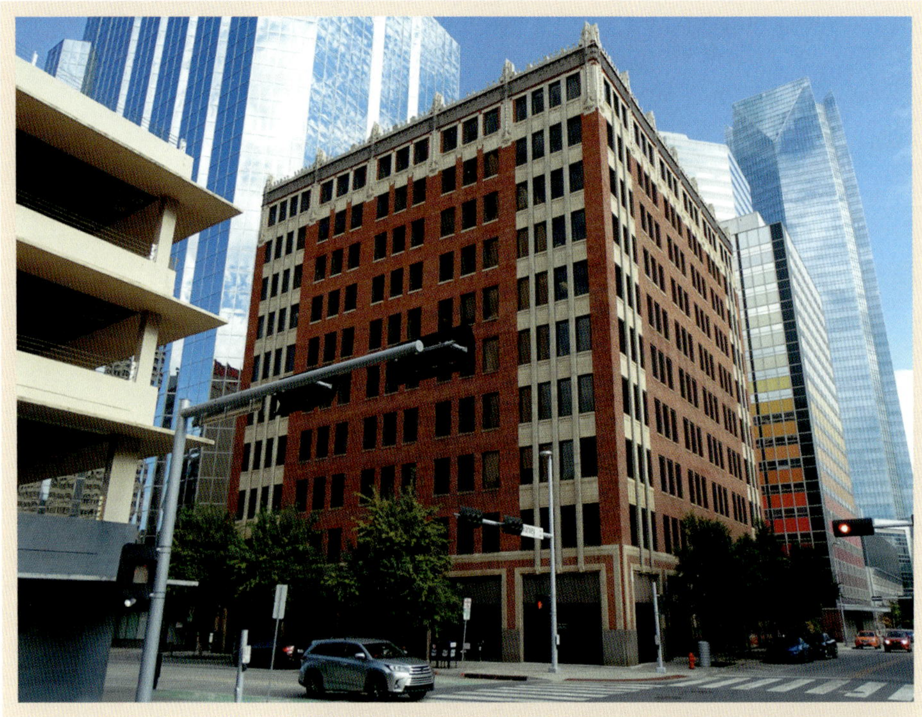

The Cotton Exchange Building at 218 North Harvey Avenue was built in 1923 as Oklahoma emerged as the third-largest cotton producer in the country. The developer sought to bring 23 cotton companies together in one place designed with skylights and windows to provide the best lighting for judging fiber quality. The cotton companies disappeared, but the building remains popular with law firms due to close proximity to the Oklahoma County Courthouse. (Past, courtesy of Oklahoma Historical Society.)

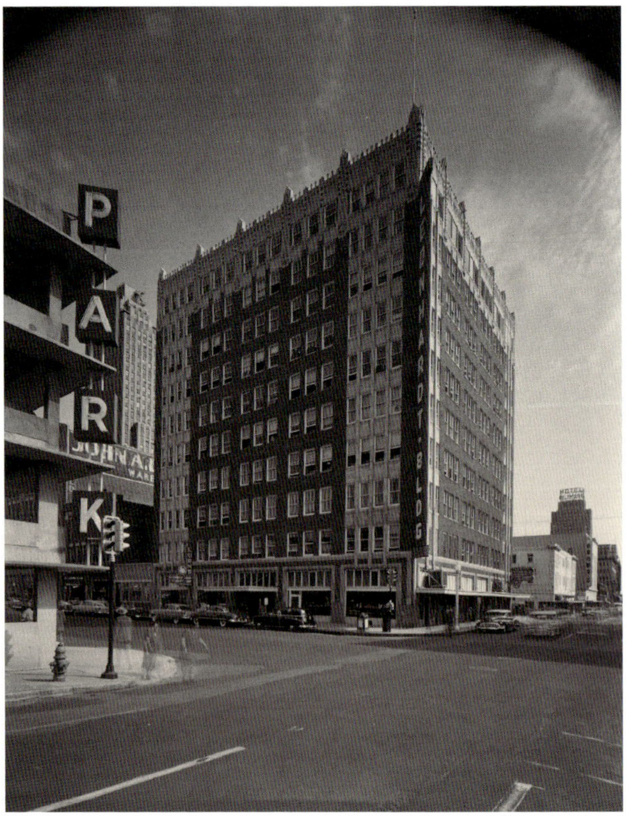

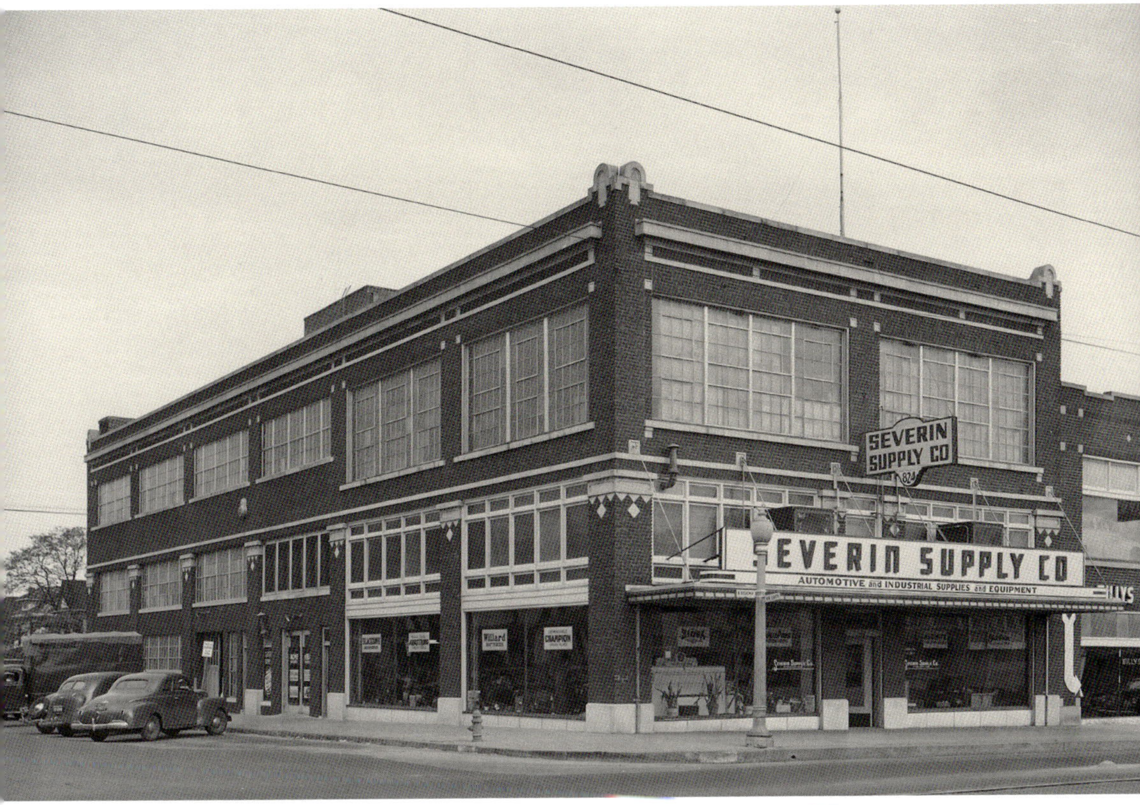

Cars were still new when Shelbourne Motor Company opened at 824 North Broadway Avenue, so the dealership advertised free driving lessons to drum up business. The three-story showroom and garage were later home to Severin Tire & Supply, which operated until 1968. In 1987, Chris Salyer purchased the building; he renovated the top floor into his residence and leased the bottom floor to retailers. (Past, courtesy of Oklahoma Historical Society.)

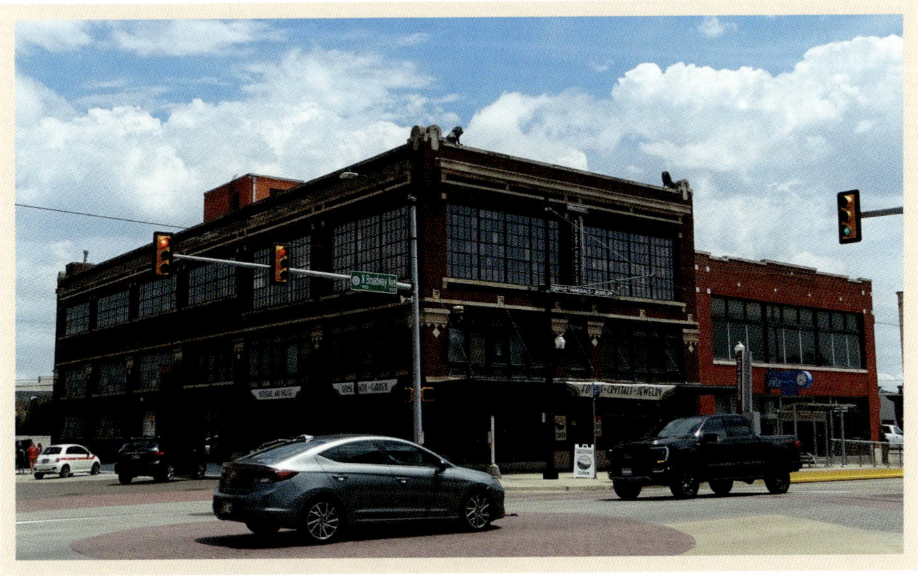

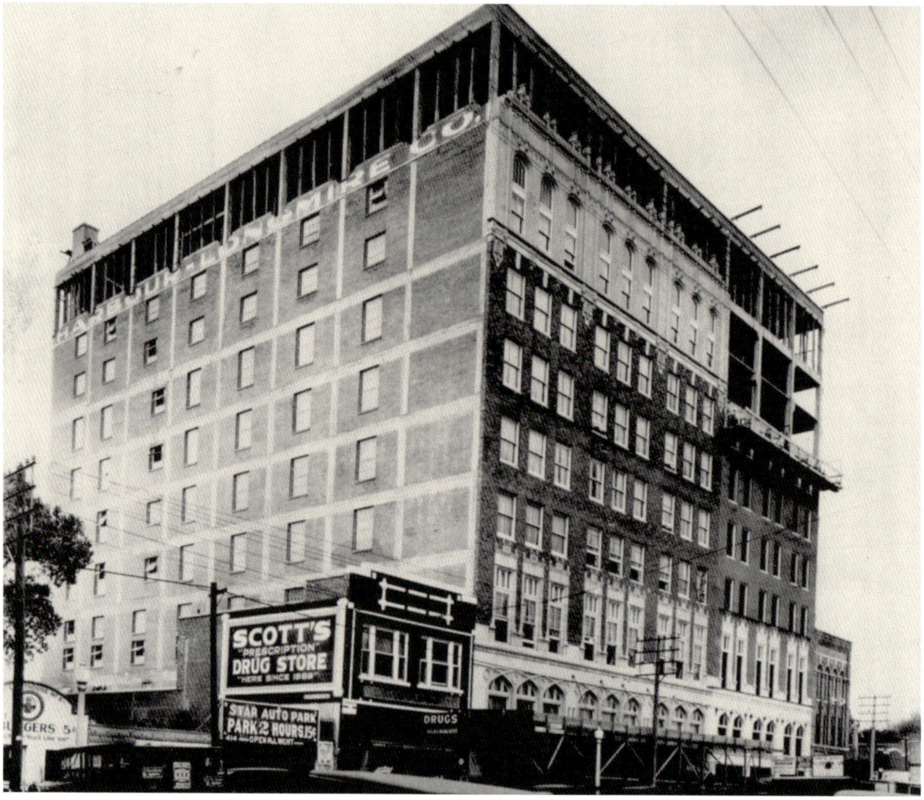

James Harbour and William Longmire started Harbour-Longmire furniture in 1910, and it was the second-largest furniture retailer in the country when they started construction in 1925 on an ornate new building at 420 West Main Street. The business was sold in 1945, and the building was empty and in danger of being torn down when it was renovated into offices in the 1980s. The building is now an annex for operations of the City of Oklahoma City. (Past, courtesy of Oklahoma Historical Society.)

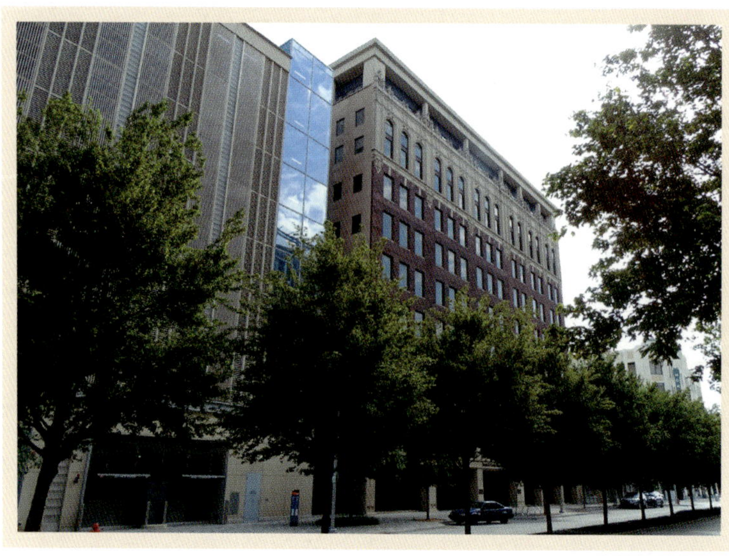

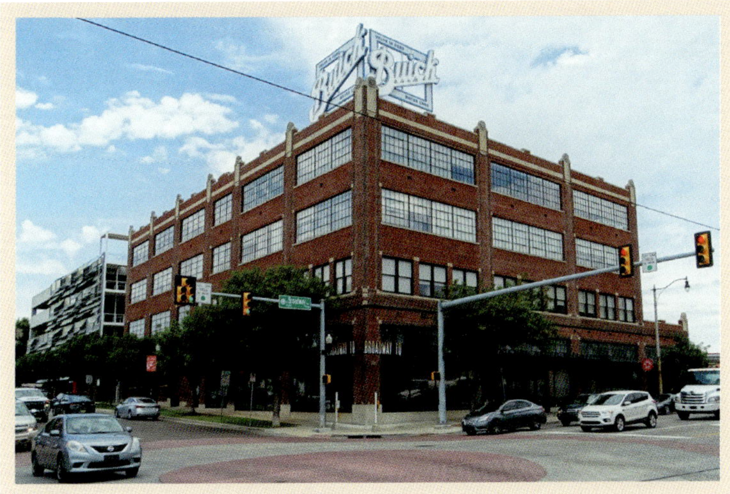

The Buick Building at 1101 North Broadway Avenue was built in 1926 as car sales along the strip known as Automobile Alley outgrew the older smaller dealerships. The Buick Building was later turned into offices but fell into disuse as downtown went into decline in the 1980s. The dealership was purchased by Midtown Renaissance Group in 2013 and renovated into restaurants and offices. Improvements included a recreated neon Buick sign added to the roof. (Past, courtesy of Oklahoma Historical Society.)

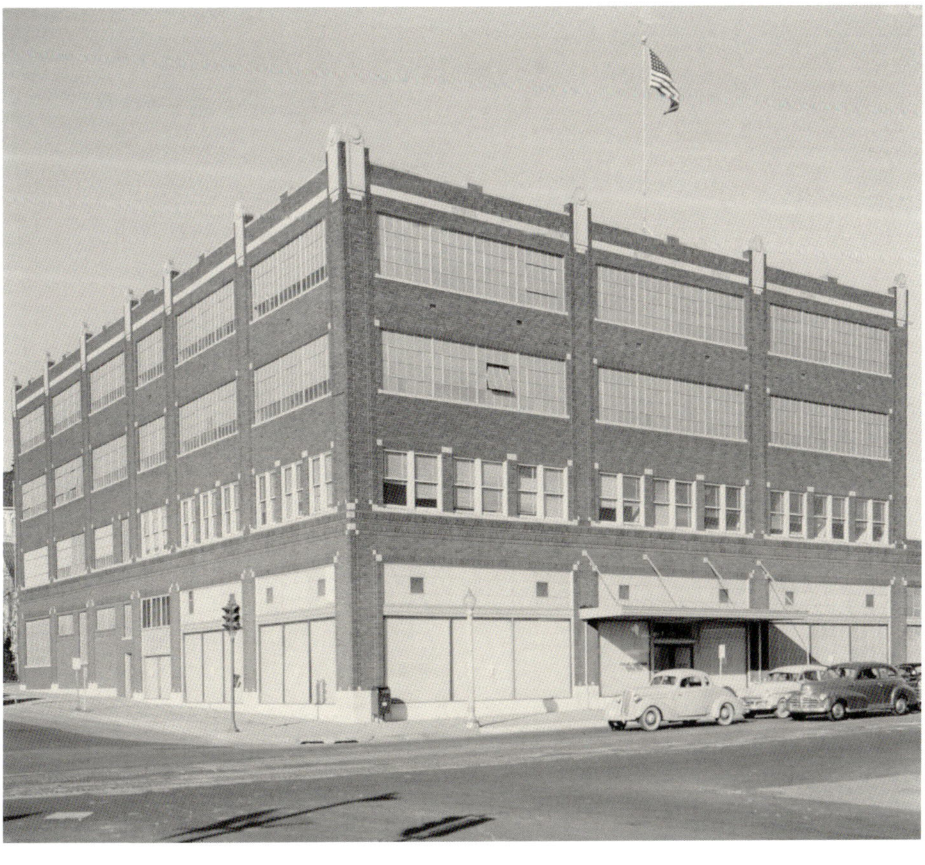

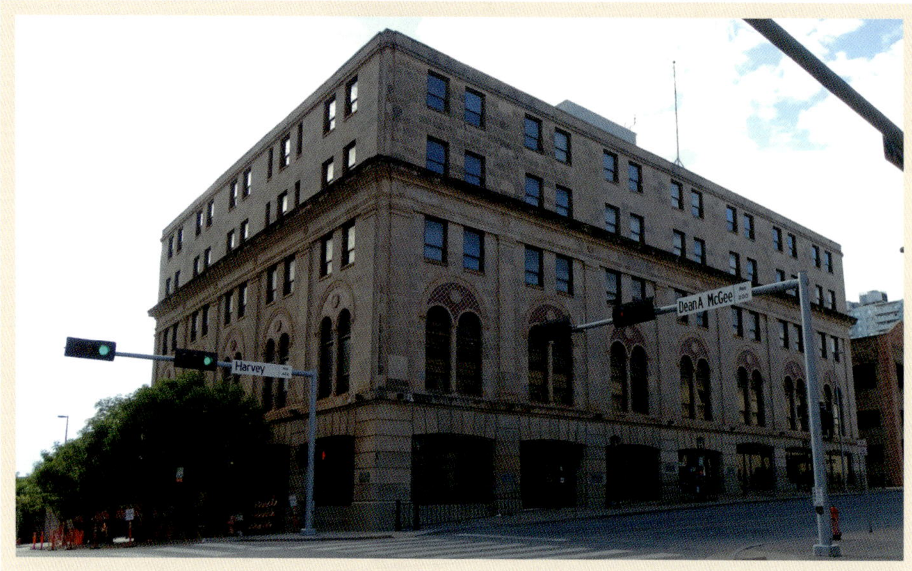

The Benevolent and Protective Order of the Elks started construction of its first Oklahoma City lodge in 1926. The 12-story Italian Renaissance building was constructed with cut limestone, double-arched windows, and wrought-iron balconies. The Elks lost control of the building to Oklahoma Natural Gas, which purchased it in 1947 and continues to use it as a base for its Oklahoma City operations. (Past, courtesy of Oklahoma Historical Society.)

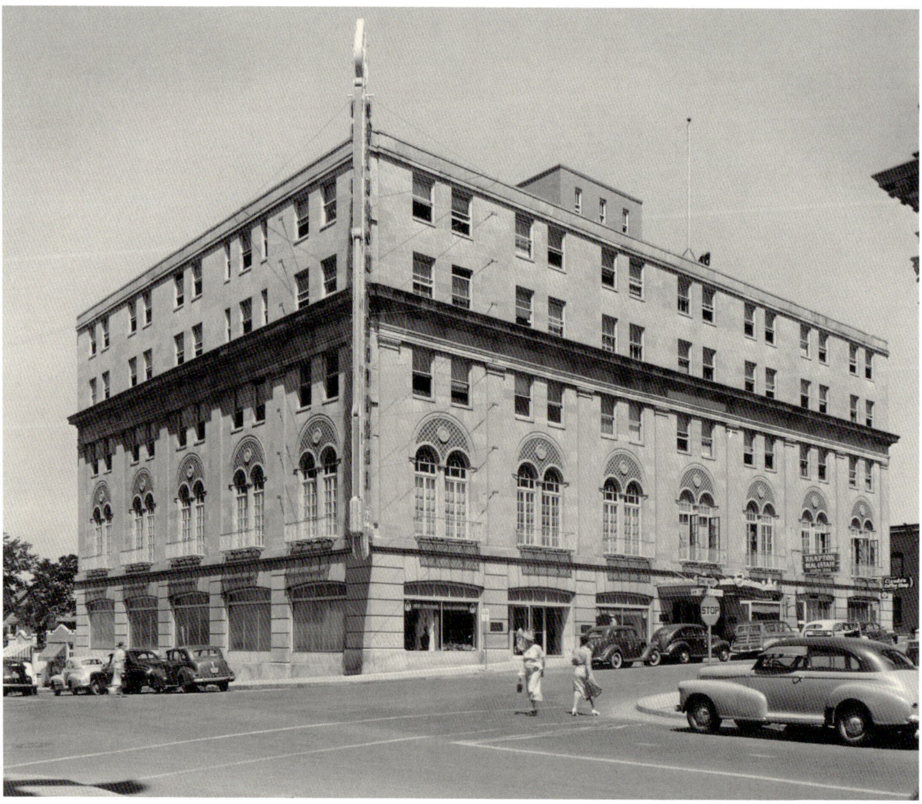

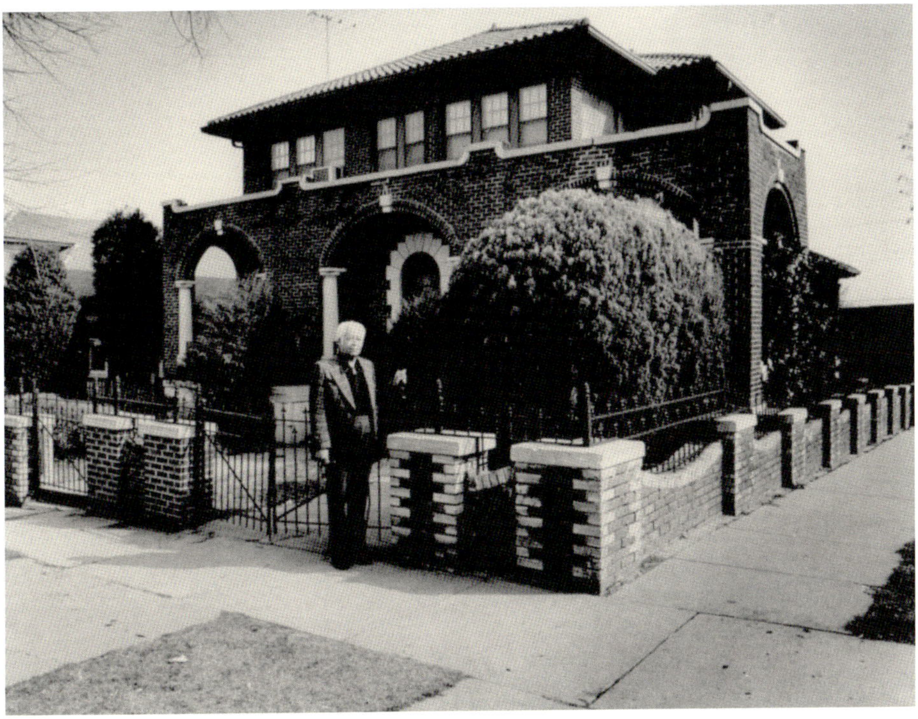

The Luster Mansion was built in 1926 by black businessman S.D. Lyons, who established the East India toiletries company in a red building next to the home. East India sold hair products and face powder to black customers worldwide. Lyons's stepson Melvin Luster, pictured, continued to maintain the family home as Deep Deuce went into a steep decline in the 1980s. The family sold the mansion to the Urban Renewal Authority in 2019. (Photos courtesy of the *Oklahoman*.)

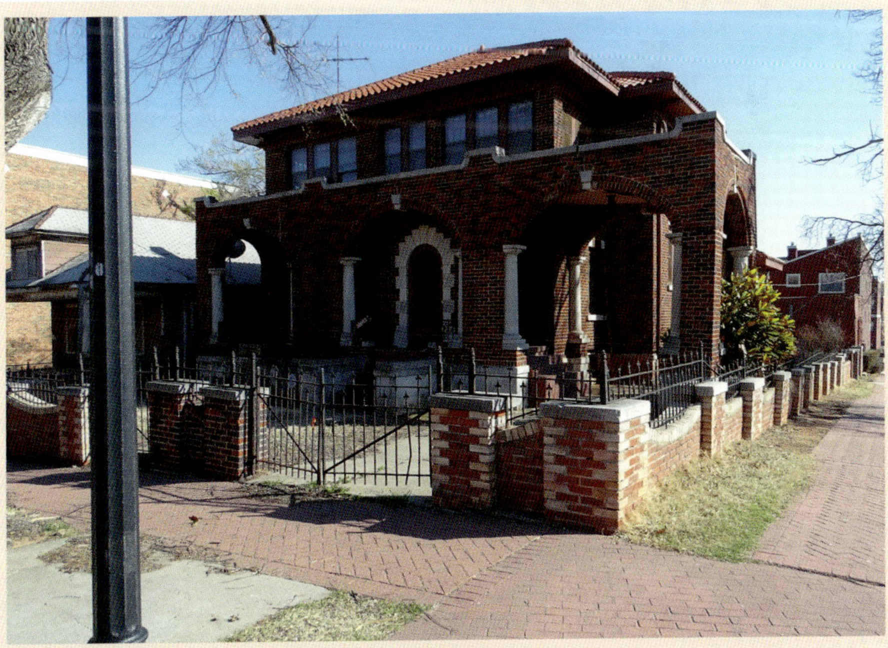

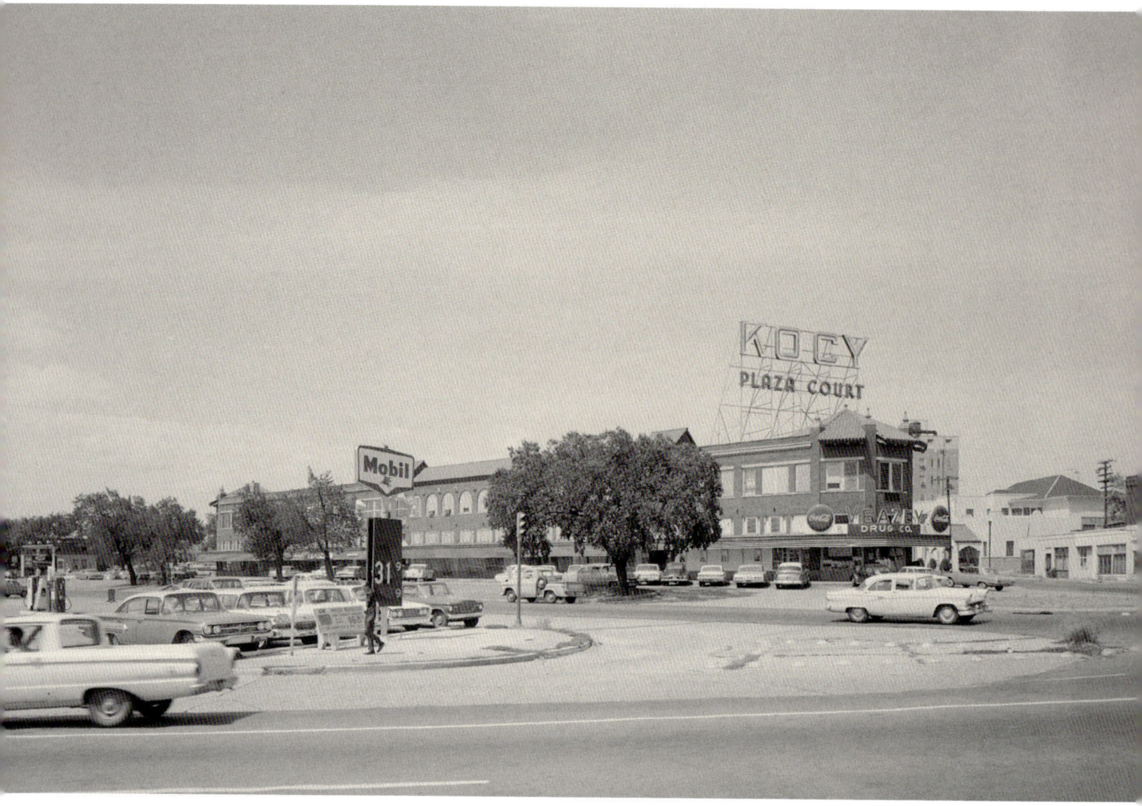

The Plaza Court Building at 1110 Classen Drive was Oklahoma City's first suburban shopping center when it was built in 1926. The two-story building's prominent tenants included Veazey Drugs, Crescent Market, and WKY, the state's first radio station. The building shut down in 1993 and stayed empty until 2006, when Midtown Renaissance bought it and restored it into a mix of shops, restaurants, and offices. (Past, courtesy of Oklahoma Historical Society.)

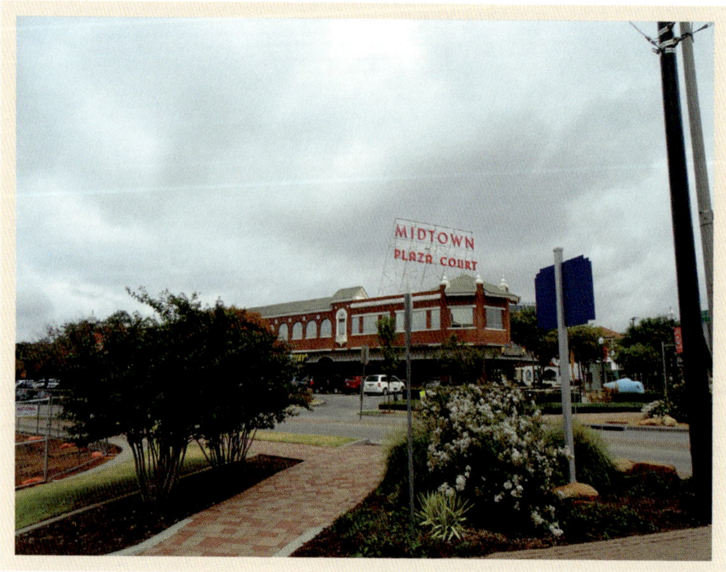

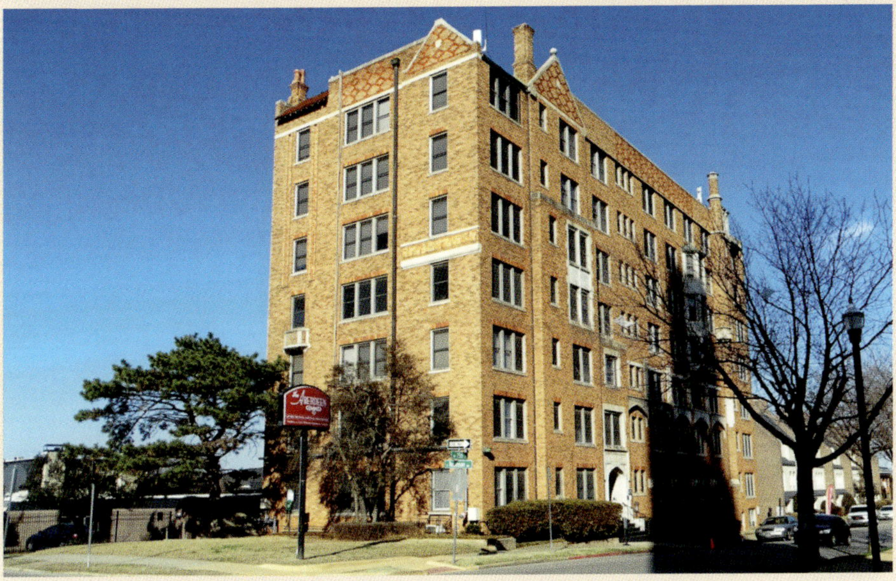

Heritage Hills was Oklahoma City's premier neighborhood, and Heritage Hills East was being promoted as an adjoining collection of smaller high-class bungalow homes when the luxury Aberdeen Apartment Hotel was built in 1927 along the dividing line between the two additions. The seven-story, Gothic Revival structure is still one of just a handful of apartment buildings in the urban core that is higher than five stories tall. (Past, courtesy of Oklahoma Historical Society.)

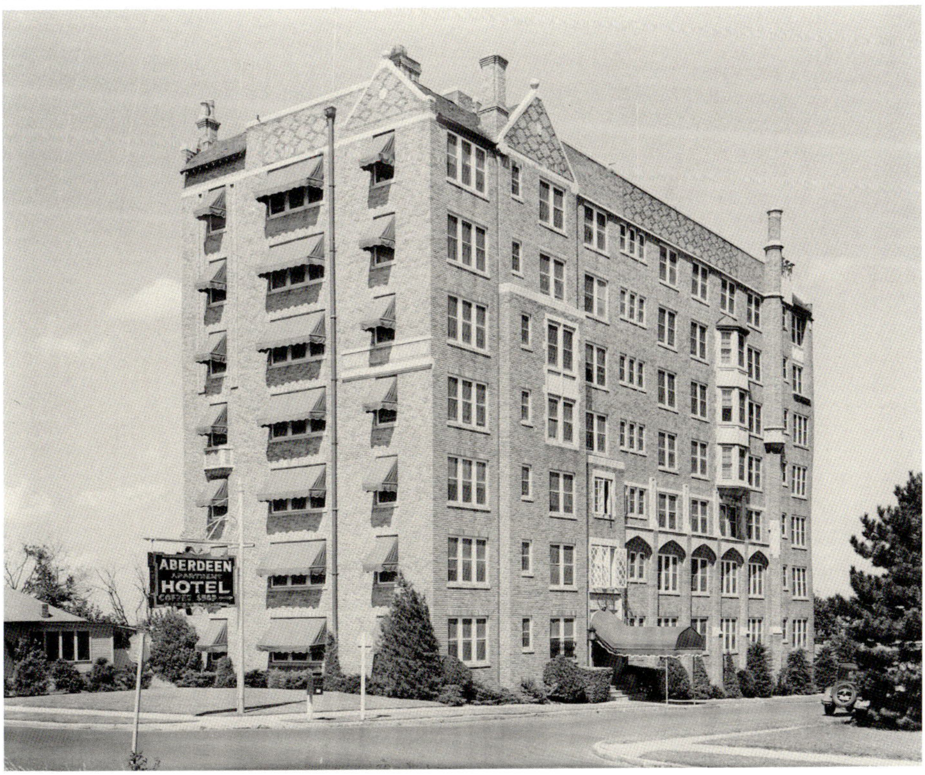

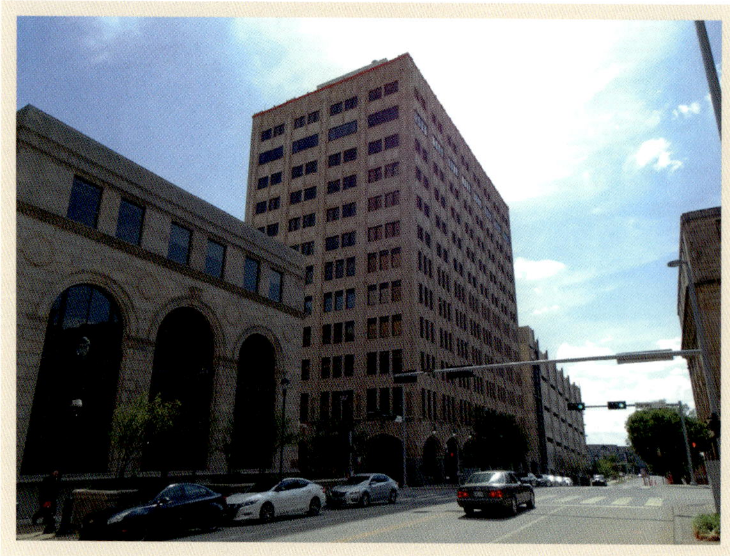

Electrical service to homes and businesses was becoming commonplace when Oklahoma Gas and Electric chose to build a new headquarters at 321 North Harvey Avenue. The Gothic structure with arched openings and columns was built to six stories but designed for an additional six stories—an expansion that was added in 1954. The utility continues to call the building home almost a century later. (Past, courtesy of Oklahoma Historical Society.)

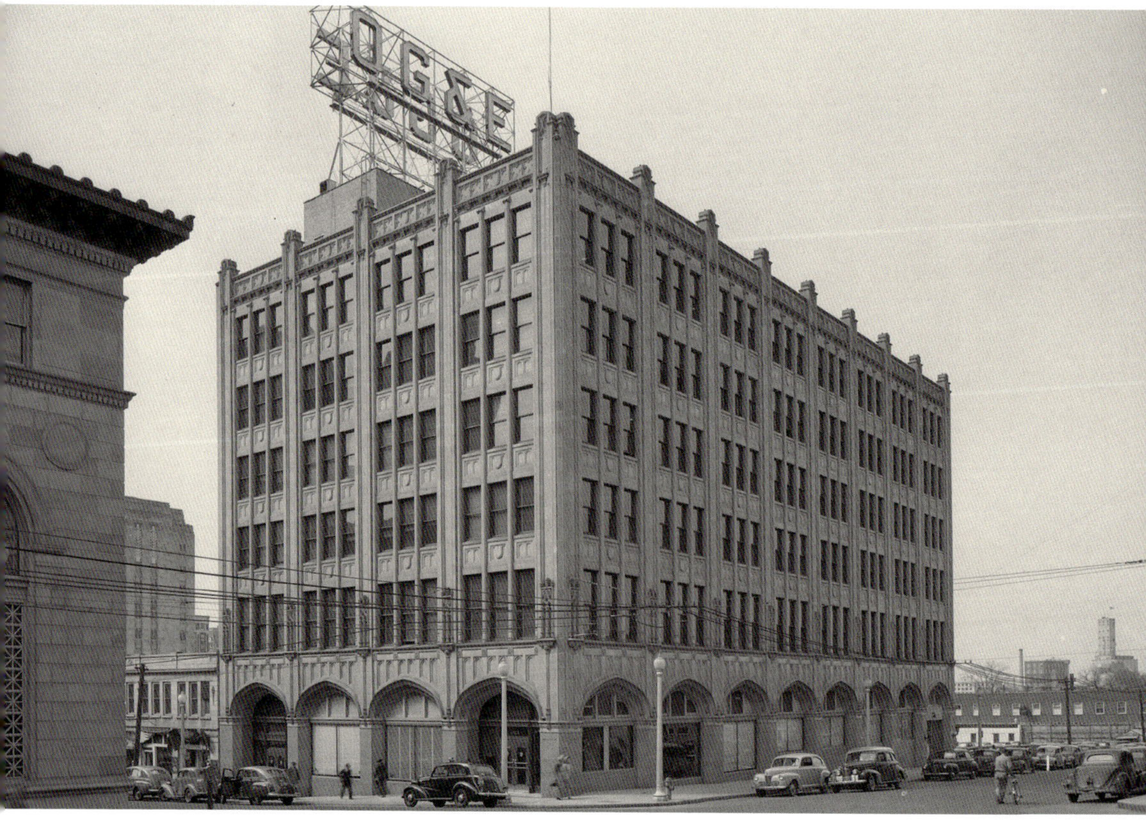

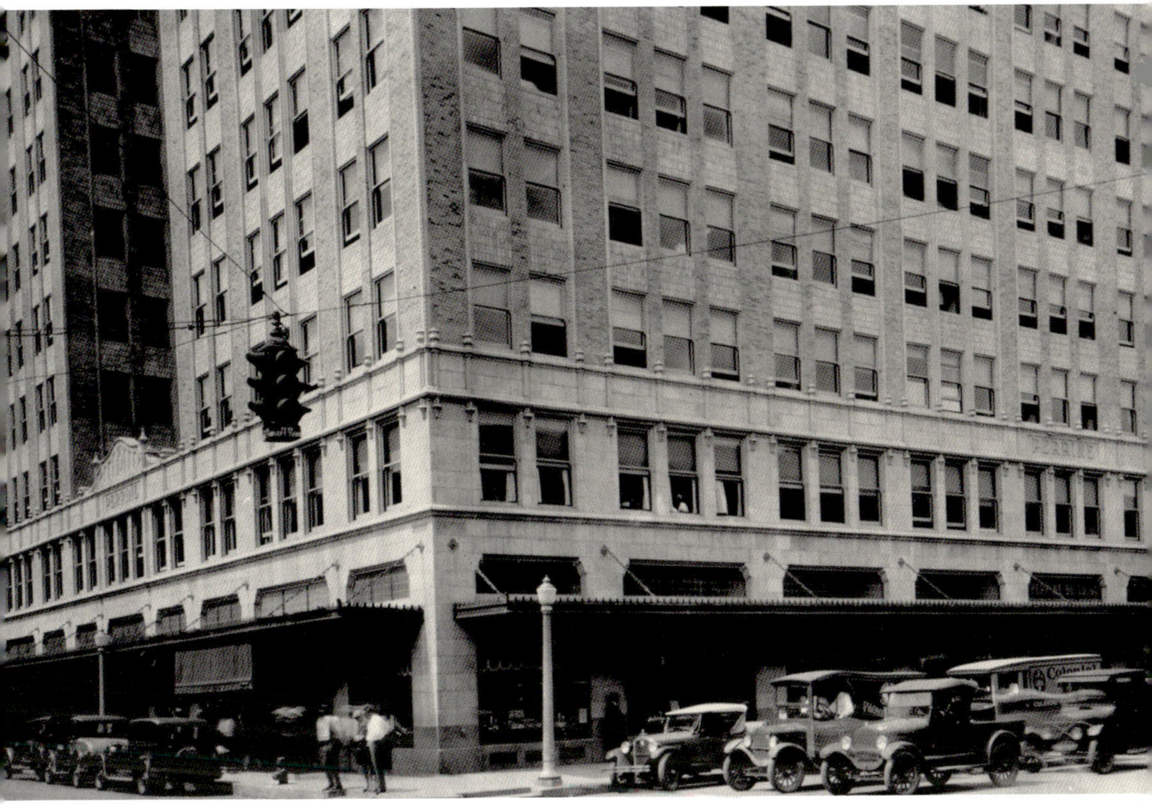

Now known as Robinson Renaissance, the 12-story Perrine Building was built in 1927 as oil money flowed and Oklahoma City saw a boom in business and population. The U-shaped building design assured that virtually every office came with a window. A renovation in 1987 removed the third floor within the U and added a glass atrium that opened up a basement and turned it into a food court. (Past, courtesy of Oklahoma Historical Society.)

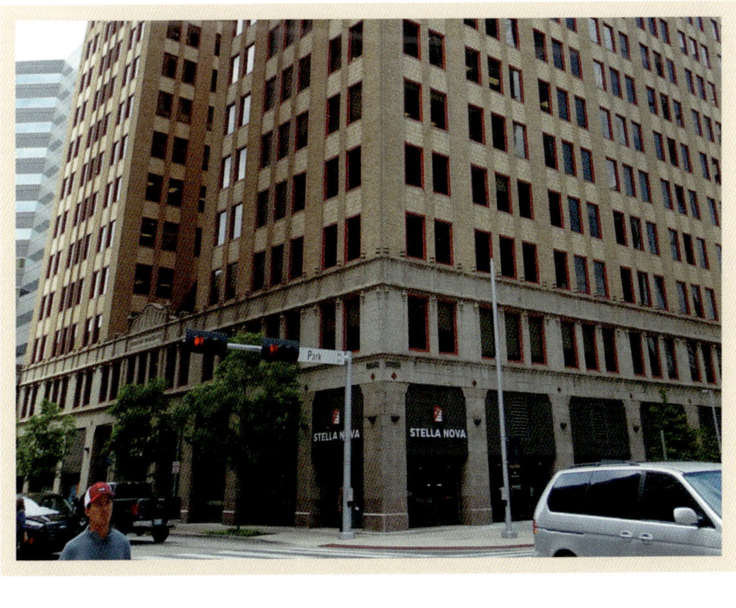

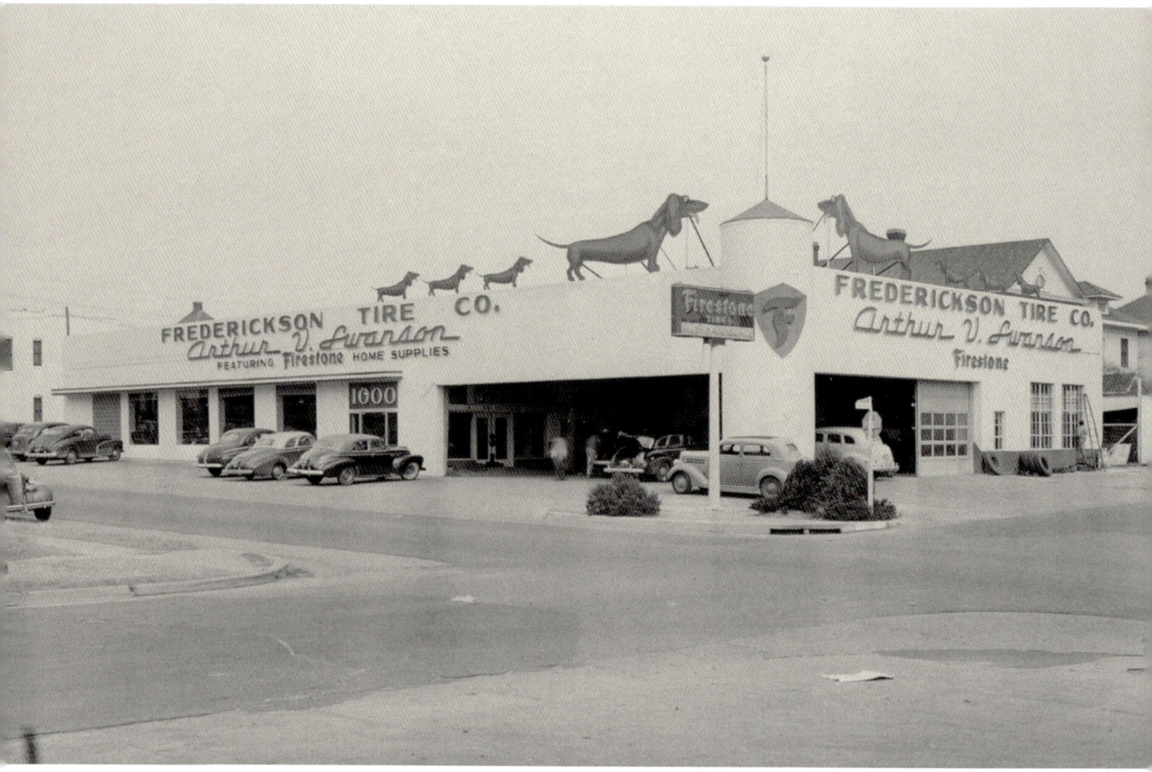

Oscar Frederickson founded what was then Frederickson Tire Co. in 1909. He married into the Swanson family, and over the years, the business morphed into Swanson's Tires at Northwest Ninth Street and Hudson Avenue. The building was renovated several times before Crouse sold it in 2015 to investors who converted it into a mix of restaurants, shops, and entertainment. (Past, courtesy of Oklahoma Historical Society.)

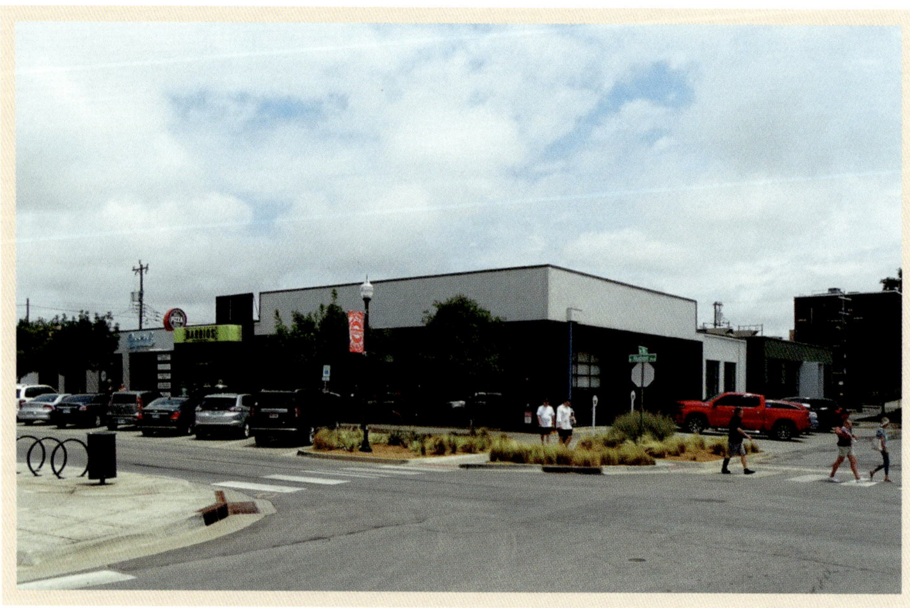

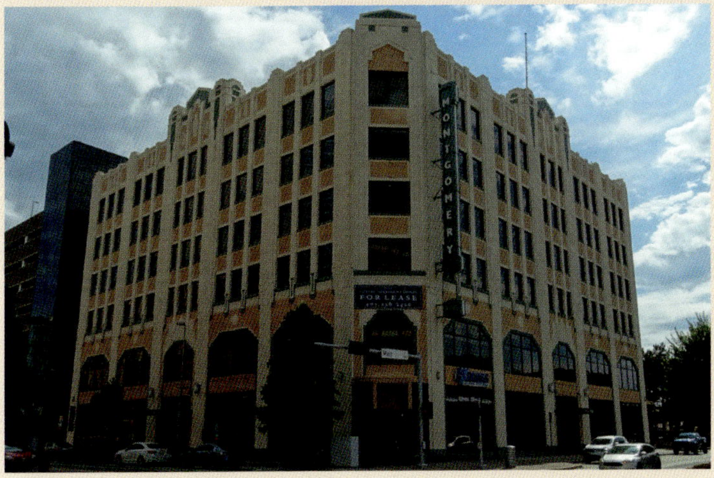

Montgomery Ward was one of ten department stores that opened downtown in the 1920s. The six-story department store opened at 500 West Main Street in 1928 and was one of the more ornate retail anchors. The store closed in 1966 as shopping moved to suburban malls. The building was converted into offices in the 1980s. Developer Dick Tanenbaum renovated the building in 2006 and turned it into apartments, naming it the Montgomery. (Past, courtesy of Oklahoma Historical Society.)

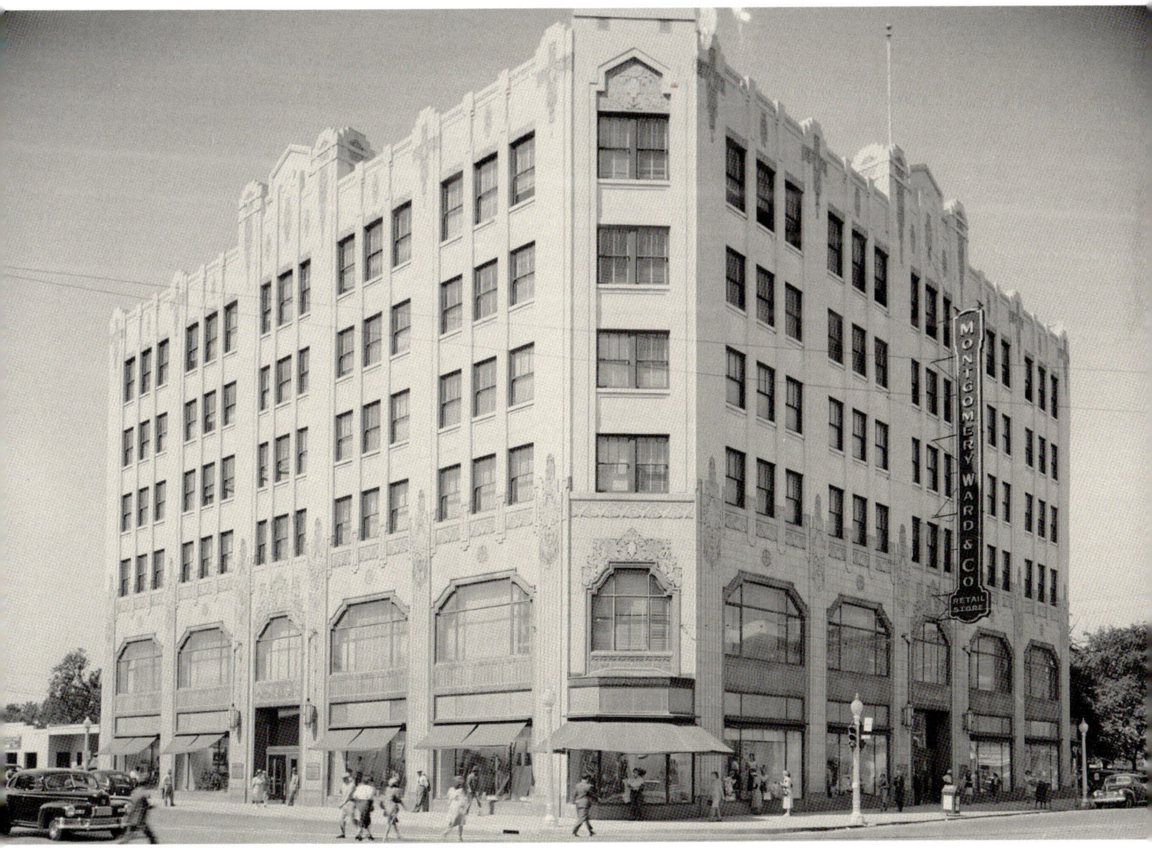

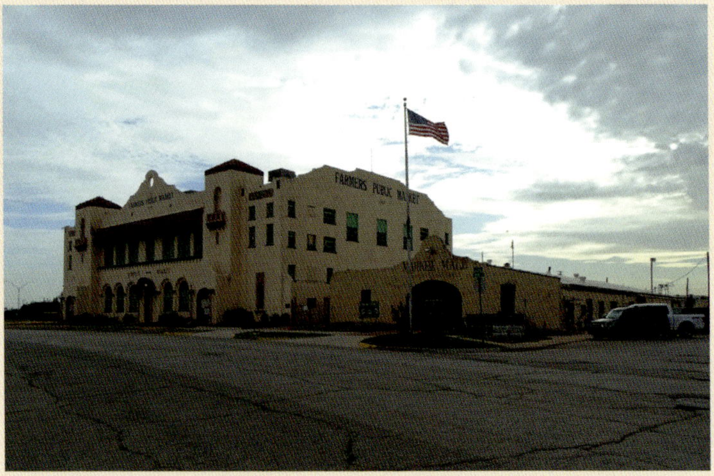

Oklahoma City was struggling with makeshift produce vendors operating in unsanitary conditions when a deal was made with John J. Harden to limit sales in a public market he would open at 311 South Klein Avenue in 1928. The two-story, 40,000-square-foot market featured a roller-skating rink and event venue upstairs but fell into disuse in the 1990s. It was purchased and renovated by Burt and Jody McAnally in 2002. (Past, courtesy of Oklahoma Historical Society.)

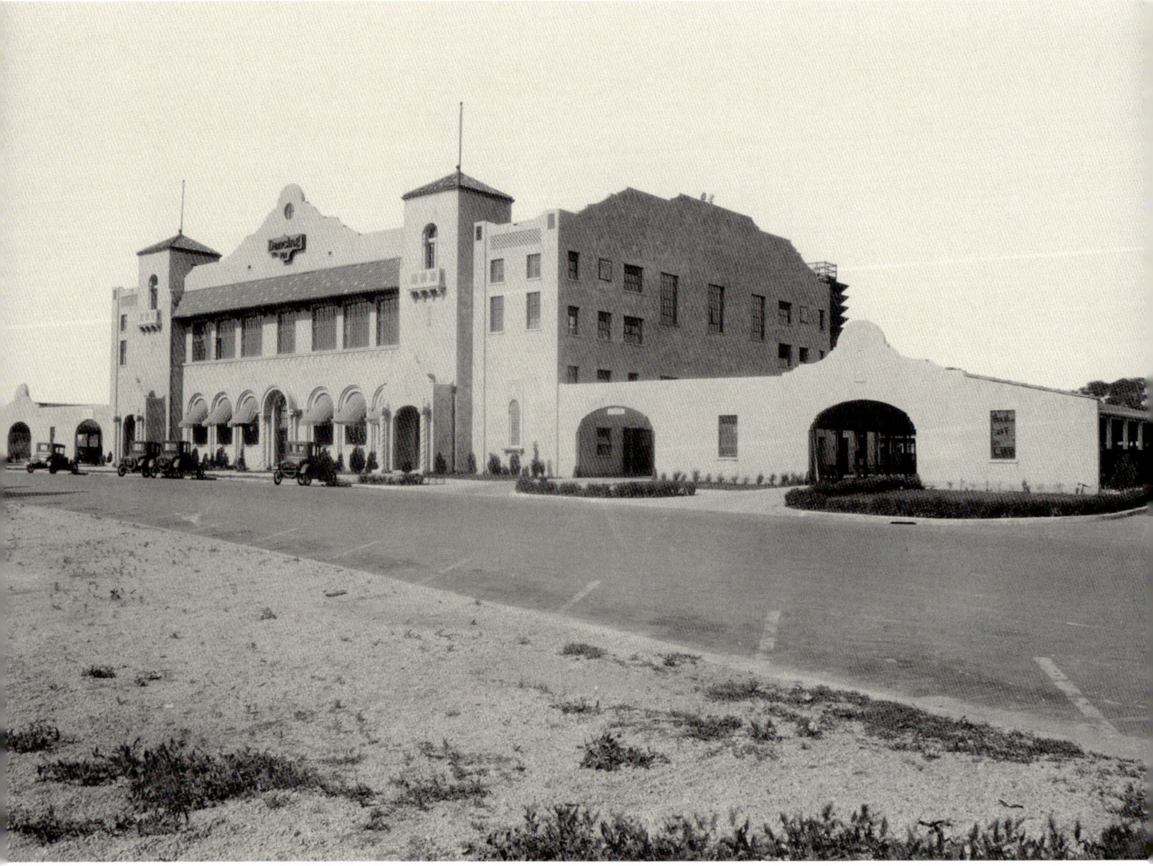

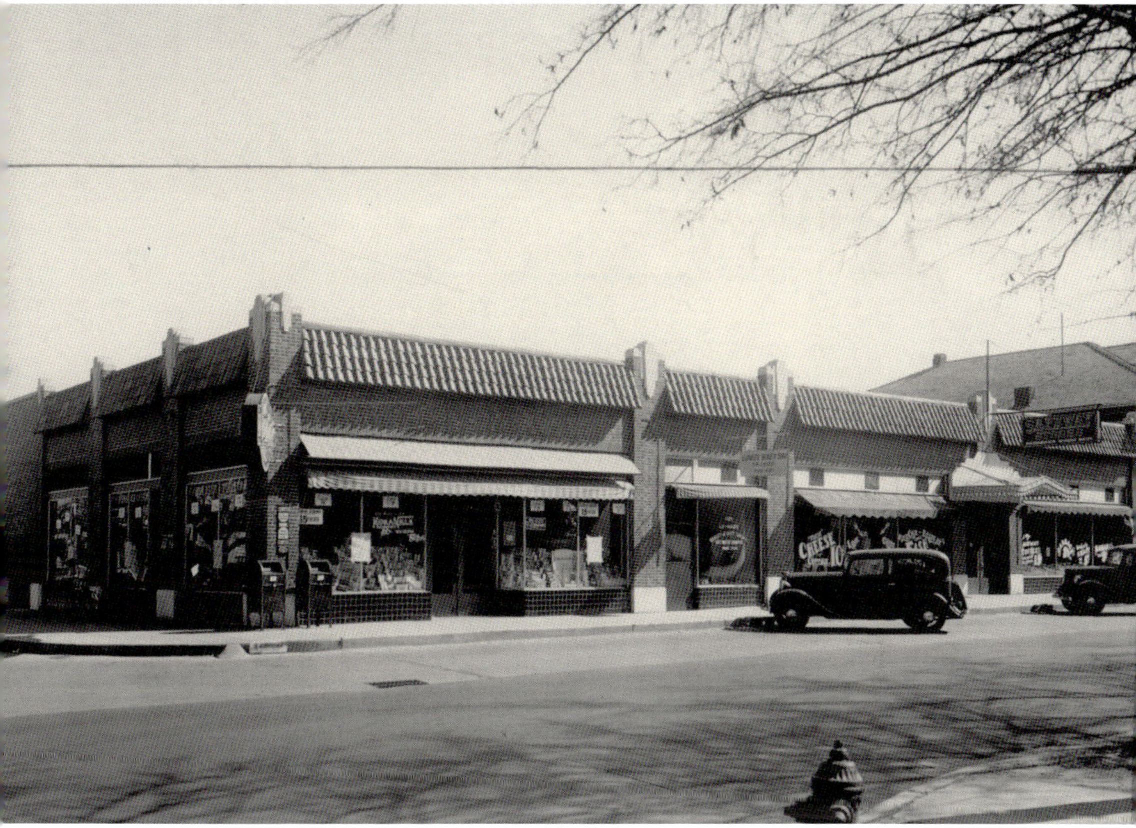

Safeway, a national grocery chain, had several locations in Oklahoma City when it opened a neighborhood store at 1120 North Robinson Avenue in 1928. The store closed in the early 1950s, and for the next 30 years, it was home to a surgical supply firm. As of 2022, the building was home to Three Circle Arts. (Past, courtesy of Oklahoma Historical Society.)

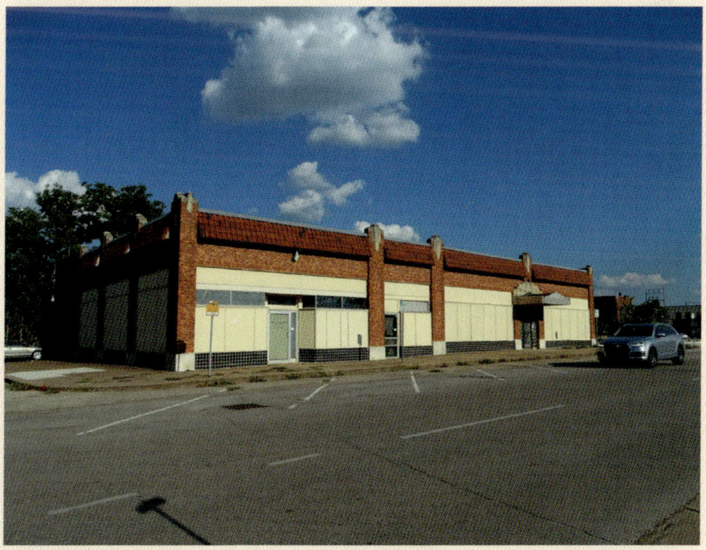

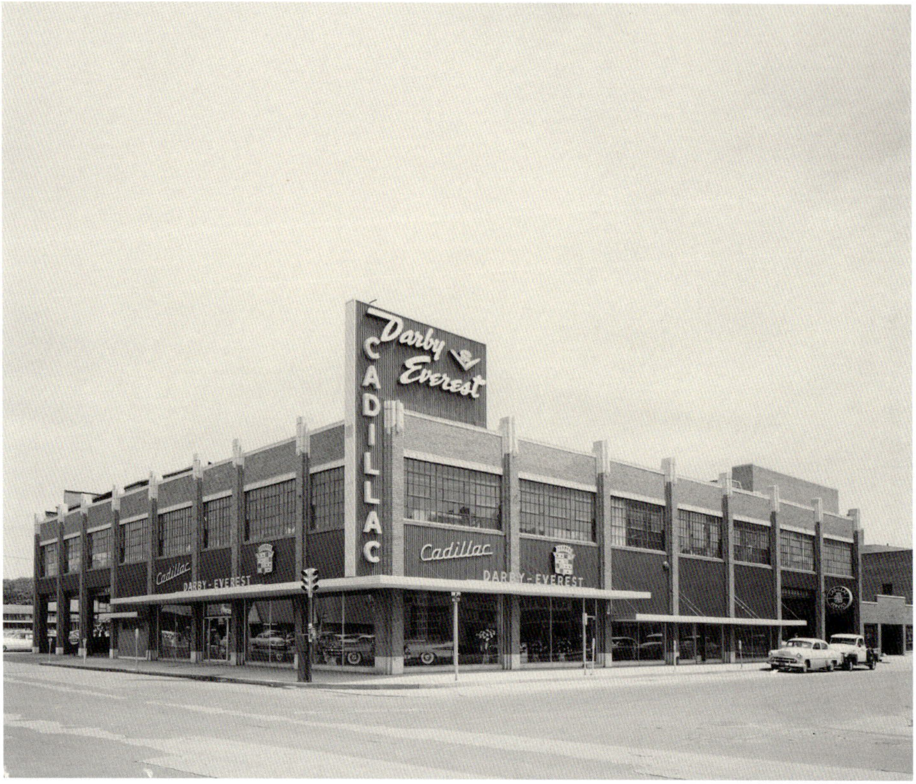

Greenlease-Moore operated several dealerships in the 1920s, including a three-story Chevrolet showroom. It was built in 1929 at 400 North Walker Avenue. The dealership switched to Cadillac sales, which continued under Darby Everest and then Bob Moore. Cadillac sales at that location ended in 1994 when the dealership moved to north Oklahoma City. The building was bought by Rick Dowell and turned into offices in 1910. (Past, courtesy of Oklahoma Historical Society.)

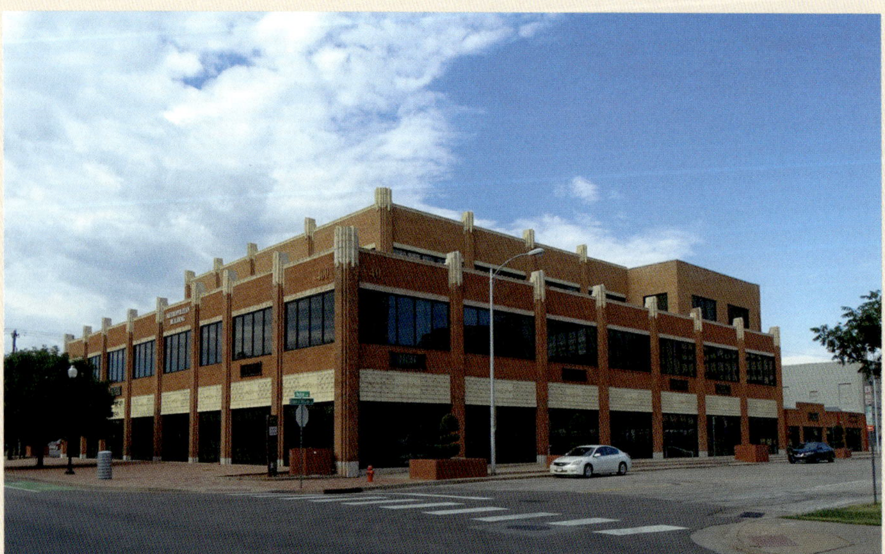

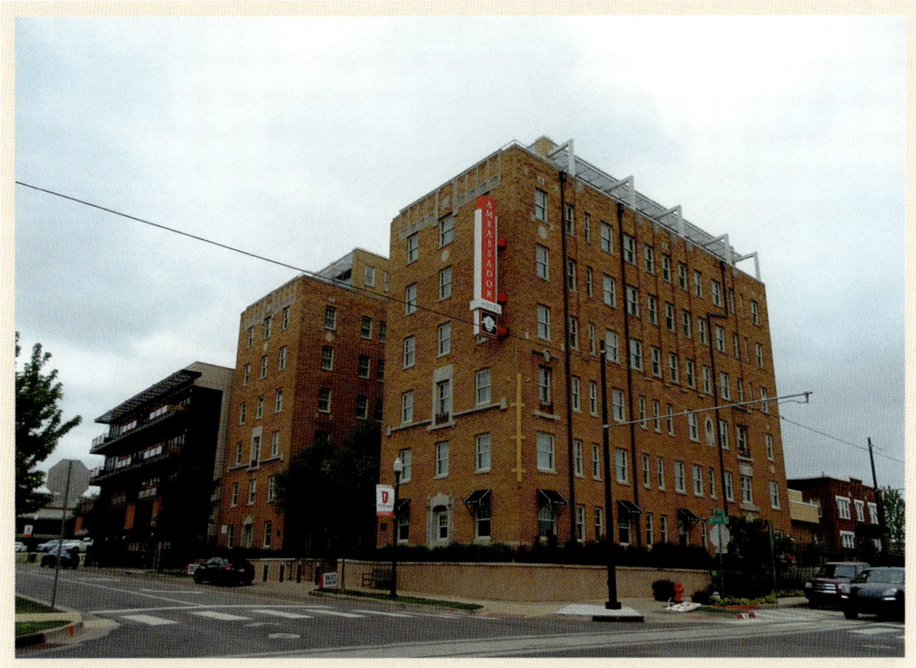

The Osler Building, 1200 North Walker Avenue, was built in 1929 as offices for doctors at nearby St. Anthony and Mercy hospitals, but it was reduced to low-end space before it was renovated into the Ambassador Hotel. The adjoining garage was renovated into apartments and retail by Midtown Renaissance Group. (Past, courtesy of Oklahoma Historical Society.)

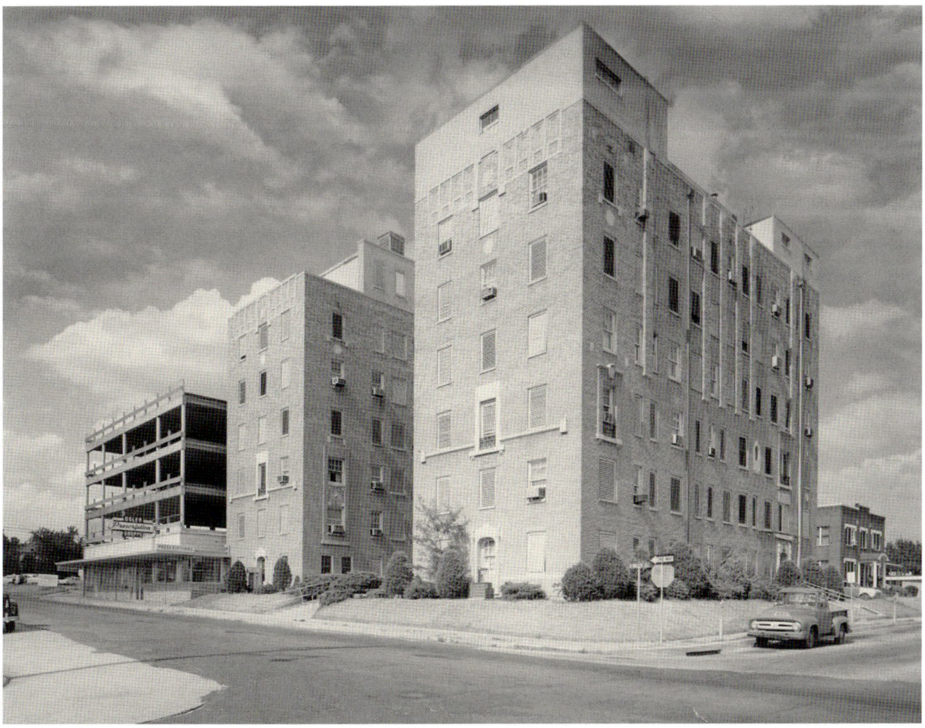

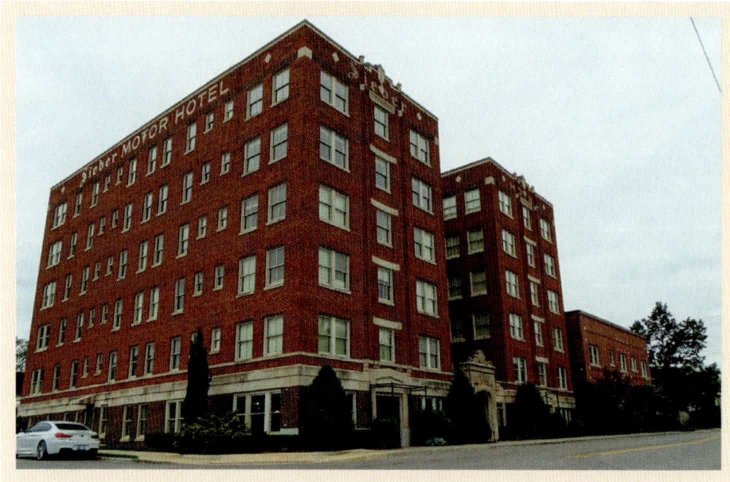

German immigrant Robert Sieber settled in Oklahoma. He erected a two-story building at 1311 North Hudson Avenue in 1922 that was home to his grocery and butcher shop and upstairs apartment and leased the remaining space to a pharmacy. Six years later, he built the six-story Sieber Apartments Hotel. The buildings were preserved into apartments by Marva Ellard in 2008. (Past, courtesy of the Oklahoma Historical Society; present, courtesy of the *Oklahoman*).

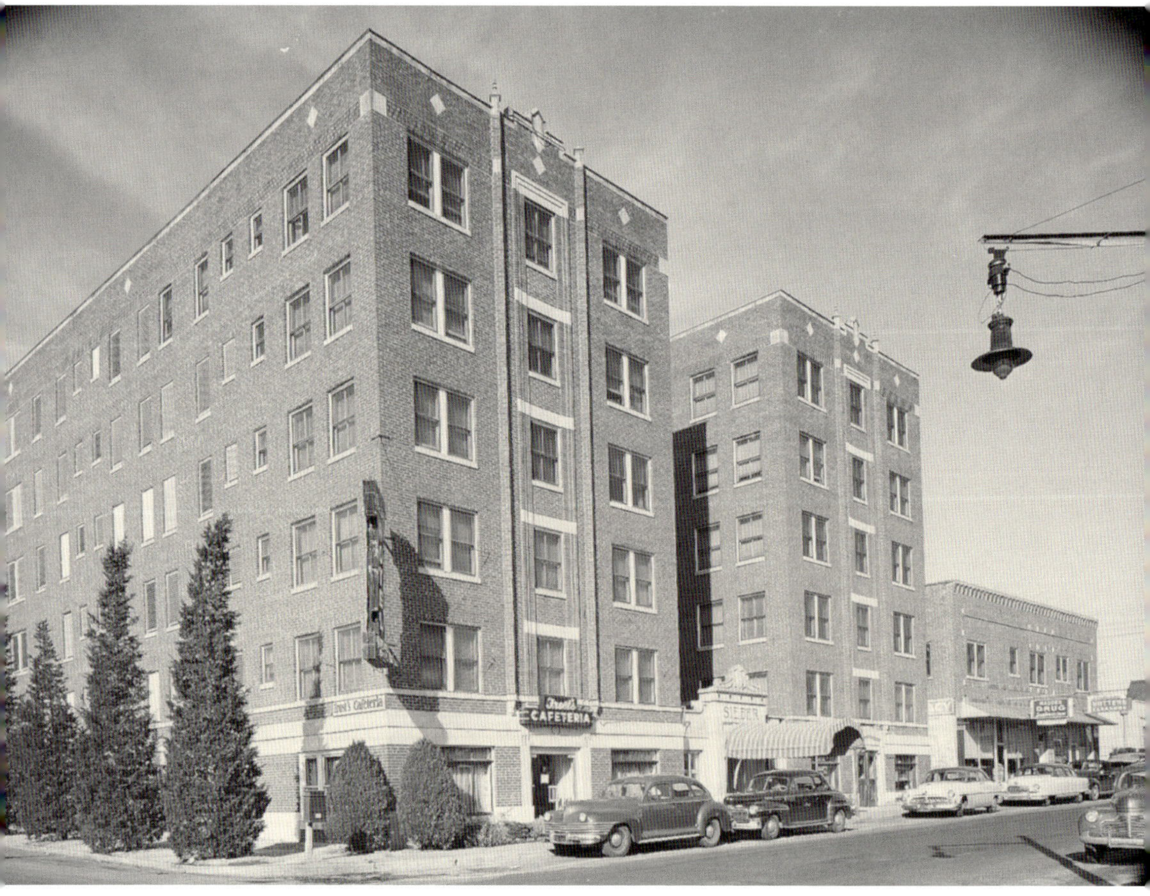

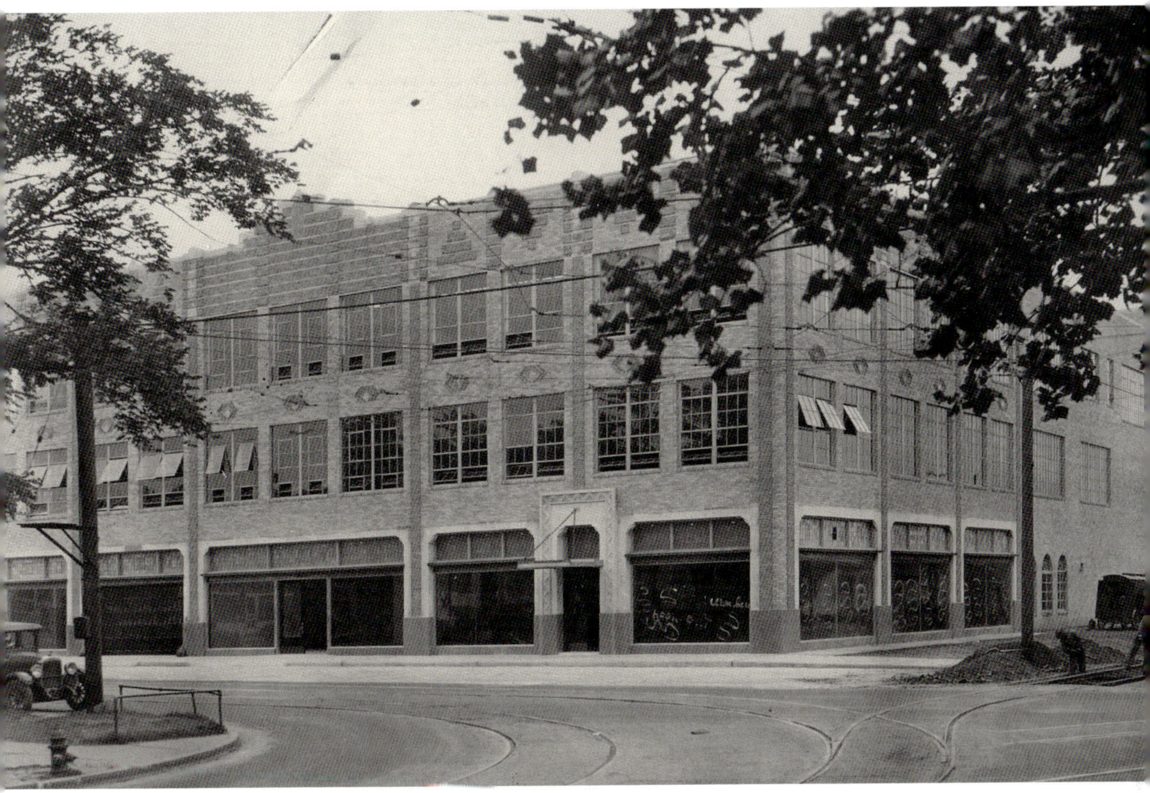

After outgrowing the first dealership opened along Automobile Alley, Norton-Johnson Buick expanded and built a larger showroom in 1930 at 113 Northwest Thirteenth Street. Developers Nick Preftakes and Mark Ruffin bought the building in 1994 from car dealer Don Bolen and converted it into the Garage Lofts. Because the building was once a car dealership, it has a parking ramp throughout, and residents are able to park indoors on the same level as their apartments. (Past, courtesy of Oklahoma Historical Society.)

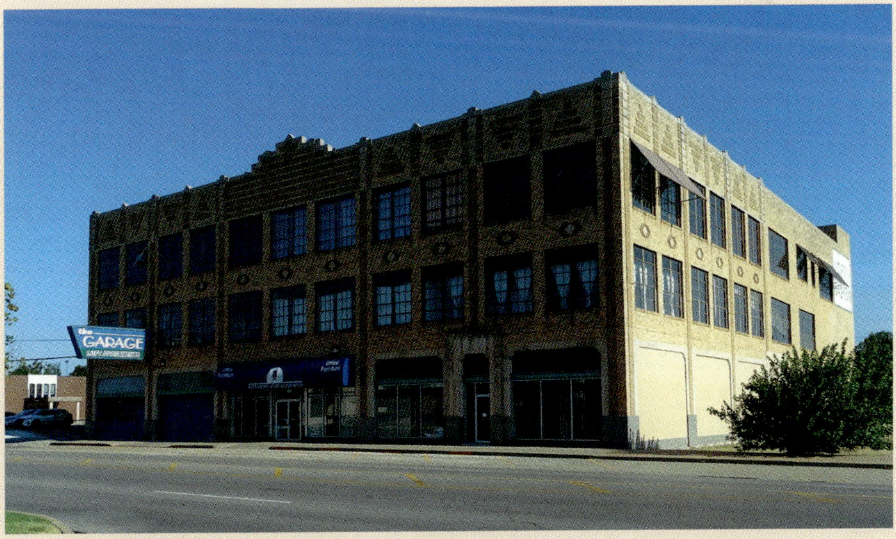

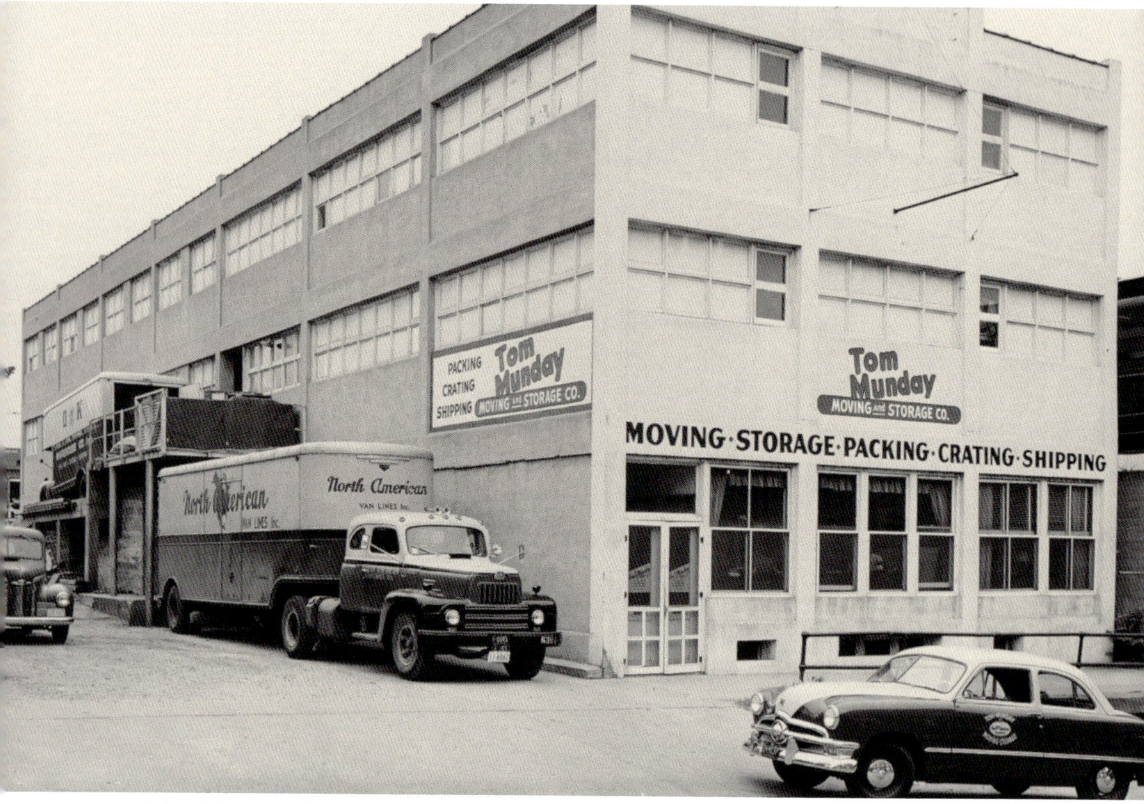

Built in 1930 along the Burlington Northern and Santa Fe (BNSF) Railway tracks, a three-story concrete and brick building at 6 Northeast Sixth Street was home for Tom Munday Moving and Storage for 44 years before it ceased operations in the 1980s. Peter and Linda Mandel bought the building in 2004 and spent the next 14 years renovating the 21,000-square-foot building and converting it into their home. (Past, courtesy of Oklahoma Historical Society.)

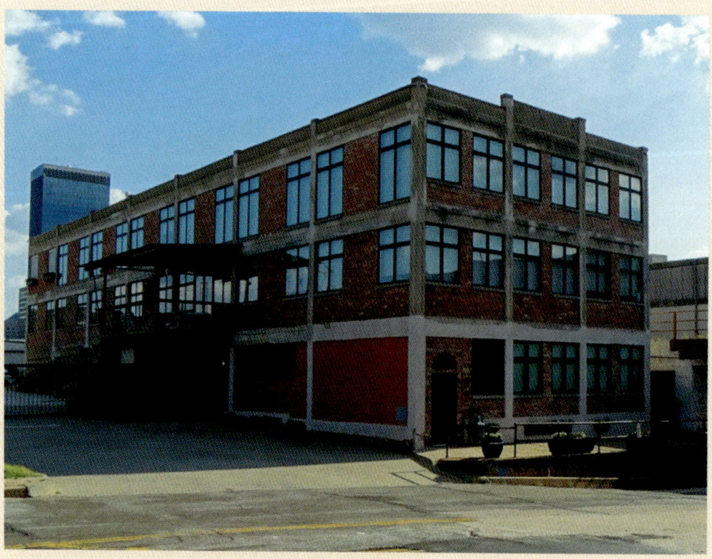

CHAPTER 2

SKYSCRAPER SKYLINE

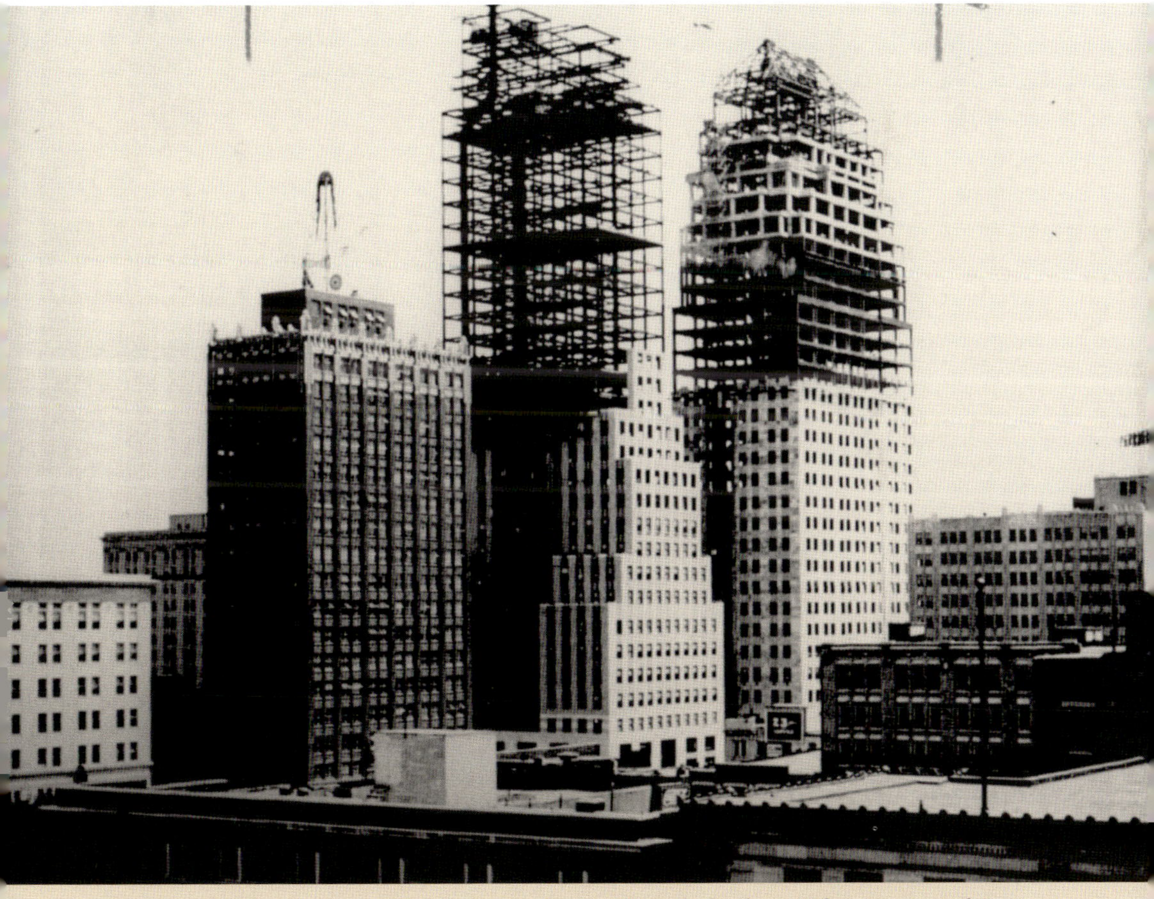

The Great Depression was wrecking the national economy in 1931, but Oklahoma City, boosted by new oil fortunes, was still thriving. Residents gathered daily to watch the "Great Skyscraper Race," in which oilman Walter Ramsey and First National Bank, flush with oil money, sought to be the first to build the city's tallest skyscraper. (Courtesy of the *Oklahoman*.)

American First National Bank and Security National Bank merged in 1930 to form First National Bank and Trust Company. Four months later, the new bank announced plans to build the city's tallest tower at 120 North Robinson Avenue. The bank succumbed in 1986 to the 1980s oil crash. After years of neglect and decline, the 33-story tower, anchored by a hotel, apartments, and retail, reopened in 2022. (Past, courtesy of Oklahoma Historical Society.)

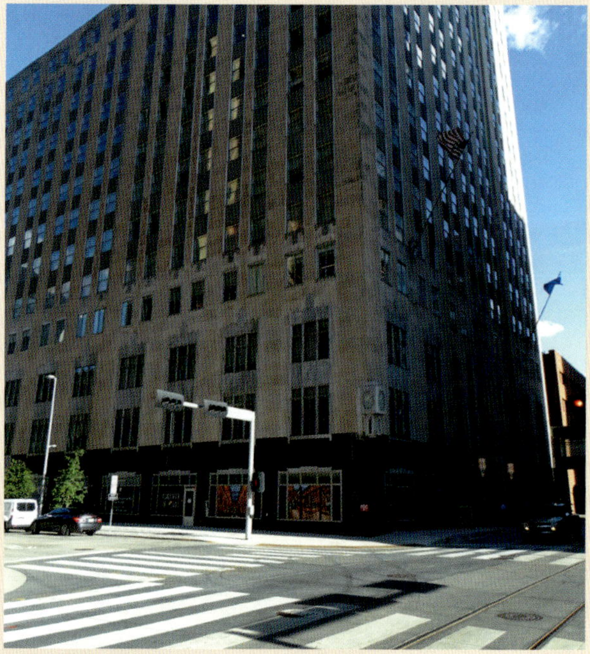

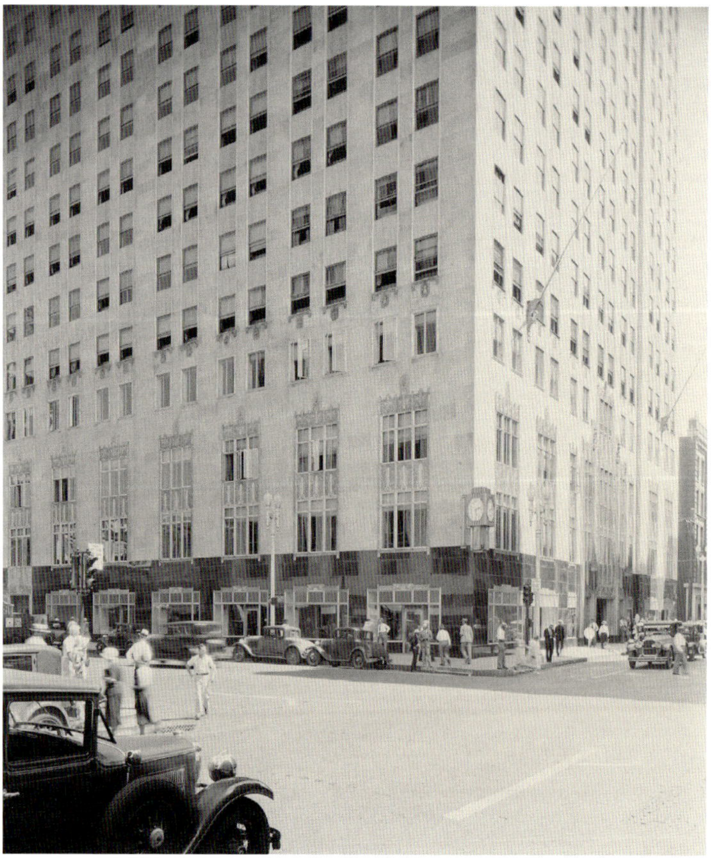

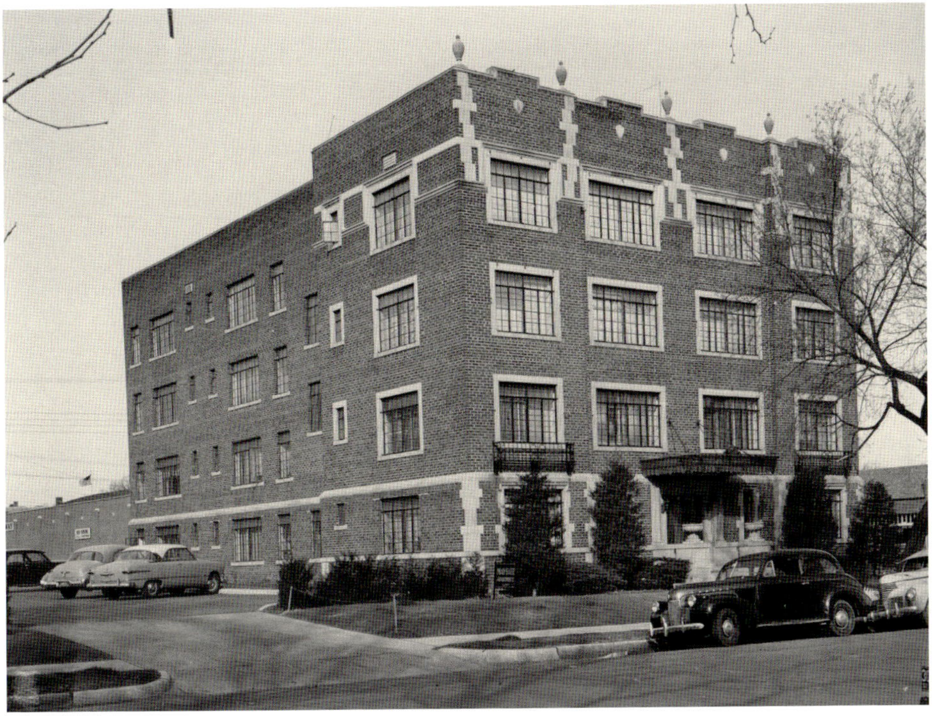

The Mayfair, 1315 North Broadway Place, was home to some of Oklahoma City's wealthiest residents when it opened in 1931. It fell into disuse in the 1970s, and in 1990, it was turned into a headquarters for the United Way of Central Oklahoma. The building was restored as apartments in 2013 by Midtown Renaissance Group. (Past, courtesy of Oklahoma Historical Society.)

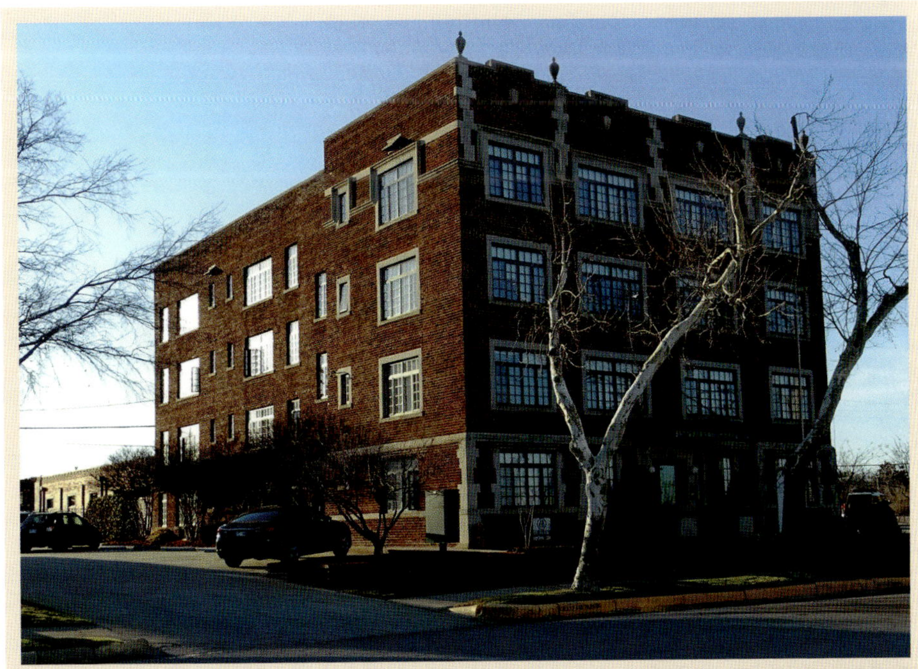

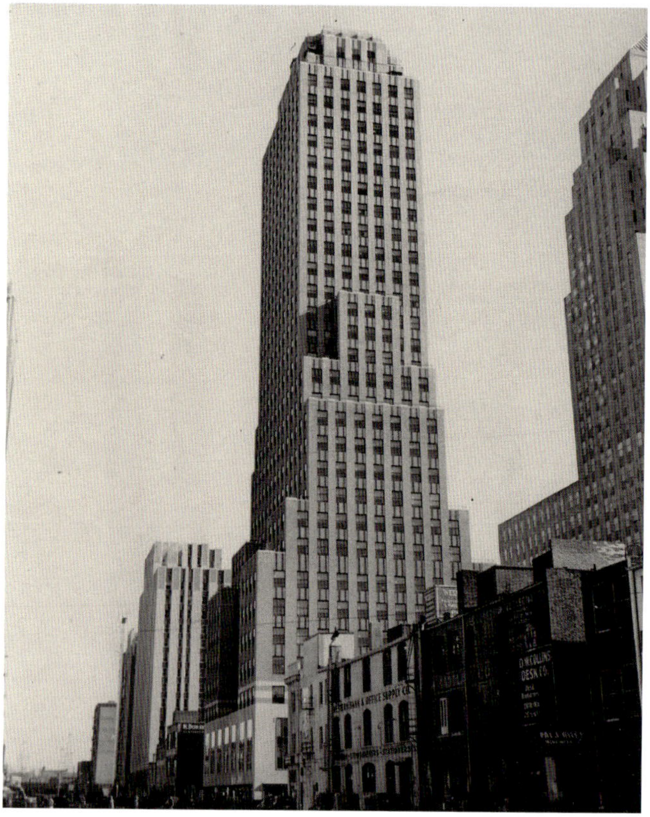

After acquiring the northeast corner of Park and Robinson Avenues, oilman Arthur Ramsey started a race with First National Bank to see which could open first. Ramsey's 33-story tower won the race, but the oilman's fortunes were short-lived due to the Great Depression. The building was later anchored by APCO, an oil and gas company, and then Liberty Bank. Now named City Place, the tower is a mix of offices and condominiums. (Past, courtesy of Oklahoma Historical Society.)

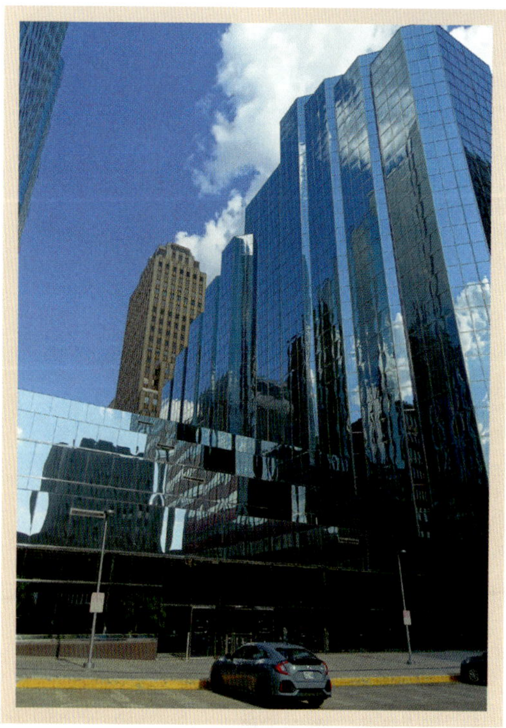

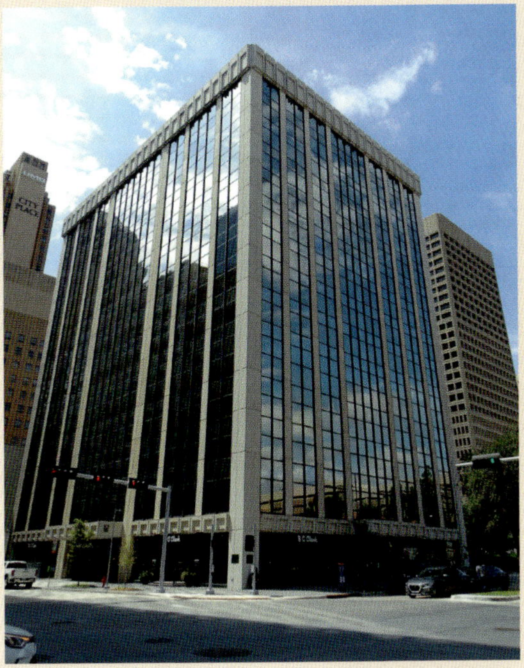

In 1931, hotelier W.B. Skirvin started building Skirvin Tower, which was intended it to be a 26-story, 700-room addition to his Skirvin Hotel across the street. The Great Depression and family disputes delayed the project several times, and construction stopped at 14 floors. A bank gutted the building and replaced a brick and marble Art Deco facade with glass and concrete. The renamed 101 Park Avenue Building is leased for offices. (Past, courtesy of Oklahoma Historical Society.)

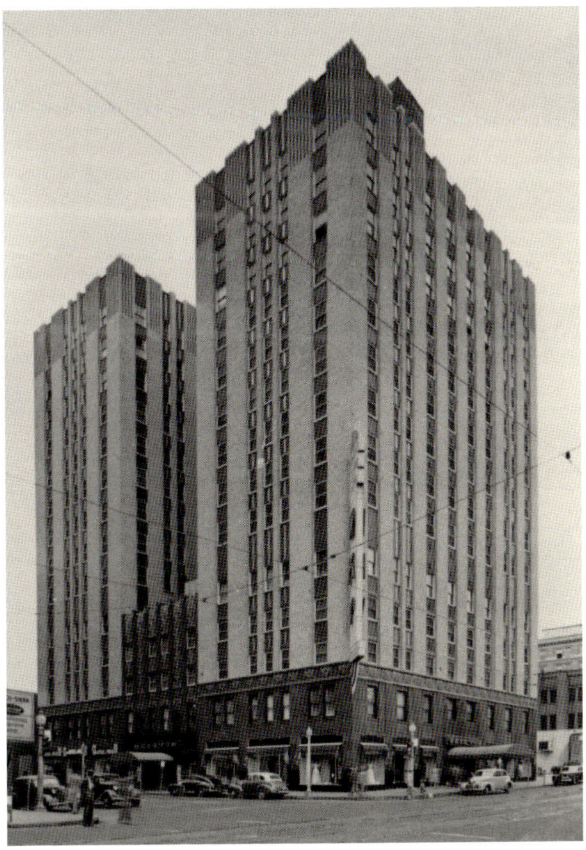

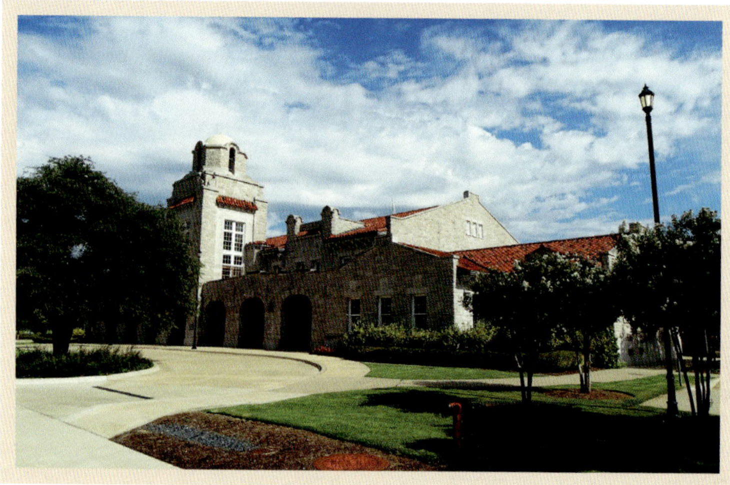

Union Station was built in 1931 for the Frisco and Rock Island Railroads when they were displaced to remove tracks that divided downtown. The expansive building opened to rave reviews and featured a large lobby with a vaulted 20-foot-high ceiling and marble walls and floor. Passenger train service ended in 1967, and the station fell into disrepair. Businessman Thurman Magbee rescued and preserved the building, which is now a part of Scissortail Park. (Past, courtesy of Oklahoma Historical Society.)

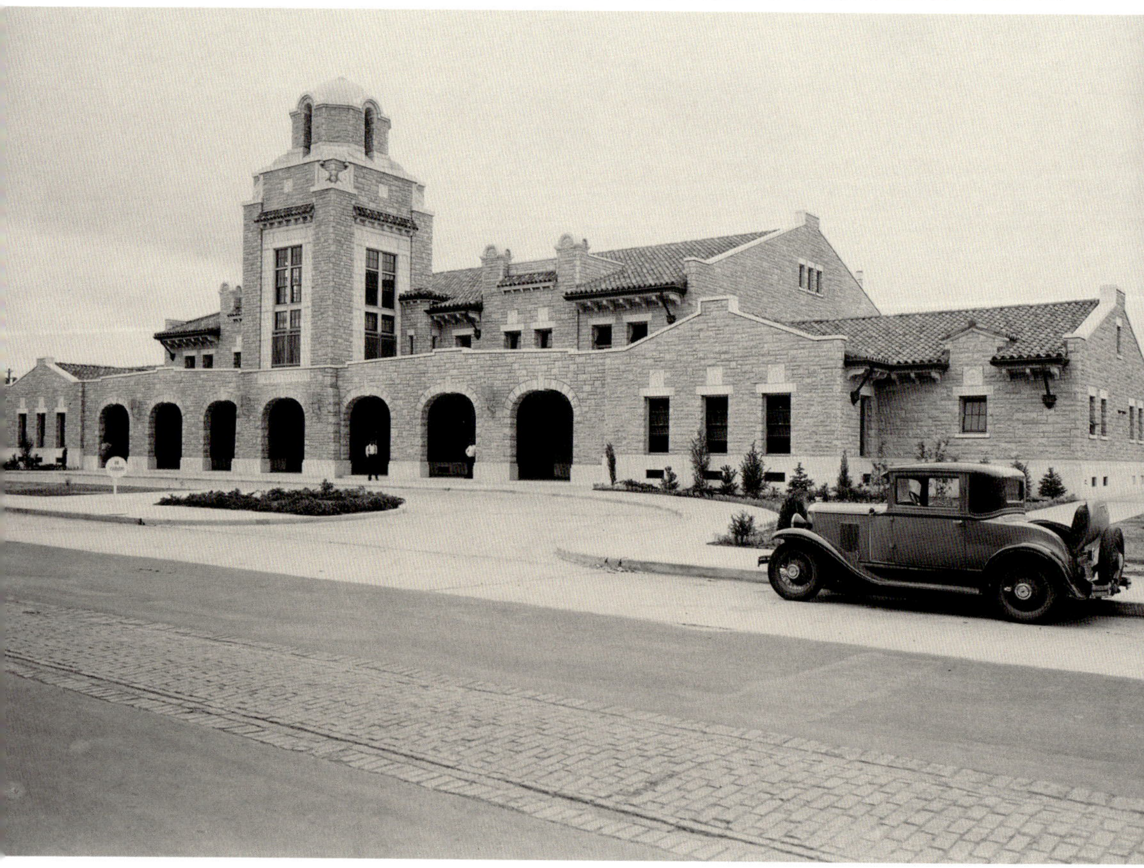

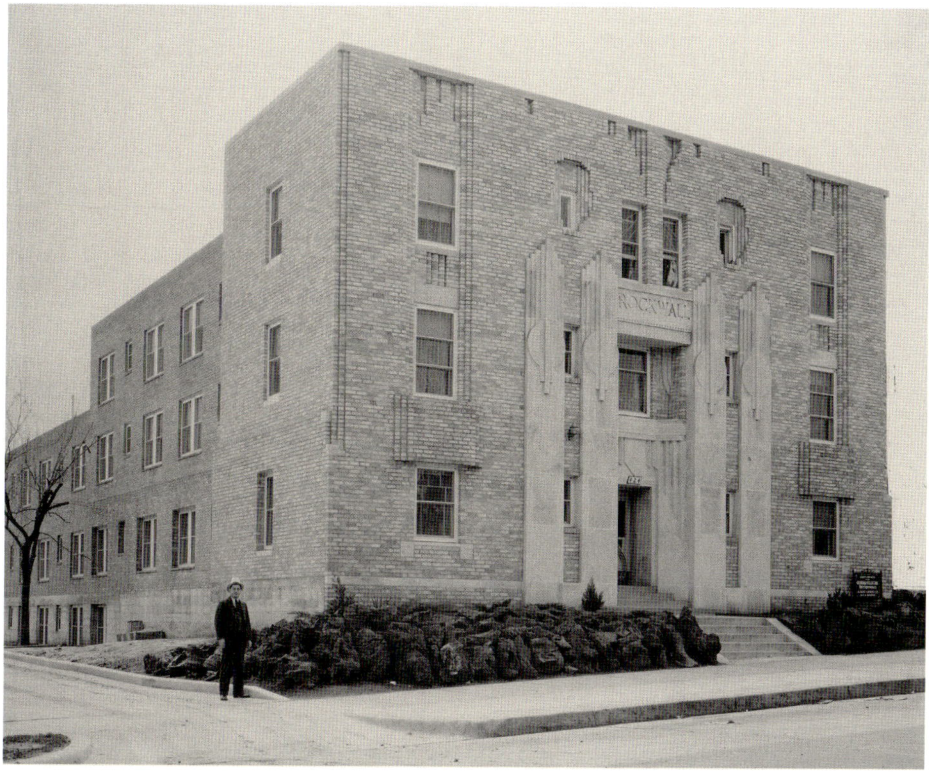

Northwest Sixth Street was a tree-lined, two-lane residential street when the Rockwall Apartments were built in the early 1930s at 424 Northwest Thirteenth Street. The street was widened and turned into a five-lane-wide commercial corridor as downtown continued to grow north to Northwest Thirteenth Street. The apartment house in 2022 was one of the last low-rent rooming houses left downtown as others were renovated into upscale housing. (Past, courtesy of Oklahoma Historical Society.)

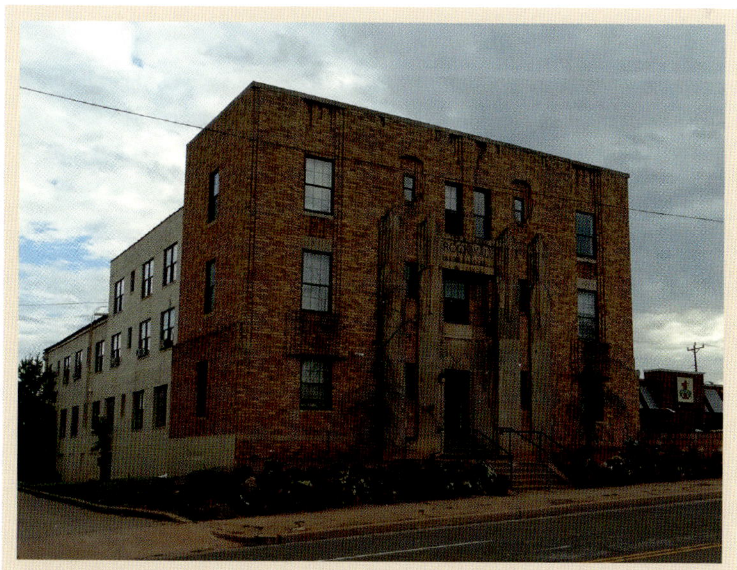

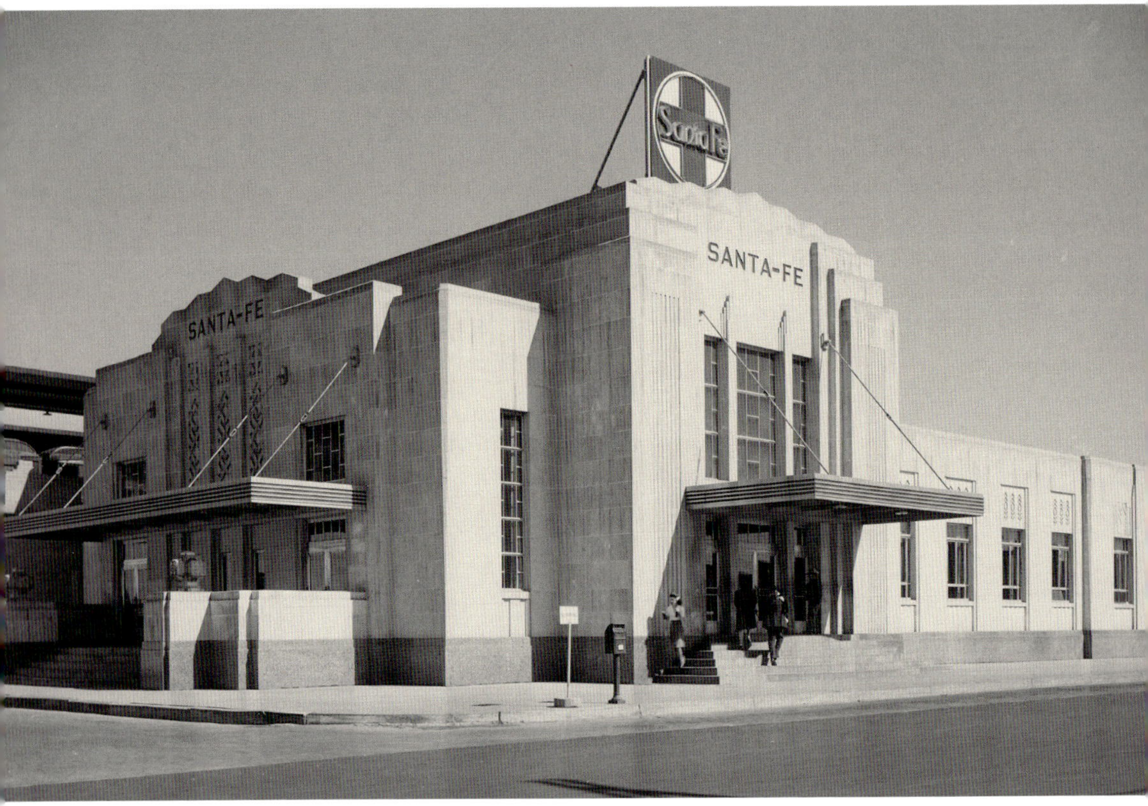

Oklahoma Station was the first rail stop in Oklahoma City, opening in 1887 two years before the area was opened for settlement in the first Land Run. The current Santa Fe Station was built on the same location in 1934. The station's Art Deco architecture is seen inside and out. The station fell into disrepair when Amtrak cut stops in 1979 but was restored when service was restored in 1999. (Past, courtesy of Oklahoma Historical Society.)

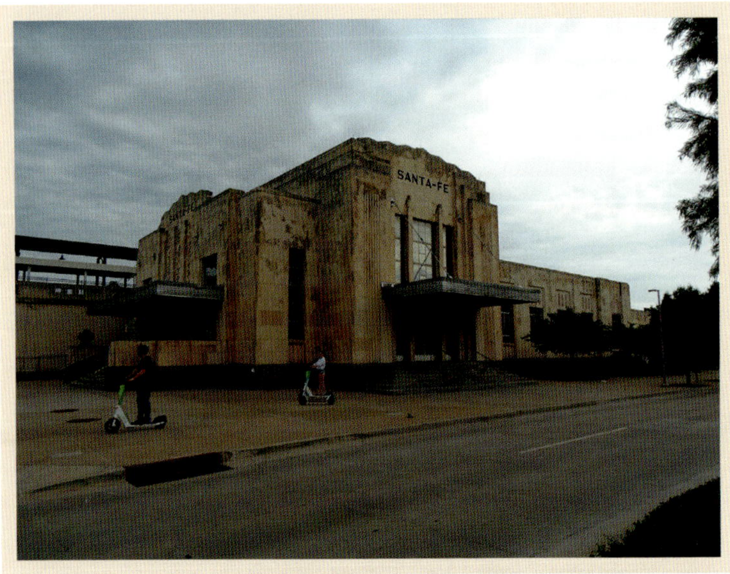

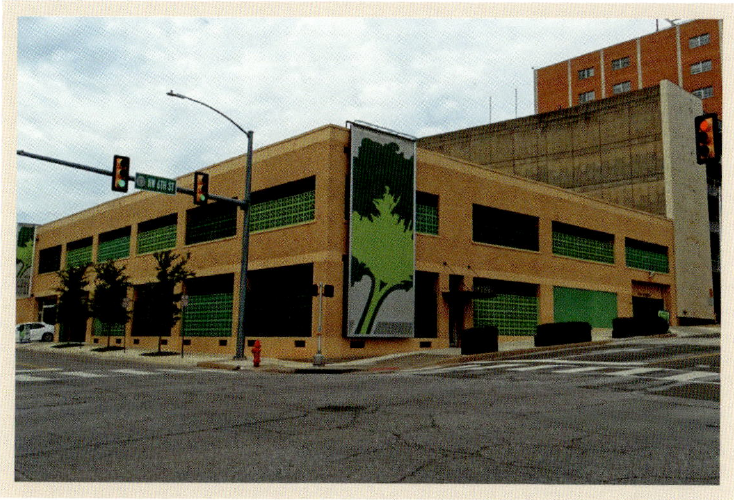

When built in 1935, the two-story building at 231 Northwest Sixth Street operated as a Packard dealership. King's Furniture opened in 1946 only to be closed a few months later. Cox Furniture Exchange took over and operated until 1954. Gibson's Discount Store followed through the 1960s until 1975, when the building was bought by John Cheek and turned into a parking garage. The garage is now operated by the Oklahoma City National Memorial. (Past, courtesy of Oklahoma Historical Society.)

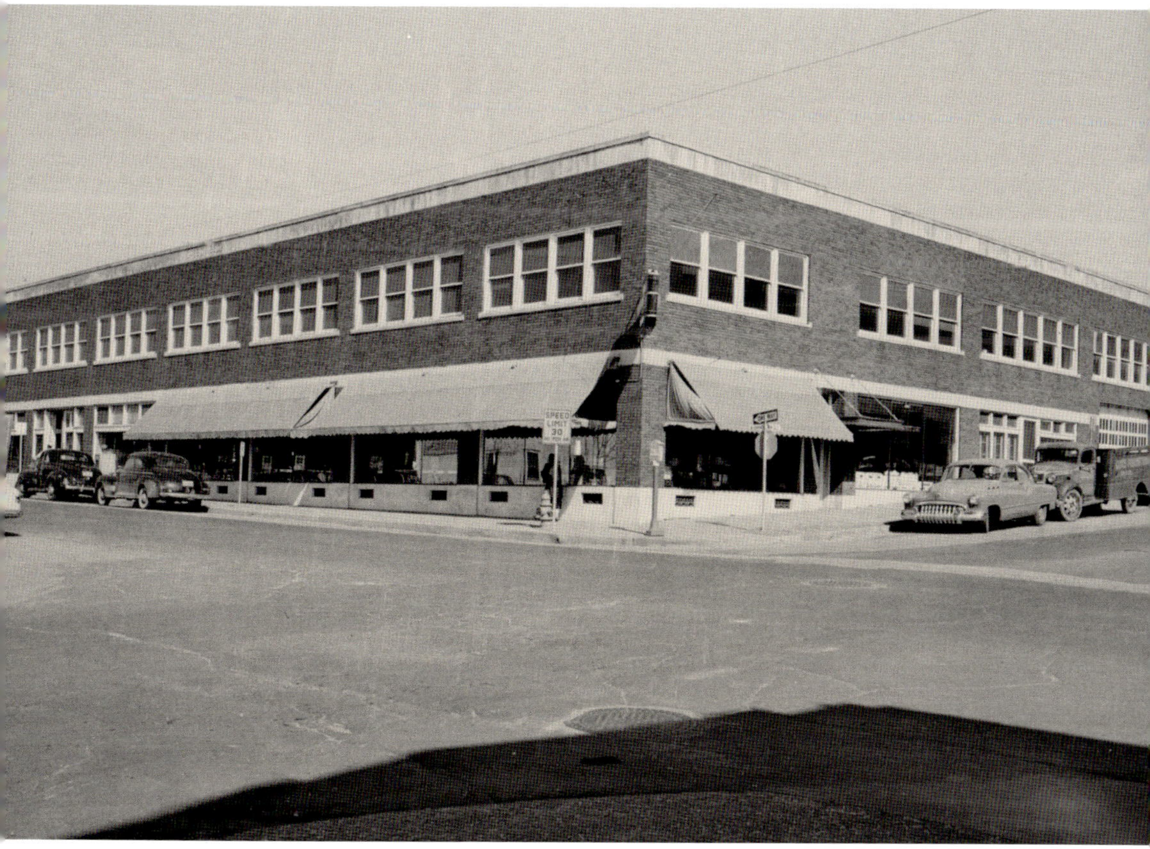

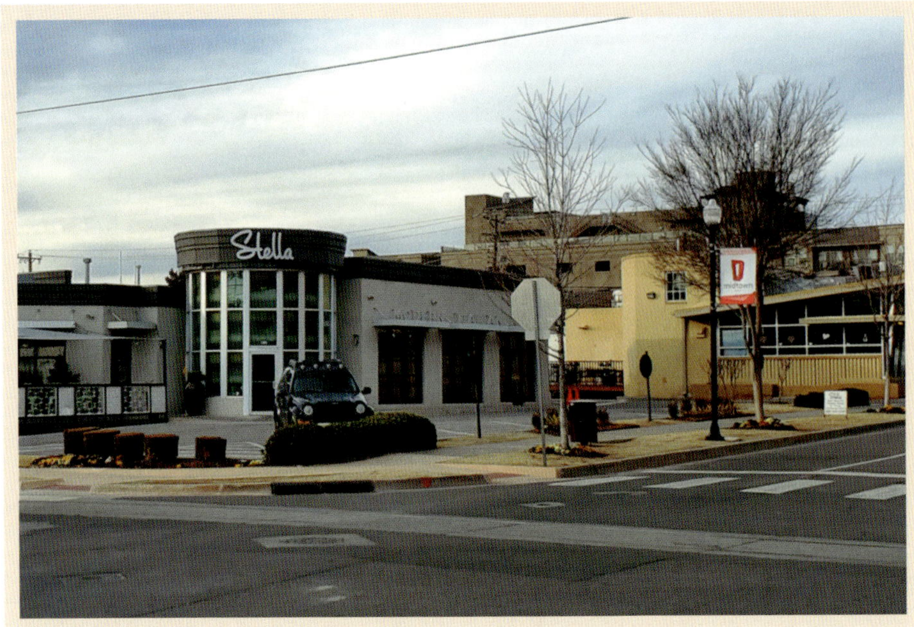

Anderson-Pritchard was a regional oil refinery operator and gasoline distributor started in Oklahoma City in 1919. The station at 1201 North Walker Avenue was built in 1936 in a futuristic style typical of the Googie movement that started the same decade. Anderson-Pritchard went defunct in 1961, and the station was home to several tenants until it was renovated into the Mexican restaurant 1492. (Past, courtesy of Oklahoma Historical Society.)

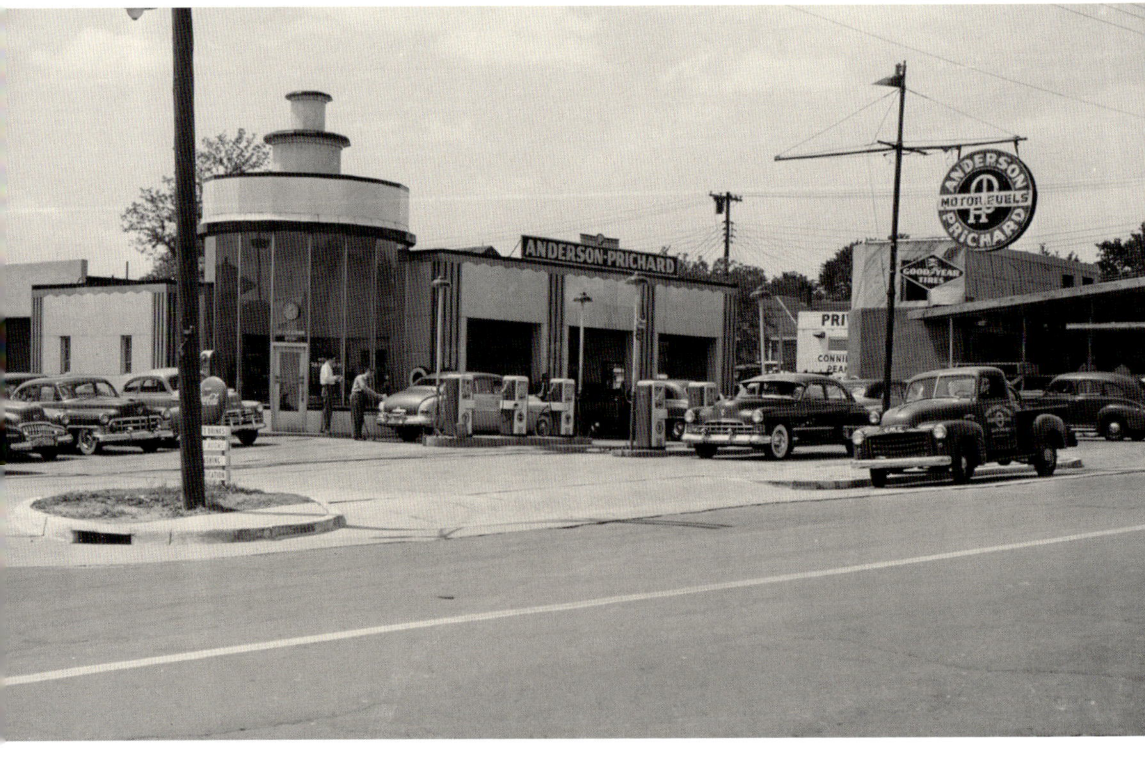

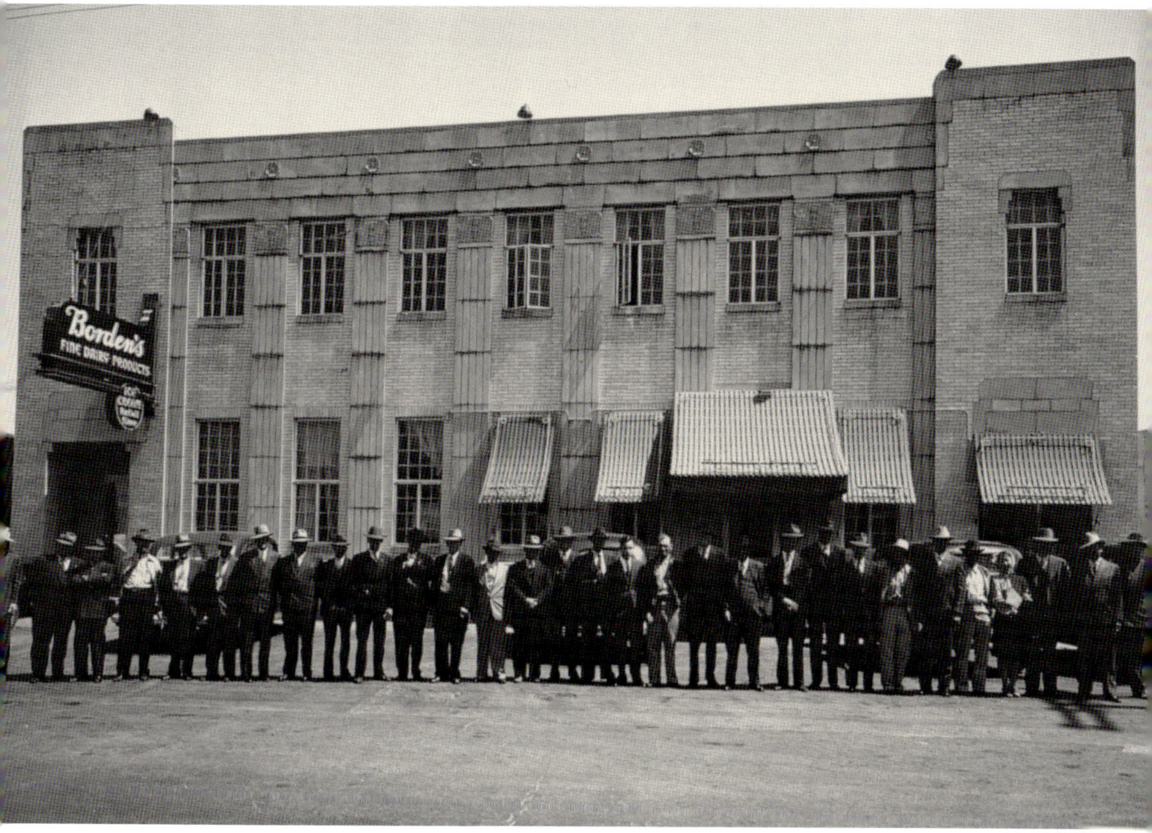

Borden Company was in the midst of a national expansion when, in 1937, it bought the Evans Dairy at Northwest Twenty-first Street and Broadway Avenue. A decade later, the company built what, at the time, was one of its largest dairies in the country. The plant closed in 1995. (Past, courtesy of Oklahoma Historical Society.)

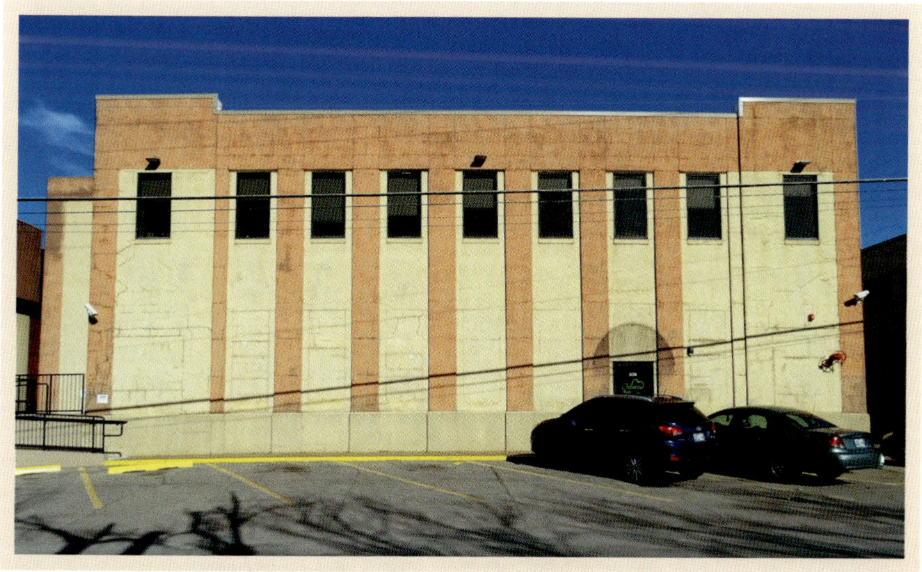

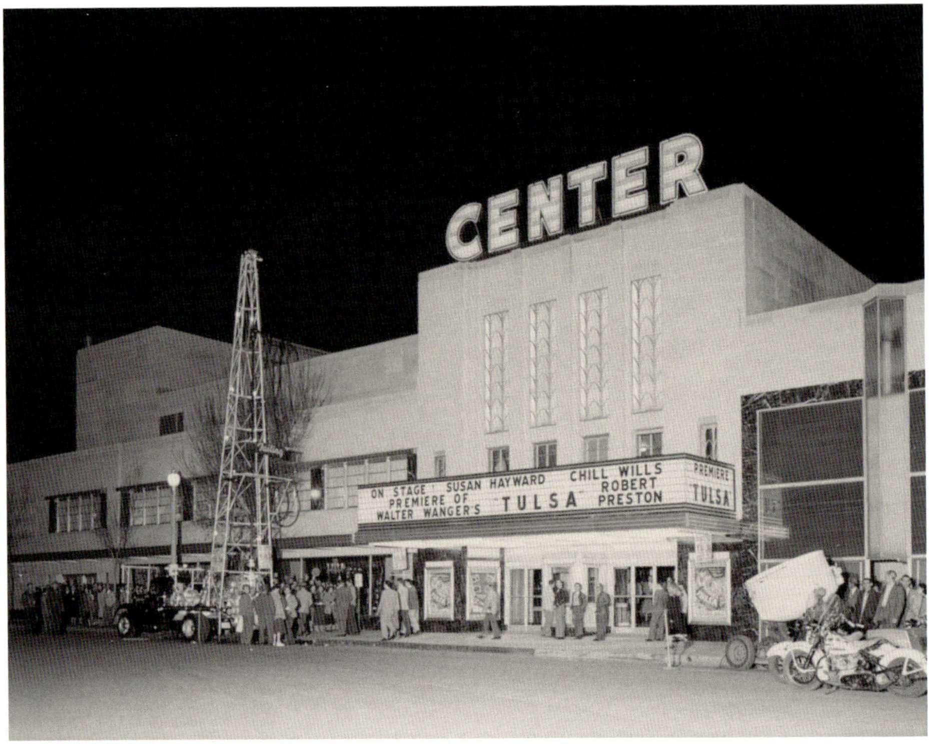

The 1,600-seat Art Deco–style Centre Theater opened on Christmas Day 1947. The theater struggled in the 1960s as it resorted to showing telecasts of sporting events and concerts. The theater closed in 1975 after the manager was arrested for showing X-rated films. It was the last-surviving movie theater downtown and facing demolition when it was bought by the Oklahoma City Museum of Art and renovated into a 250-seat theater. (Past, courtesy of the *Oklahoman*.)

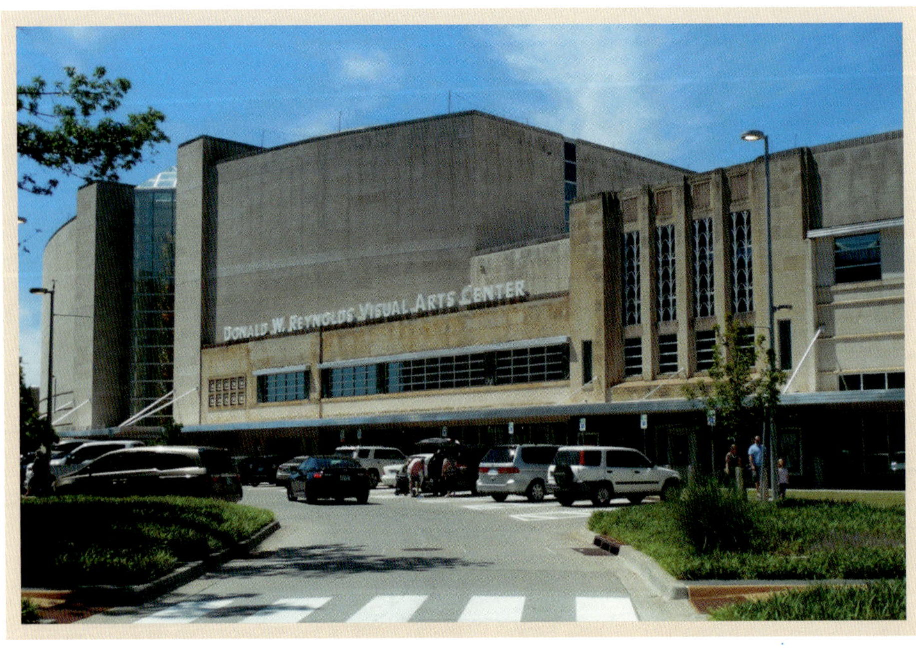

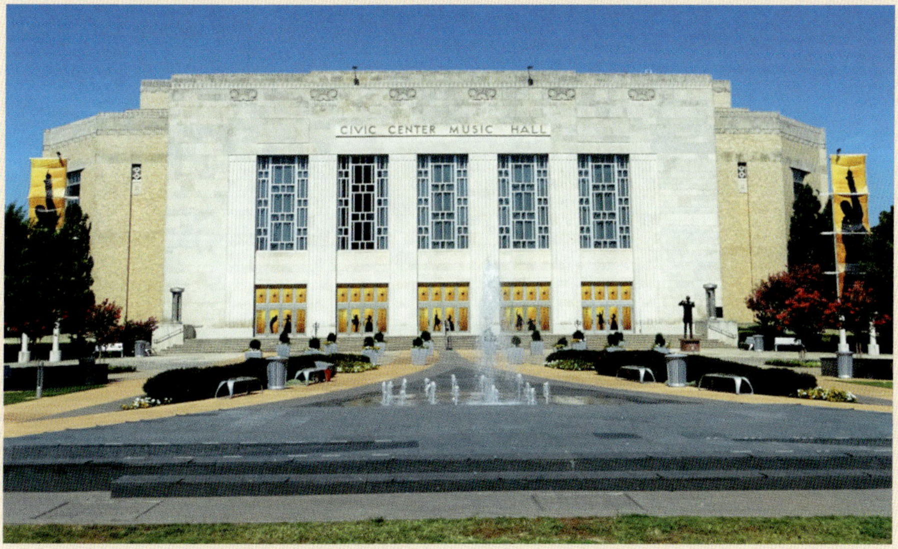

In 1937, Municipal Auditorium was built as part of the Civic Center, a public improvements package funded by the Public Works Administration and through bonds passed by voters. The original auditorium hosted conventions, basketball games, concerts, and plays. The building was turned into the Civic Center Music Hall in 1967. The auditorium was gutted in 2022 and replaced with a music hall while preserving the exterior and adjoining historic spaces. (Past, courtesy of the Oklahoma Historical Society.)

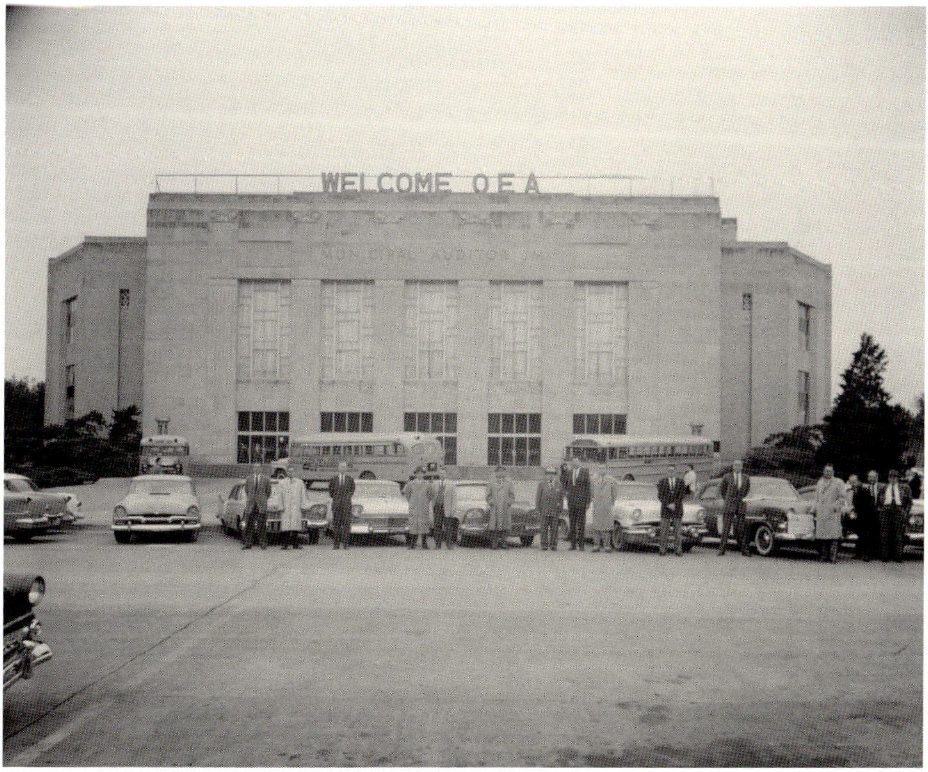

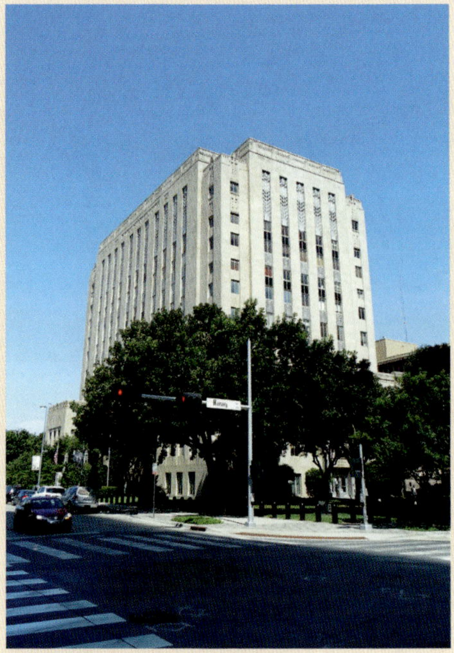

The Oklahoma County Courthouse on Park and Hudson Avenues was built in 1937 as one of four buildings constructed as part of the Civic Center. The courthouse was built with funds from the Public Works Administration, matched by a city bond issue, for a total of $1.1 million. Designed by architects Layton and Forsythe, the six-story building also housed the jail in the top two floors until the current jail was built in 1991. (Photo courtesy of the Oklahoma Historical Society.)

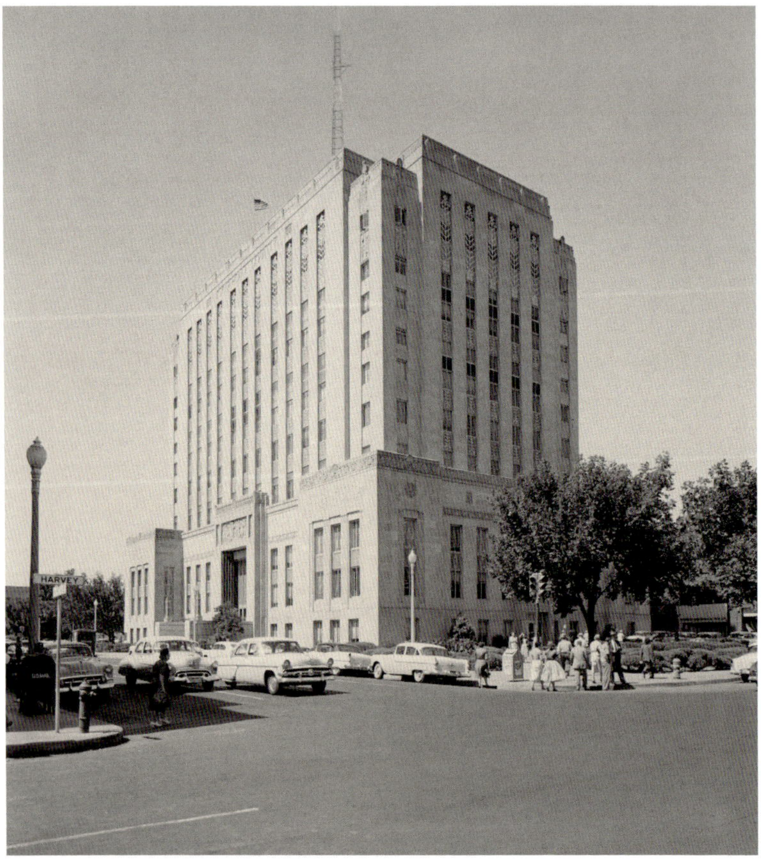

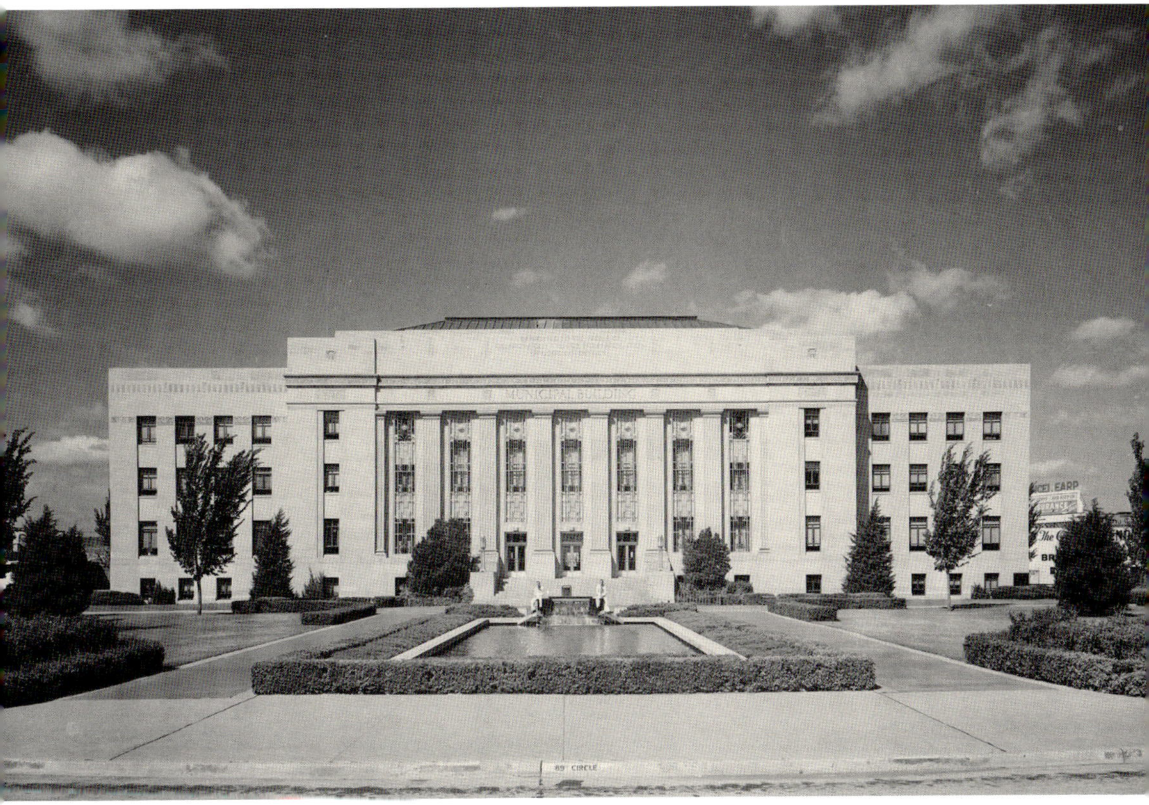

City hall is one of four structures that was considered part of the Civic Center complex; the others were the Civic Center Music Hall, county courthouse, and the police headquarters, all built in the mid-1930s. The Art Deco building was extensively renovated and historically restored in the late 1990s. The structure still serves its original purpose and maintains much of its original hardware and decor. (Photo courtesy of the Oklahoma Historical Society.)

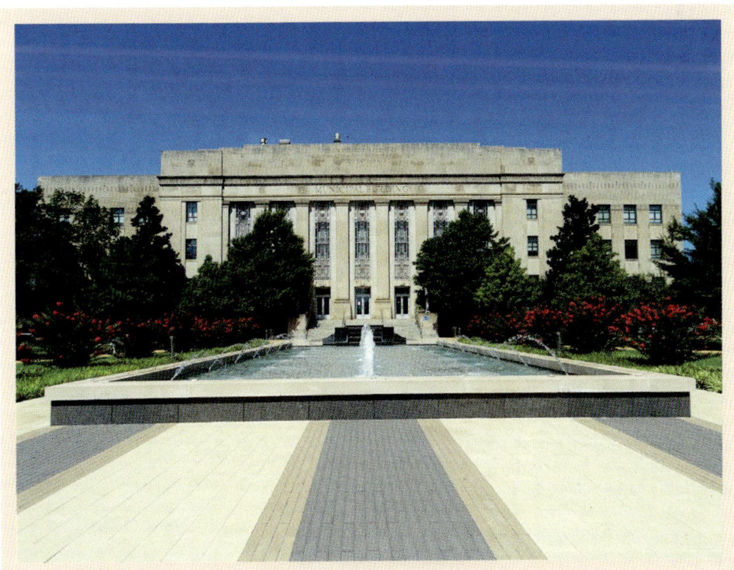

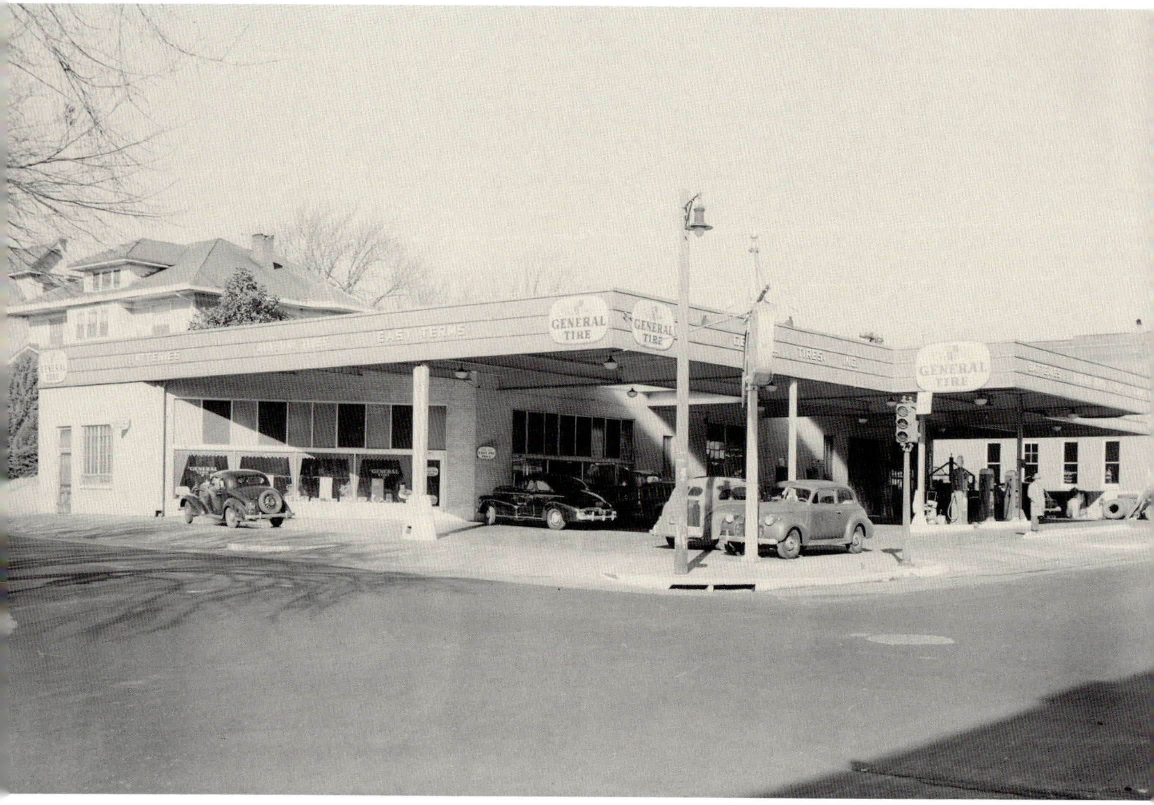

General Tire Company, 401 Northwest Tenth Street, opened in 1937 and as a 24-hour service station until 1982, when it was taken over by Johnny's Tire, which relocated from 300 North Walker Avenue. The service station closed around 1997. The former service station was redeveloped in 2021 into an 11,000-square-foot restaurant, bar, and outdoor patio. (Past, courtesy of the Oklahoma Historical Society.)

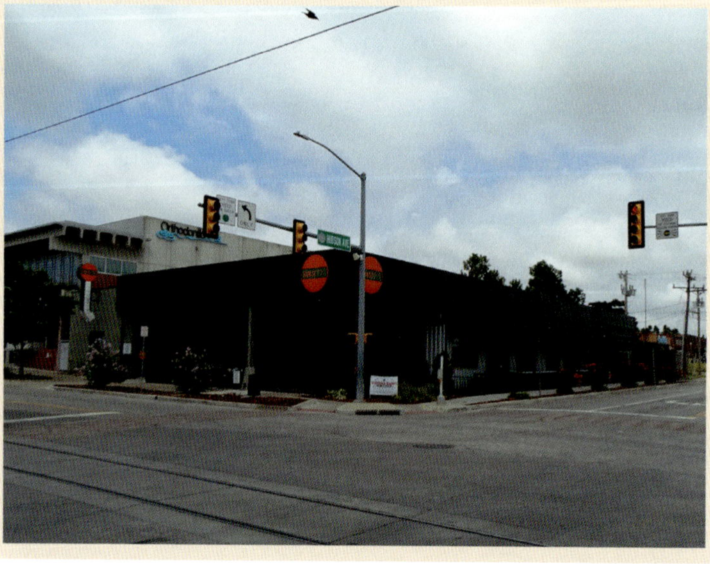

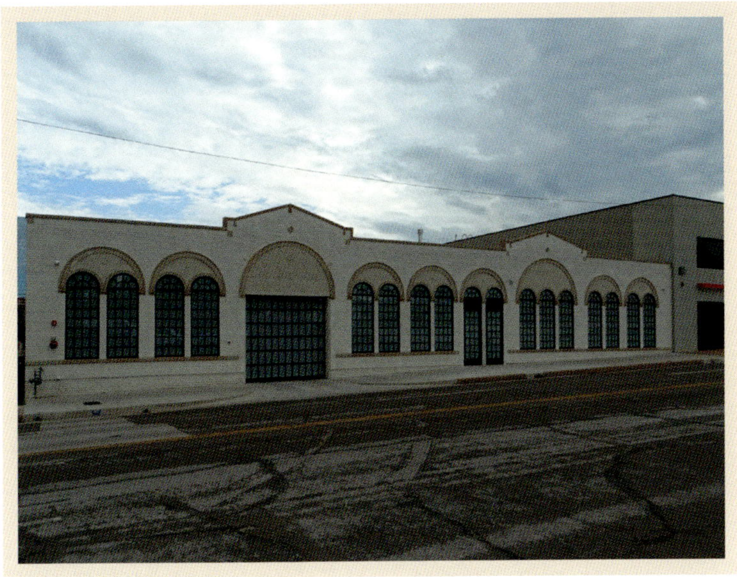

Trave-Taylor Printing Company was a growing operation when it built a new operation in 1939 at 408 Northwest Sixth Street. The company was sold to Southwestern Stationery and Bank Supply Company in 1947 and continued to operate on Northwest Sixth Street until it moved to a bigger building in 1956. The building on Northwest Sixth Street was converted into a parking garage but was renovated into a mix of offices and attached parking in 2021. (Past, courtesy of Oklahoma Historical Society.)

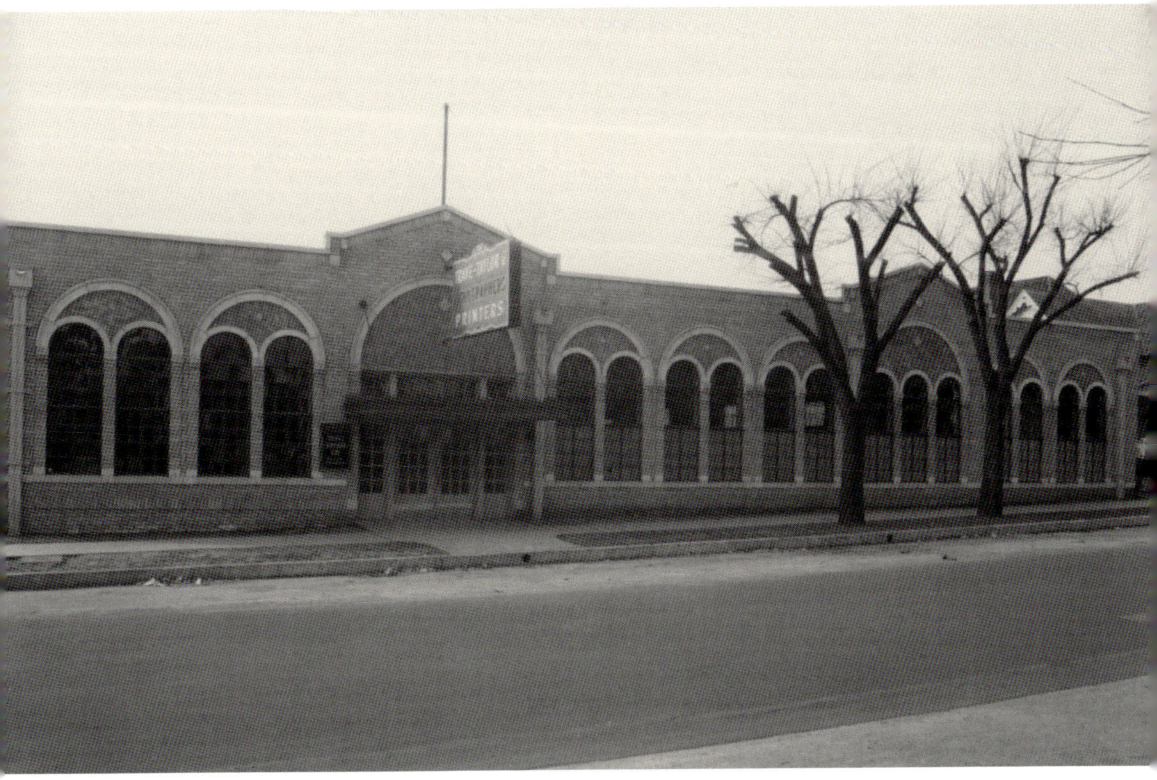

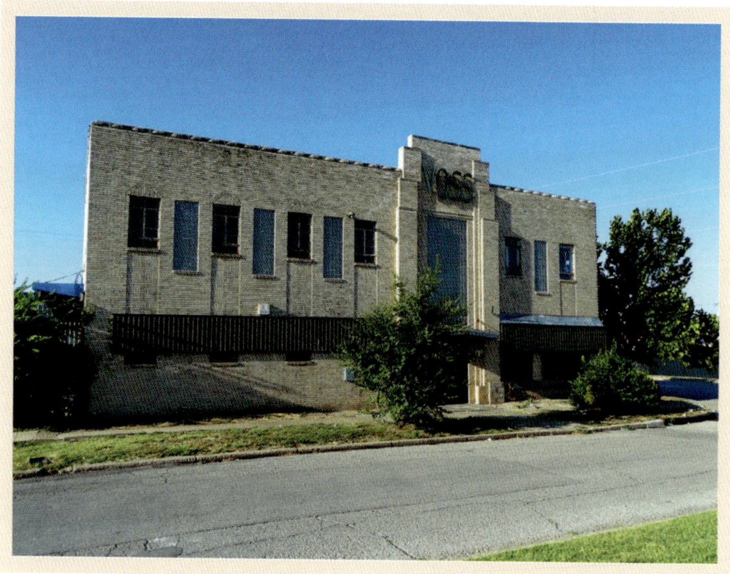

Leslie and Ina Voss started Voss Truck Lines in 1920, and it survived the Great Depression well enough to build a new shipping yard and headquarters in 1939 at 900 Southwest Second Street. The two-story building was designed in the International Style by Gaylord Noftsger, who also designed the nearby Farmers Public Market. The Voss family sold the building in 1989, and the property was largely forgotten as the area fell into decline. (Past, courtesy of Oklahoma Historical Society.)

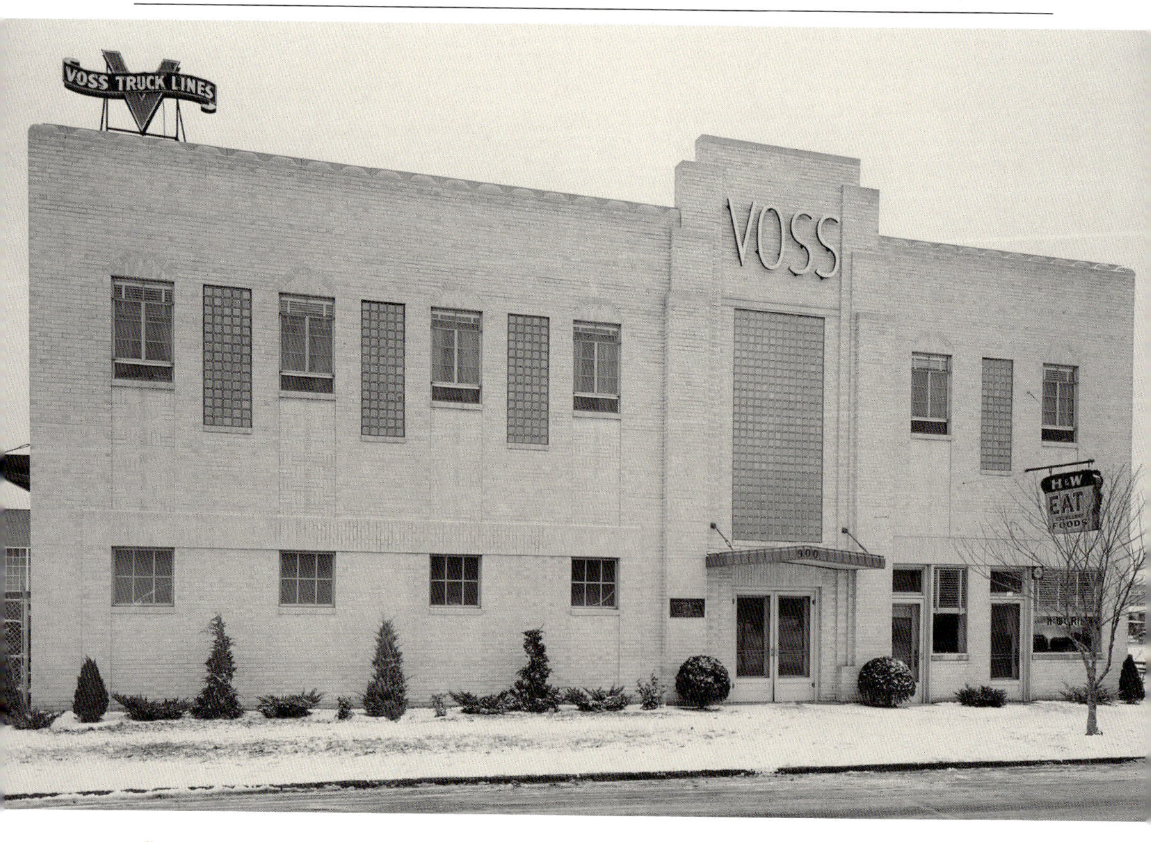

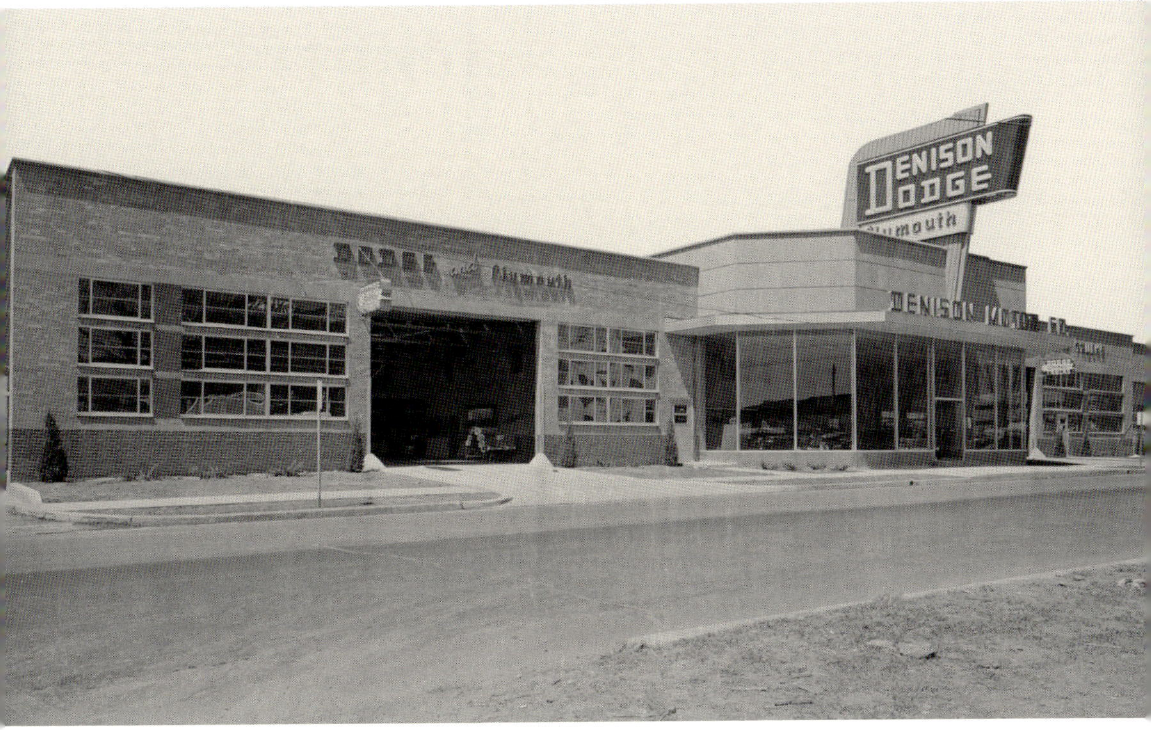

W.K. "Doc" Denison was a veterinarian when he moved to Oklahoma City and bought a car dealership in 1939. A few years later, he built and opened a new Dodge-Plymouth dealership at Main Street and Shartel Avenue. The dealership was taken over by Frank Clark and his son Jack in 1951. Jack Clark closed the dealership in 1980 and sold it to Oklahoma City, which continues to operate it as a fleet garage. (Past, courtesy of Oklahoma Historical Society.)

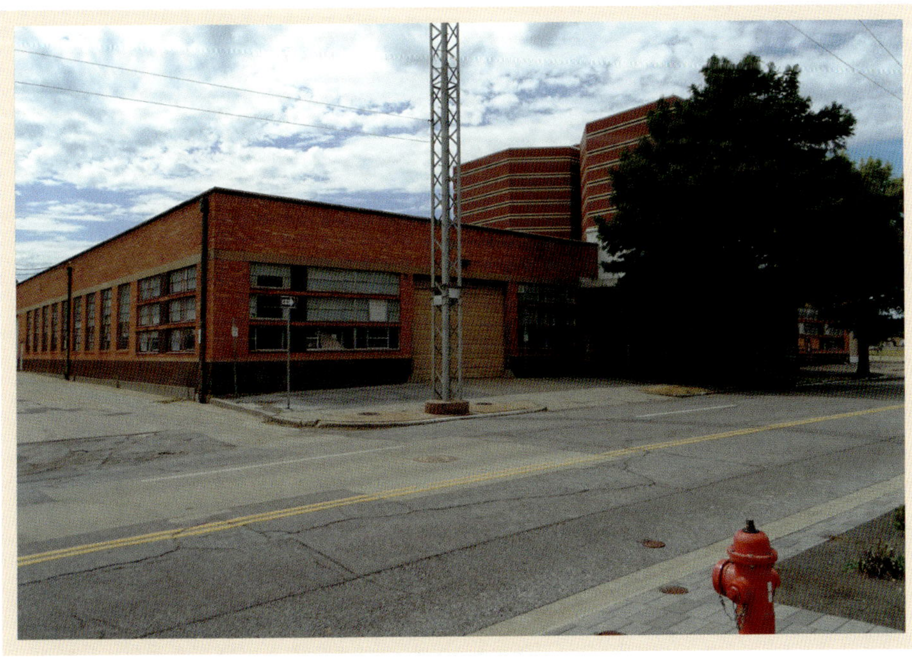

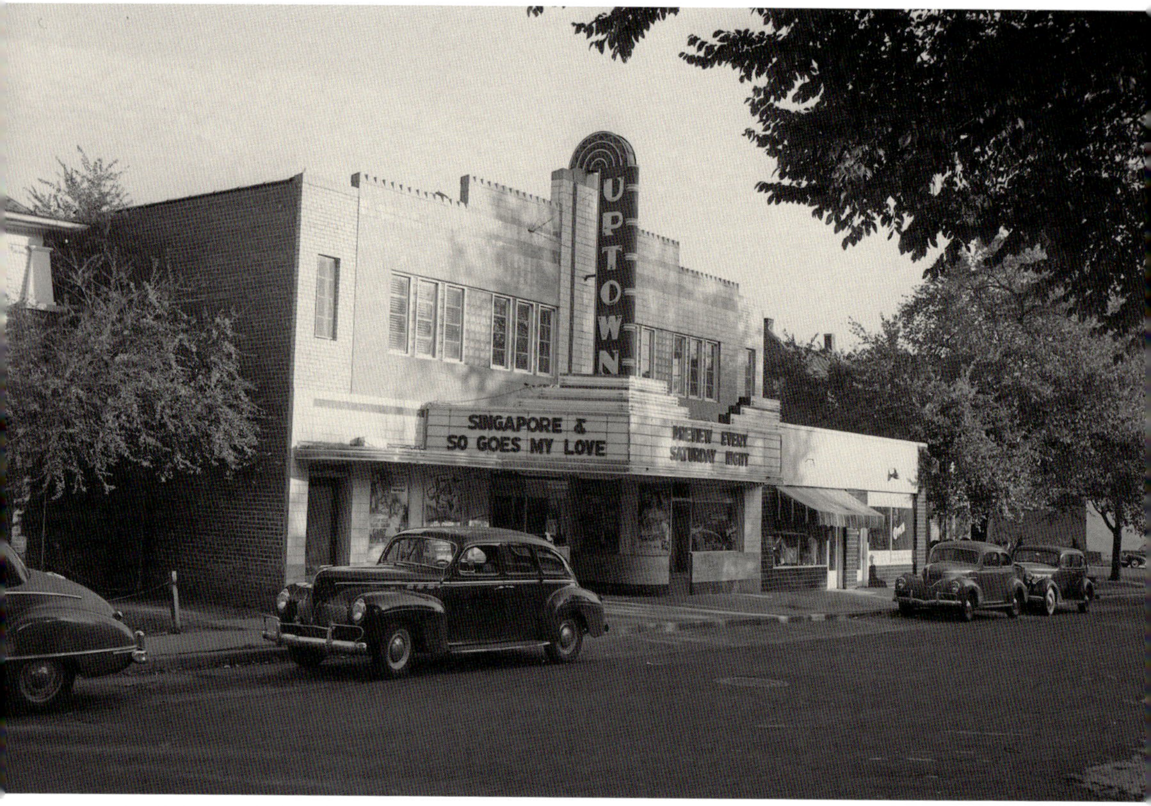

The Uptown Theater at 1212 North Hudson Avenue was built in 1941 by grocer Robert Sieber and operated until 1956, when his daughter Delrose removed the marquee, closed up half the first-floor windows and storefront, and converted it into medical office space. The theater was converted into retail space while the office annex was leased to a law firm in 2022. (Past, courtesy of Oklahoma Historical Society.)

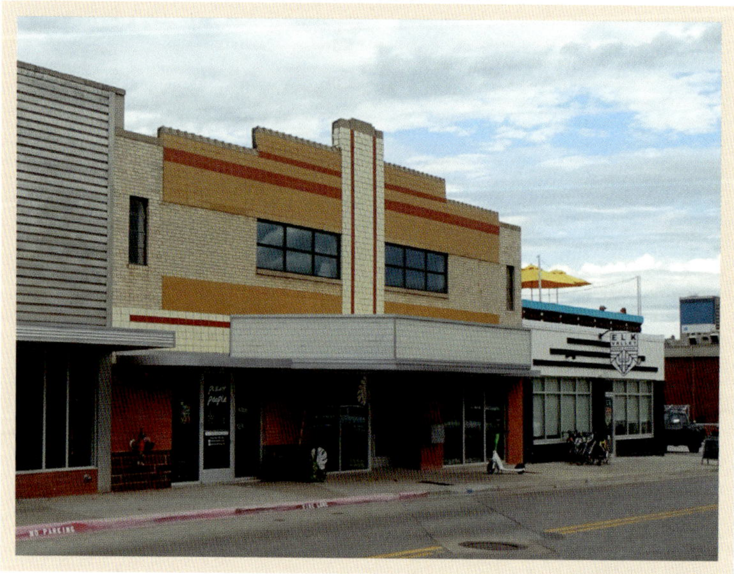

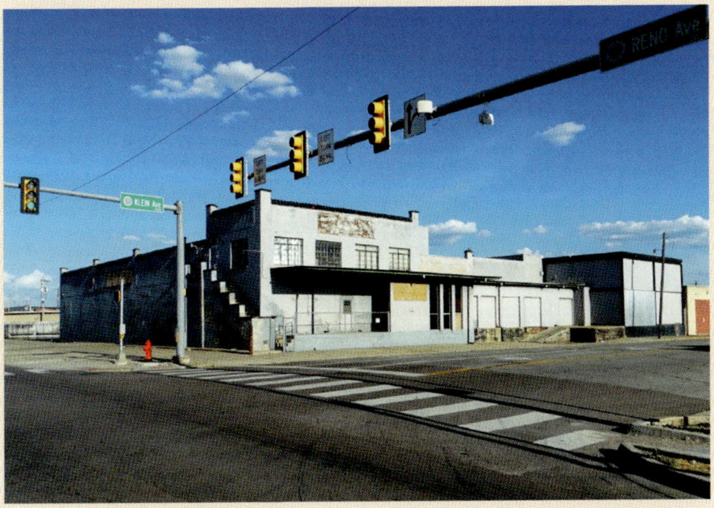

Brothers Earnest and Paul Liebmann were German immigrants who built the first ice-making plant in Oklahoma Territory in 1902. As they expanded across Oklahoma and Texas, lawmakers declared ice production was a utility. Competitors sued to put Liebmann Ice out of business, but in 1932, the US Supreme Court ruled in favor independent operators. Liebmann Ice moved out in 1965, and the building was owned by the Oklahoma City Meat Company in 2022. (Past, courtesy of Oklahoma Historical Society.)

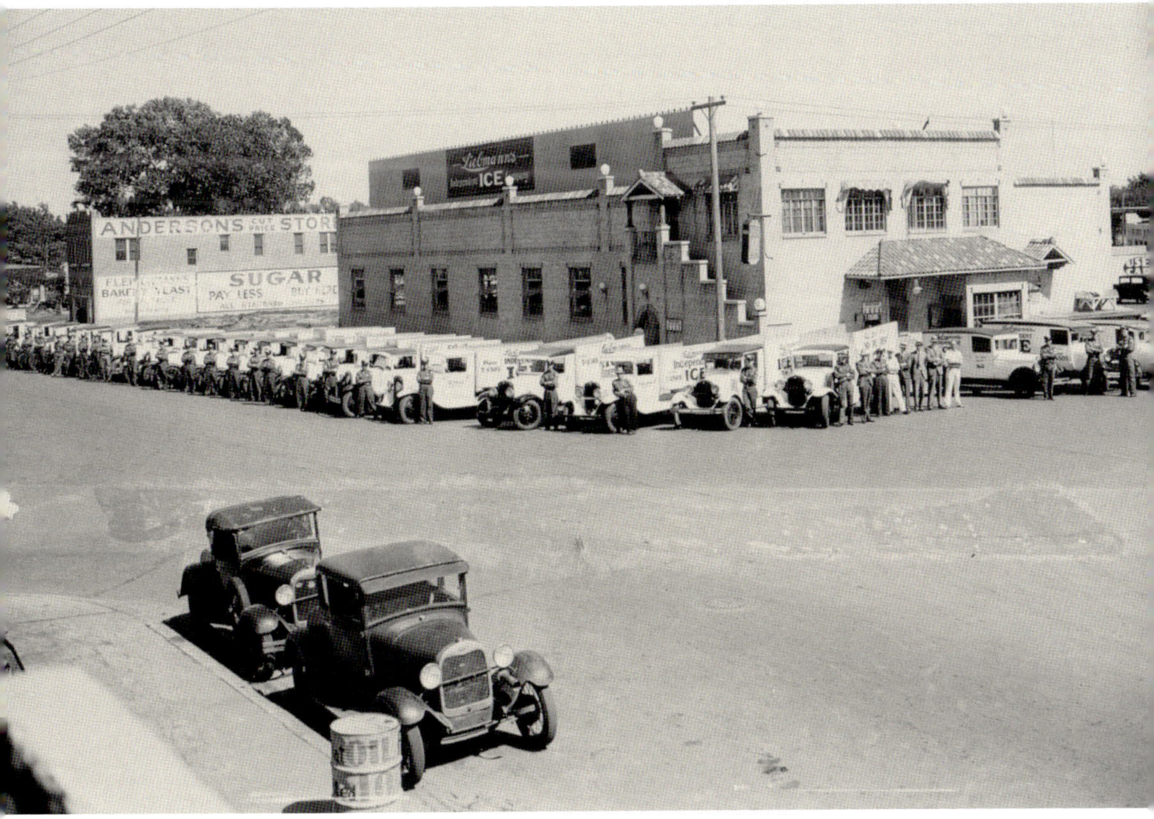

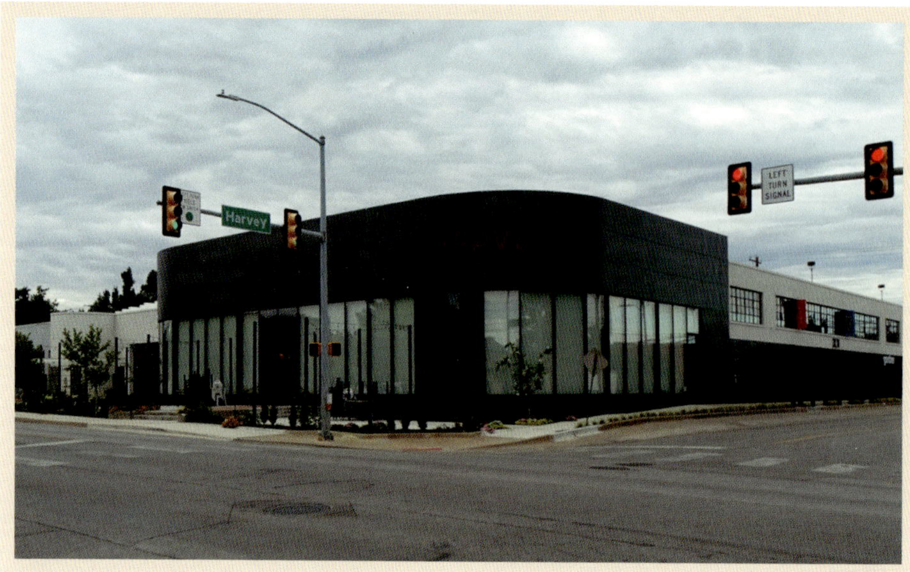

Walter E. Allen was a Detroit native who moved to Oklahoma City in 1940. He built a futuristic garage and showroom at Northwest Thirteenth Street and Harvey Avenue until he went bankrupt in 1955. The building was later home to Able Rents until developers bought the building and renovated it into a bakery, offices, and work space. The garage, separately owned, was also turned into offices. (Past, courtesy of Oklahoma Historical Society.)

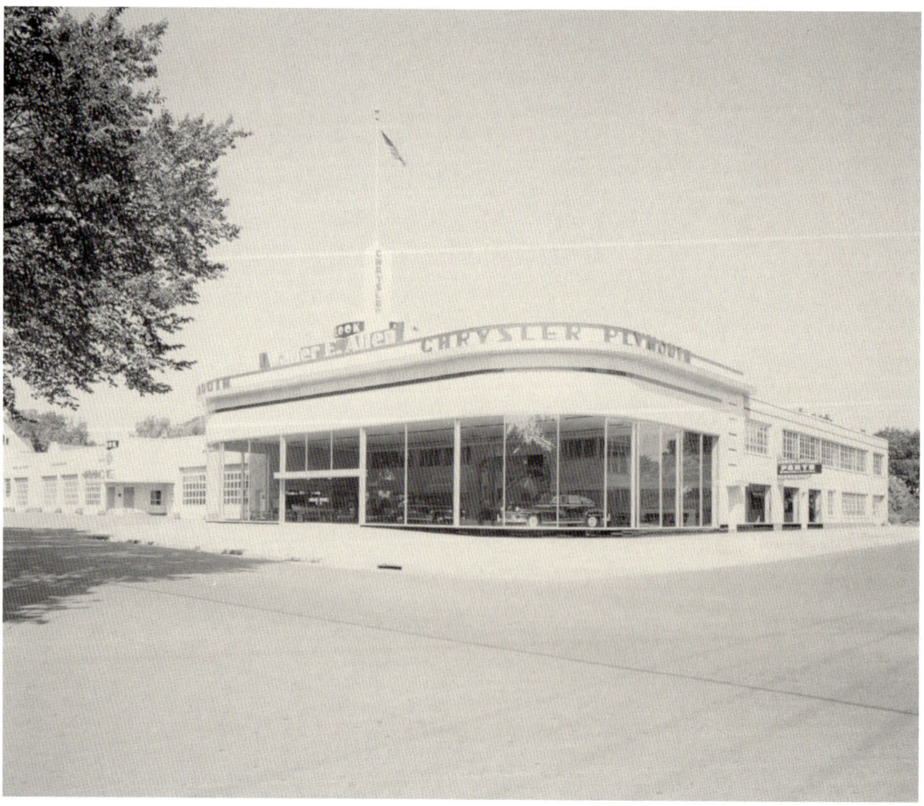

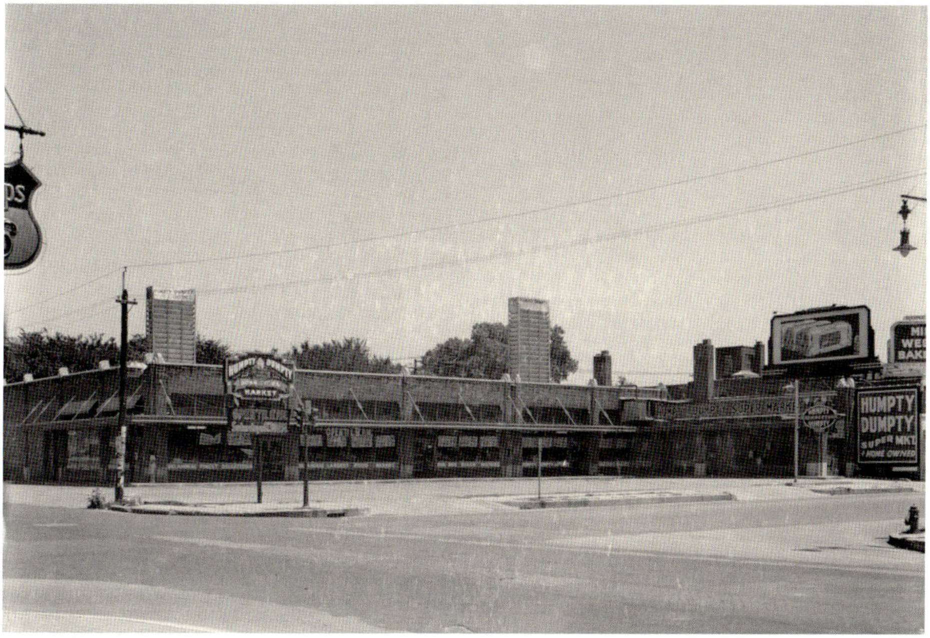

This Humpty Dumpty at Northwest Fourth Street and Walker Avenue was built in the early 1930s and was part of a failing grocery chain when it was bought in 1934 by Sylvan Goldman. Two years later, Goldman invented the shopping cart, which paved the way to self-shopping. The chain closed its Oklahoma stores in 1985. The Northwest Fourth Street location was later used as storage by OG&E (Oklahoma Gas & Electric) and then redeveloped into offices in 2001. (Past, courtesy of Oklahoma Historical Society.)

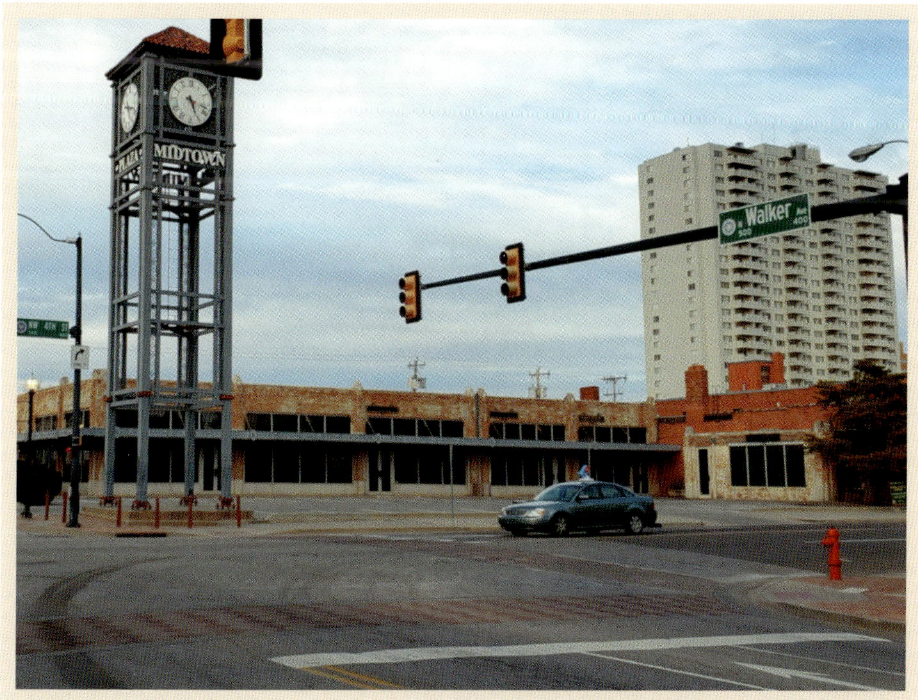

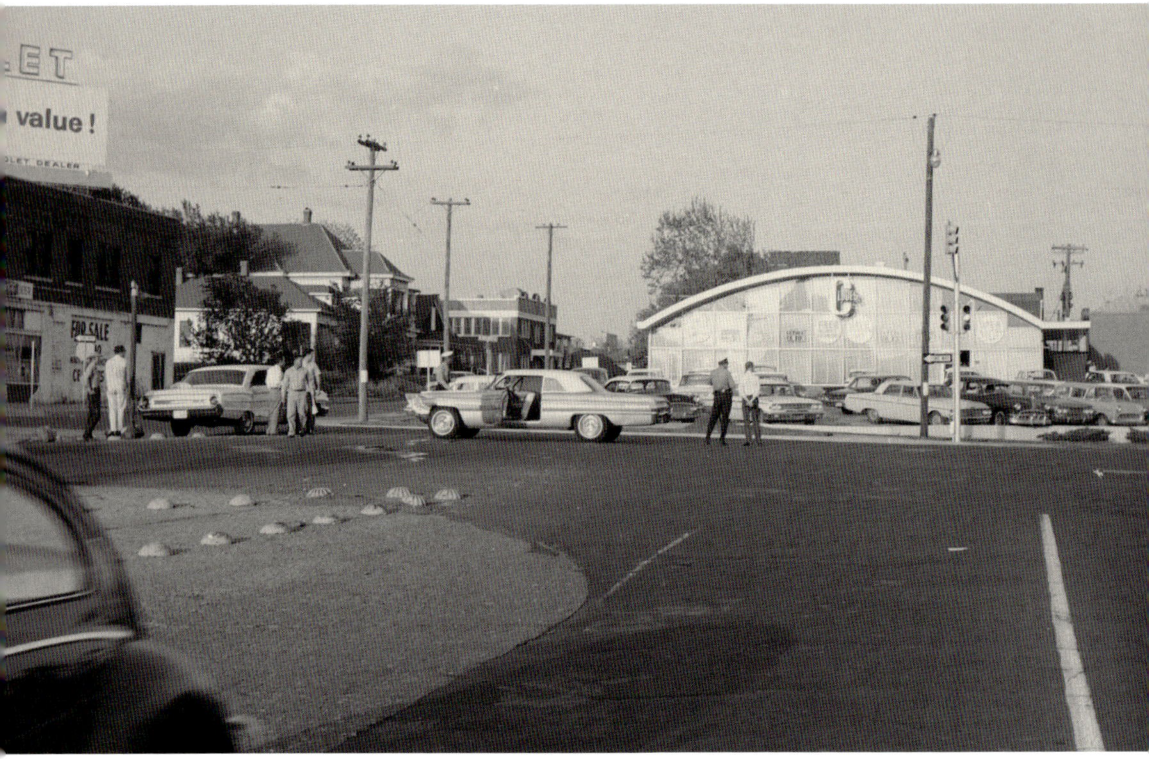

Clyde's Grocery was opened by Clyde Brewer in 1946 in the heart of Midtown and continued to operate it until he retired in 1968. The store sold twice more and changed names to Family Foods Friendly Market before closing in the 1980s. Brown's Bakery, also started in 1946, moved to the store in 1992 after its prior longtime home was torn down to make way for a Buick car sales lot. (Past, courtesy of Oklahoma Historical Society.)

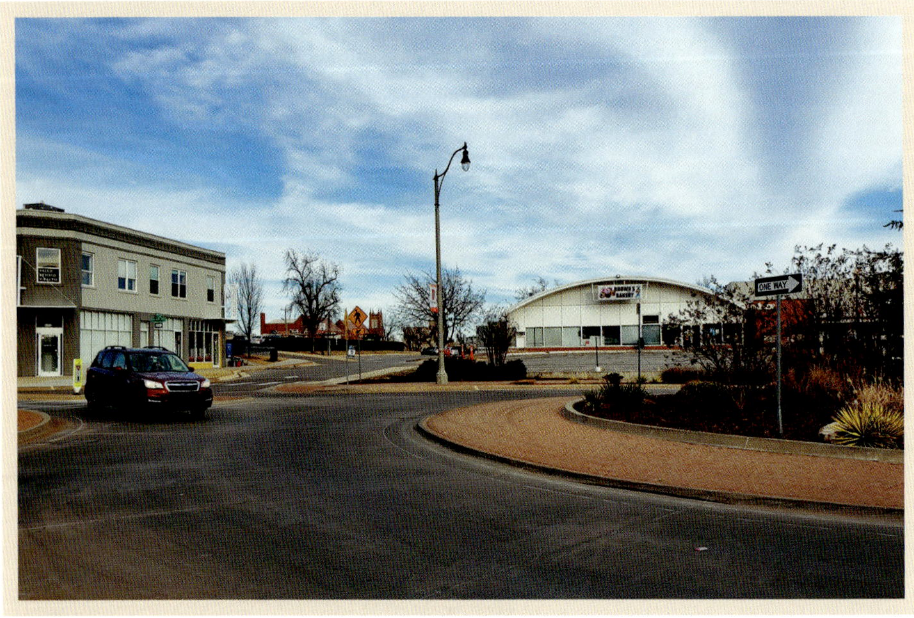

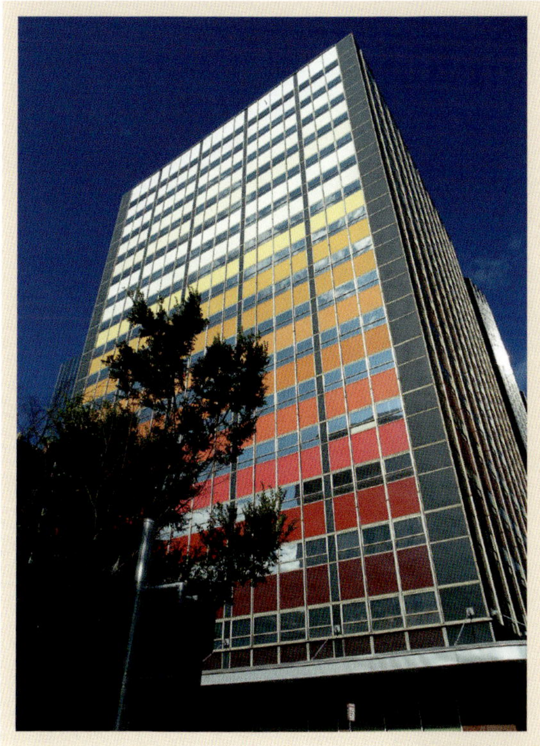

Downtown Oklahoma City was losing retail and office tenants to the suburbs when Fidelity Bank chose to build a 17-story International-style headquarters at 200 North Harvey Avenue. When Fidelity moved out in 1972, the building was renamed Park Harvey Center and occupancy dwindled. The building was bought by Dick Tanenbaum in 2006 and converted it into apartments with restaurants and retail on the first floor. (Past, courtesy of Oklahoma Historical Society.)

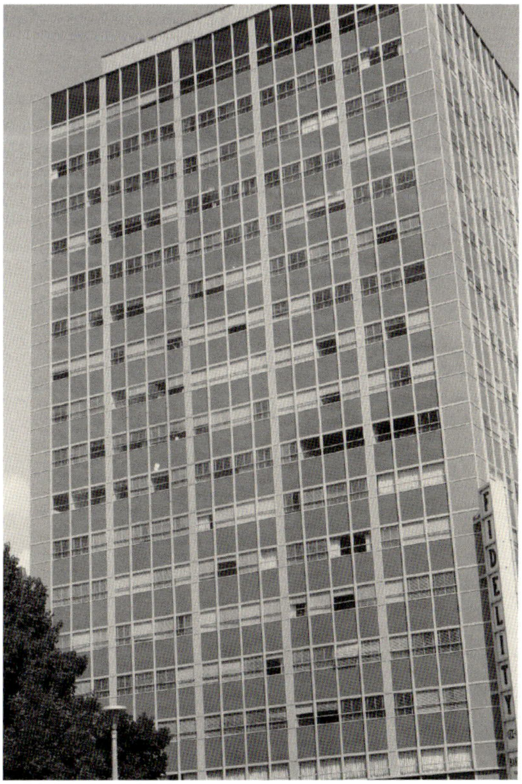

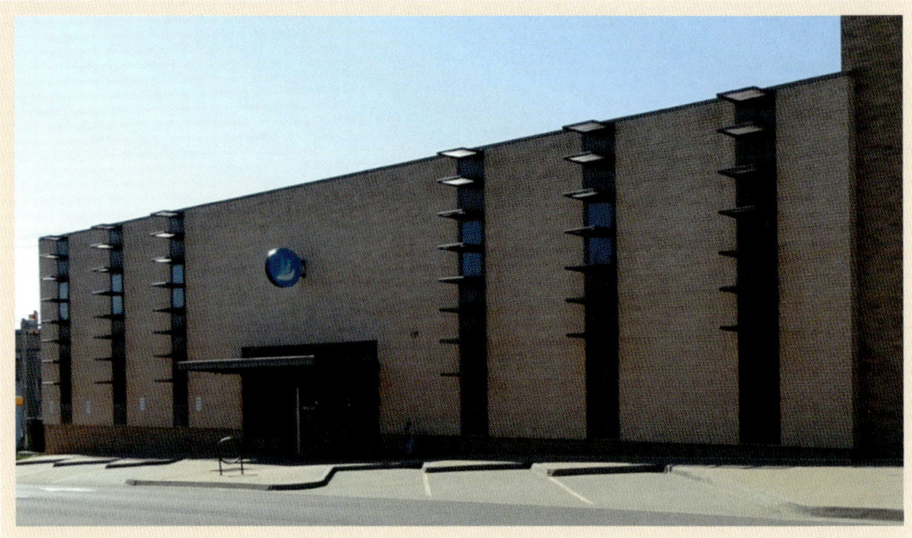

The Oklahoma Publishing Company, which printed the *Oklahoman* and *Oklahoma City Times*, started Mistletoe Express in 1931 to deliver papers. The business expanded to include other customers, and a new office and warehouse building was built at 111 Harrison Avenue in 1956. The company went out of business, and the building was renovated by Bert Belanger and reopened as offices in 2006. The building was home to digital marketing firm Tailwind in 2022. (Past, courtesy of Oklahoma Historical Society.)

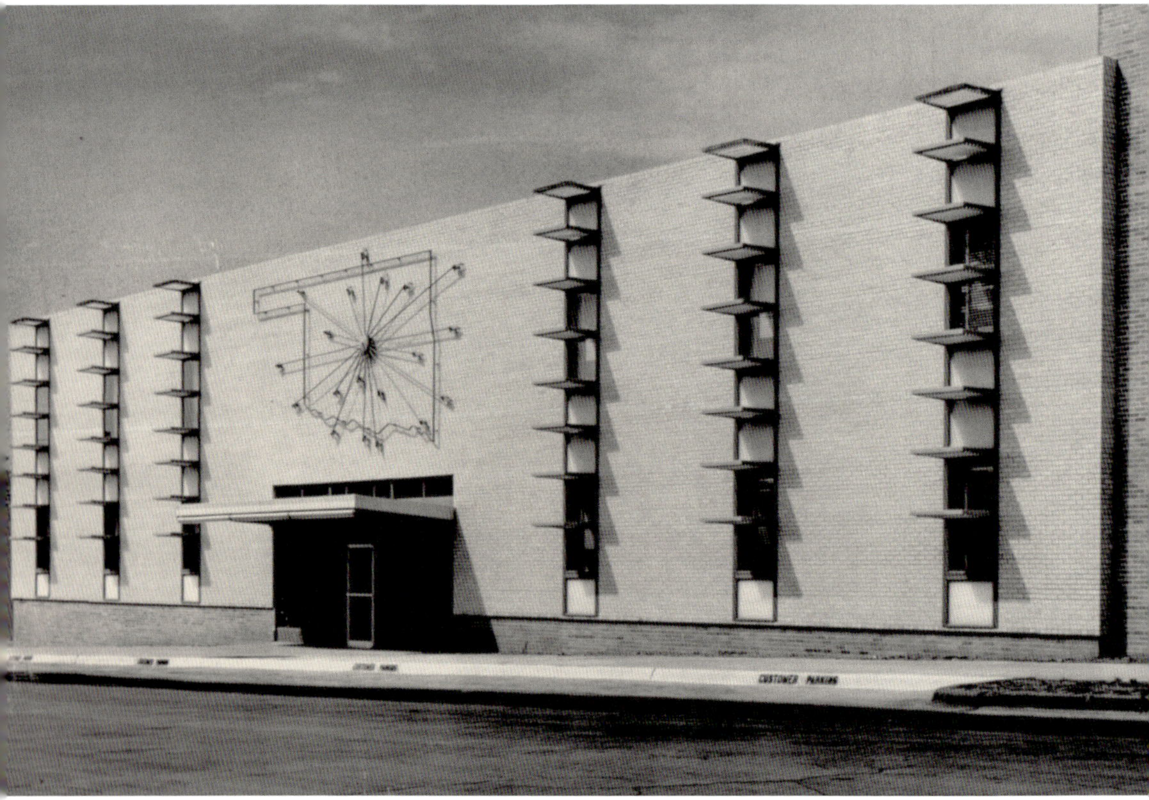

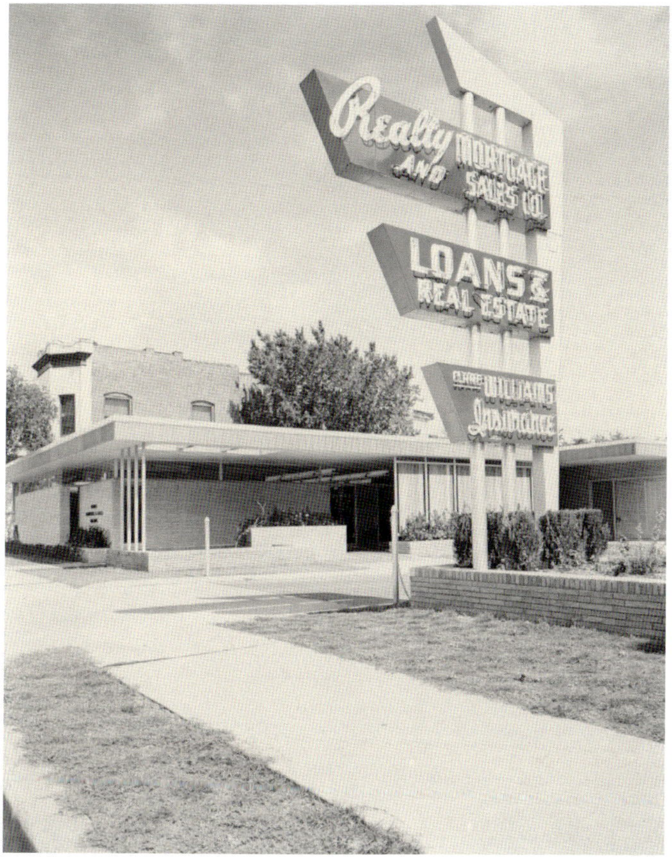

Williams Insurance and Mortgage Sales was the city's oldest independent mortgage company when it built its new Mid-Century Modern home at 230 Northwest Tenth Street. The company relocated in 1982, and the building was later home to a counseling center and then a printing shop. The building is now home to the *Mad Men*–vibe RJ's Supper Club and locally sourced restaurant Ludivine. (Past, courtesy of Oklahoma Historical Society.)

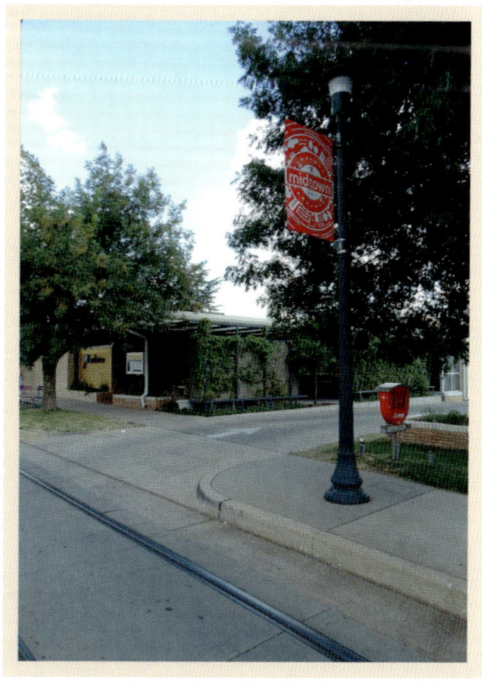

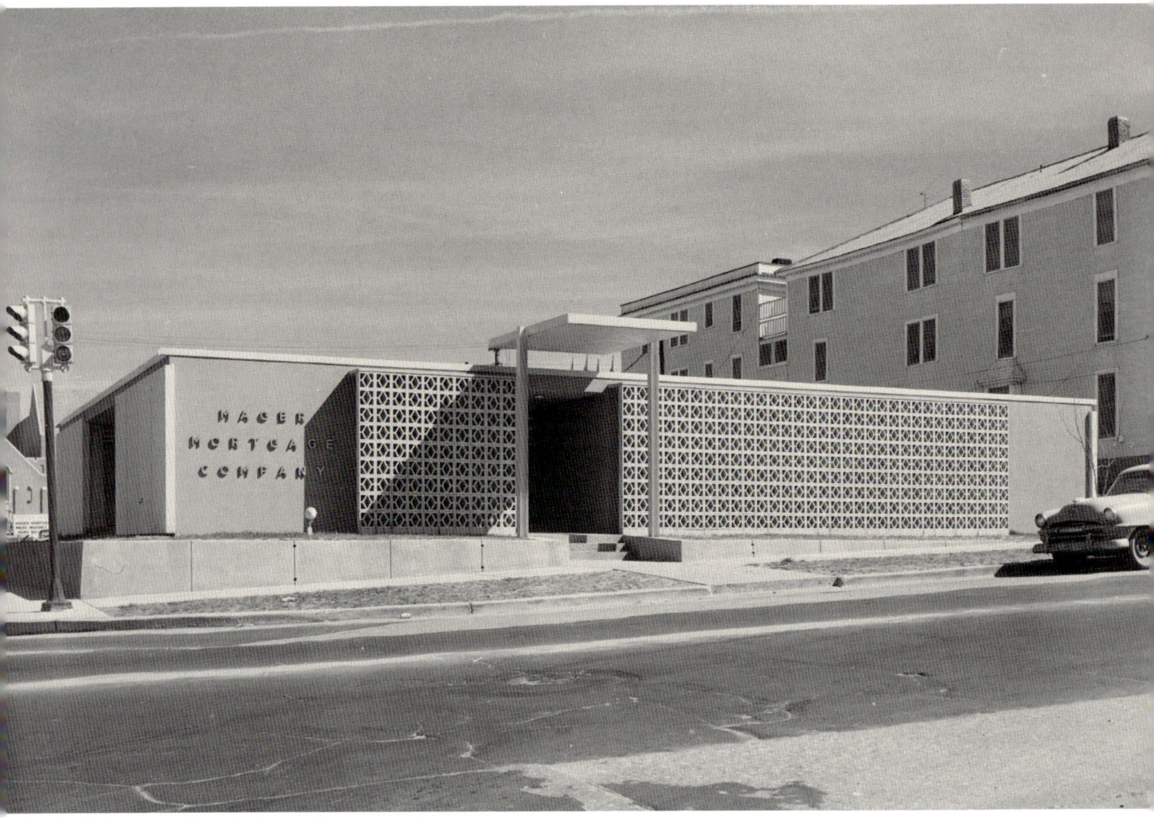

Mager Mortgage was in business for 47 years when the company built a Mid-Century Modern office building at 231 Northwest Tenth Street in 1959. Women's Clinic of Oklahoma City took over the building in 1973 when the mortgage company moved to northwest Oklahoma City. The building changed ownership several times until it was purchased and renovated by Midtown Renaissance Group. The building in 2022 was home to Midtown Vets. (Past, courtesy of Oklahoma Historical Society.)

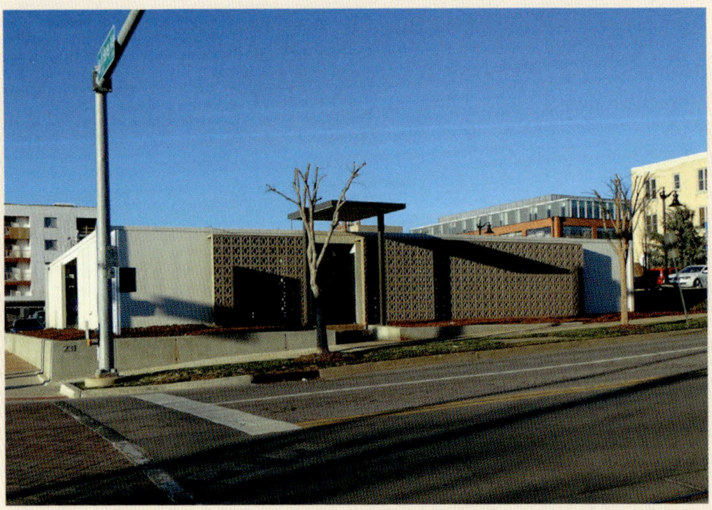

CHAPTER 3

Renewal

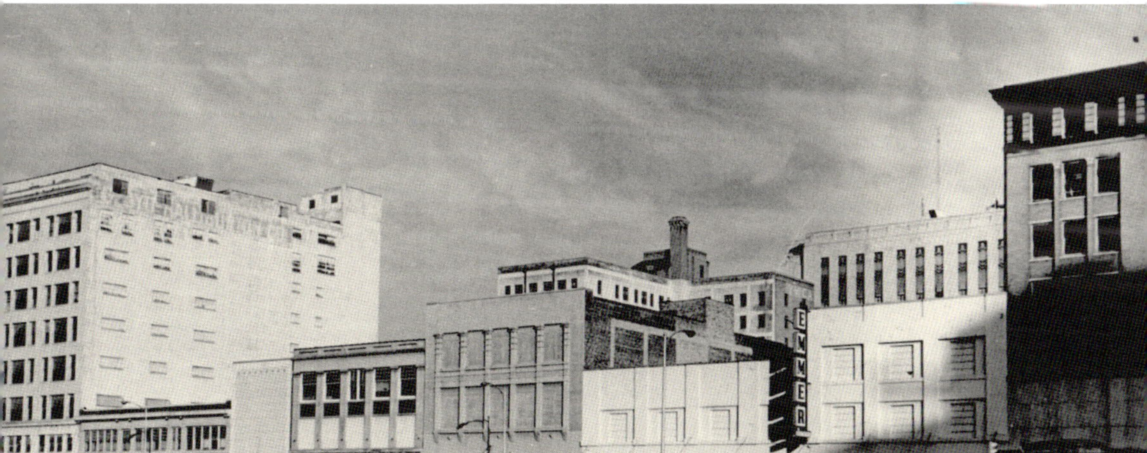

Only a few remnants of the old downtown skyline remained by the early-1970s with the demolition of hundreds of old buildings and construction of new garages and towers. The destruction of Main Street west of Harvey Avenue is shown in this photograph. (Past, courtesy of Oklahoma Historical Society.)

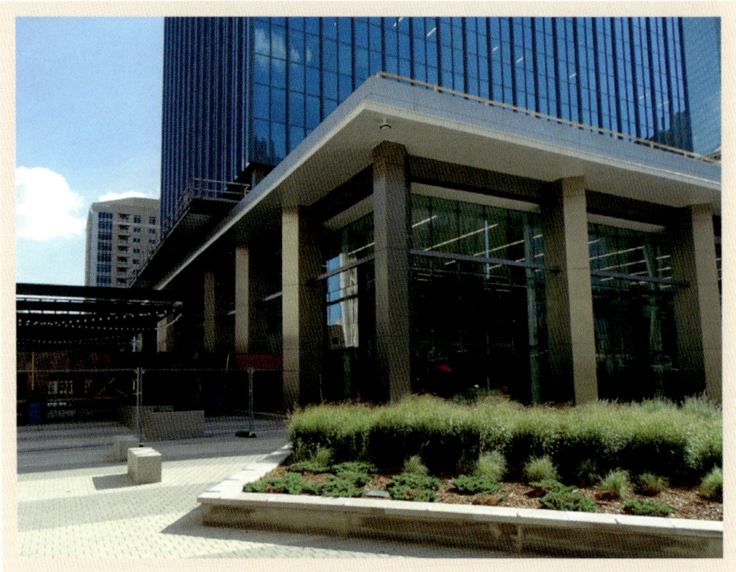

Liberty National Bank was launched in 1918 and was second in size and power to First National Bank. Liberty Tower was built in 1971 to present a modern image in contrast to First National's 1931 home down the street. Liberty survived the 1980s oil bust but was acquired by an Ohio bank in 1997. The tower was purchased by BancFirst in 2018 and underwent an extensive makeover. (Past, courtesy of Oklahoma Historical Society.)

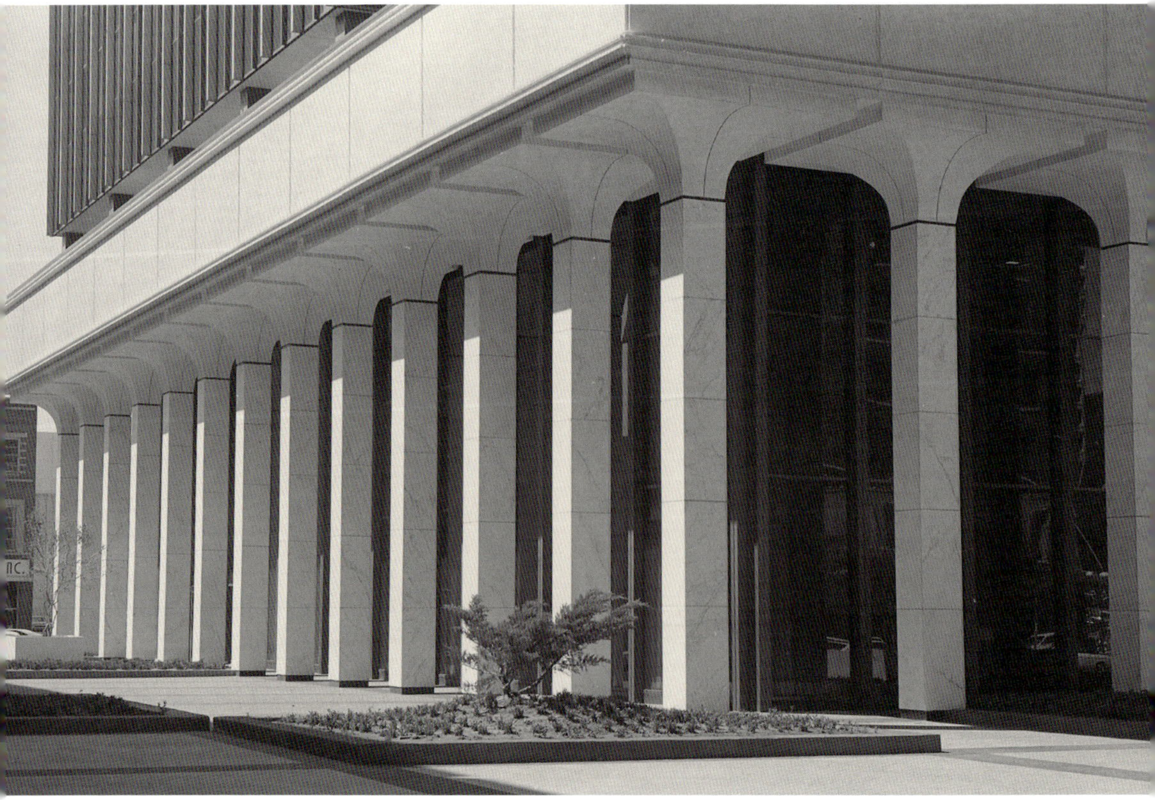

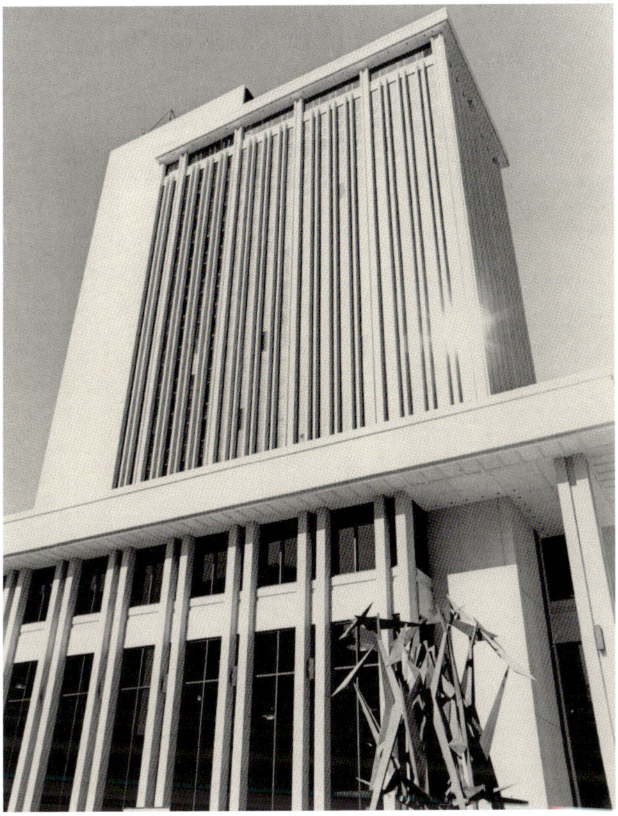

Fidelity Bank, founded in 1908, saw its fortunes boosted when oilmen Robert S. Kerr and Dean A. McGee bought controlling interest shortly after the bank opened a new 17-story headquarters in 1955. In 1972, the bank opened a new headquarters at 201 Robert S. Kerr Avenue, featuring elaborate fountain, "Falling Waters," an aquamobile by Lin Emery. The fountain was later turned off, and the building was anchored by Arvest Bank in 2022. (Past, courtesy of Oklahoma Historical Society.)

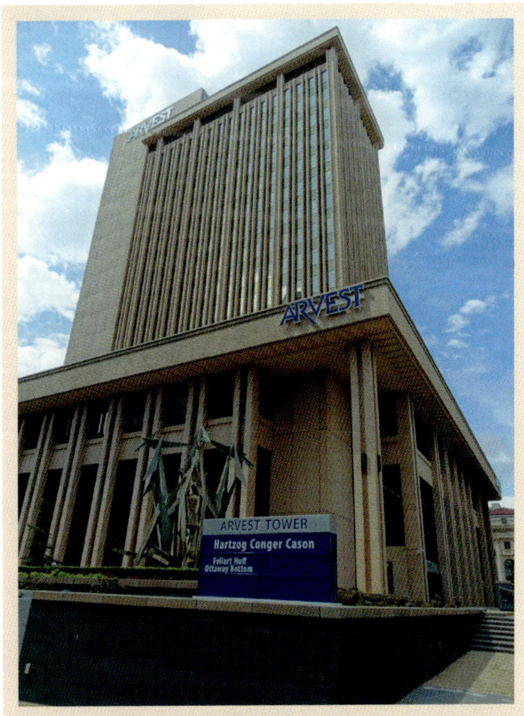

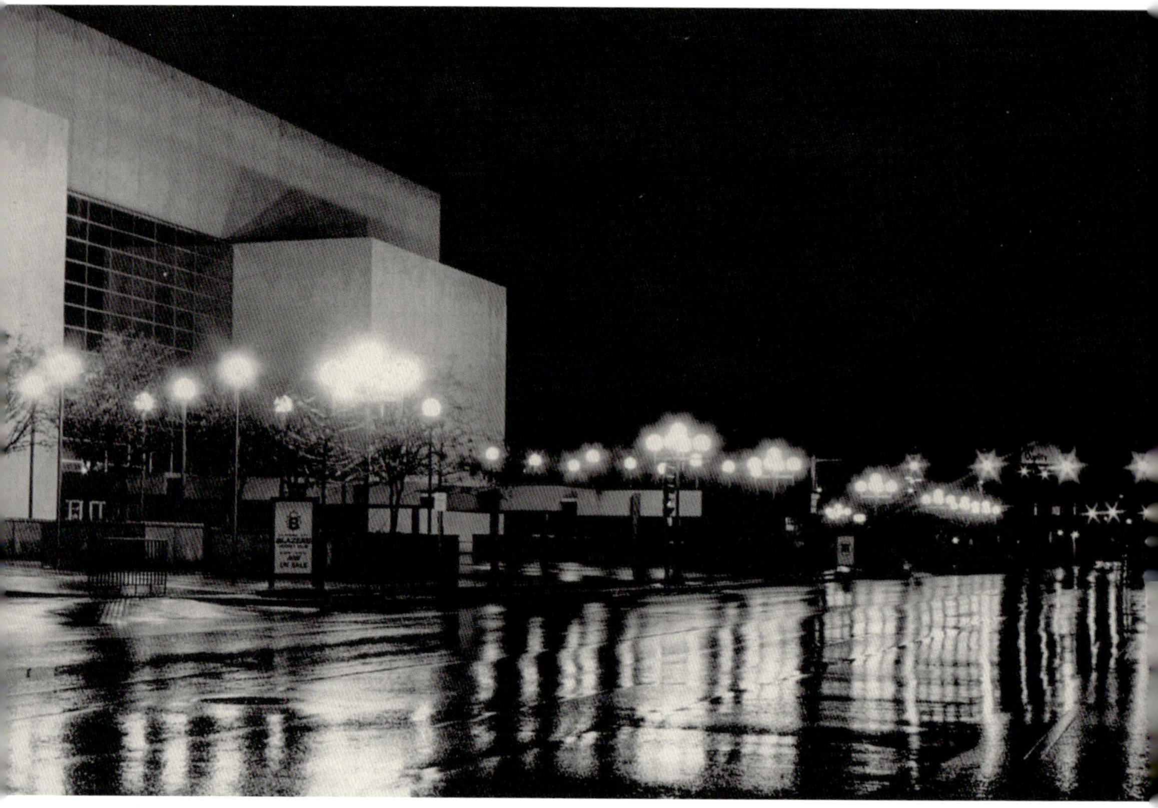

The Myriad Convention Center opened in 1972, but despite its name, it was largely a 13,000-seat arena surrounded by meeting rooms and large trade show exhibit halls. The arena hosted a semiprofessional basketball team, an arena football team, and performances by acts including Elvis Presley. The Myriad was transformed into Prairie Surf Studios after it was replaced by a new convention center in 2020. (Past, courtesy of Oklahoma Historical Society.)

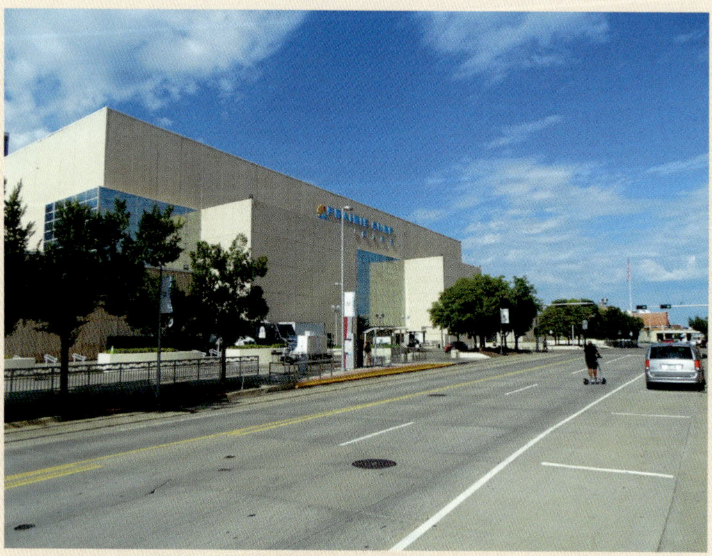

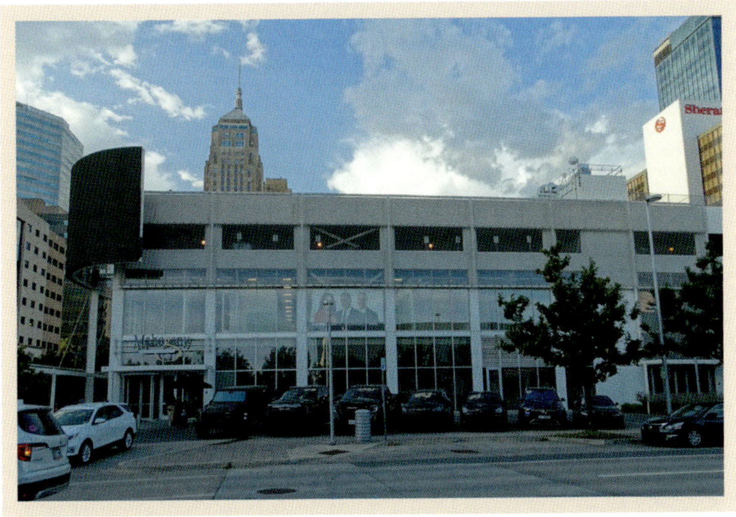

Century Center, 100 West Main Street, was built as a retail mall that started leasing in the late 1970s. It was briefly successful with a mix of clothing and gift shops, an FAO Schwartz toy store, florist, restaurants, and fitness center. The retail mix collapsed during the 1980s oil bust, and the mall stagnated until 2015, when it was redeveloped into offices and restaurants. In 2022, it was home to the *Oklahoman*. (Past, courtesy of the *Oklahoman*.)

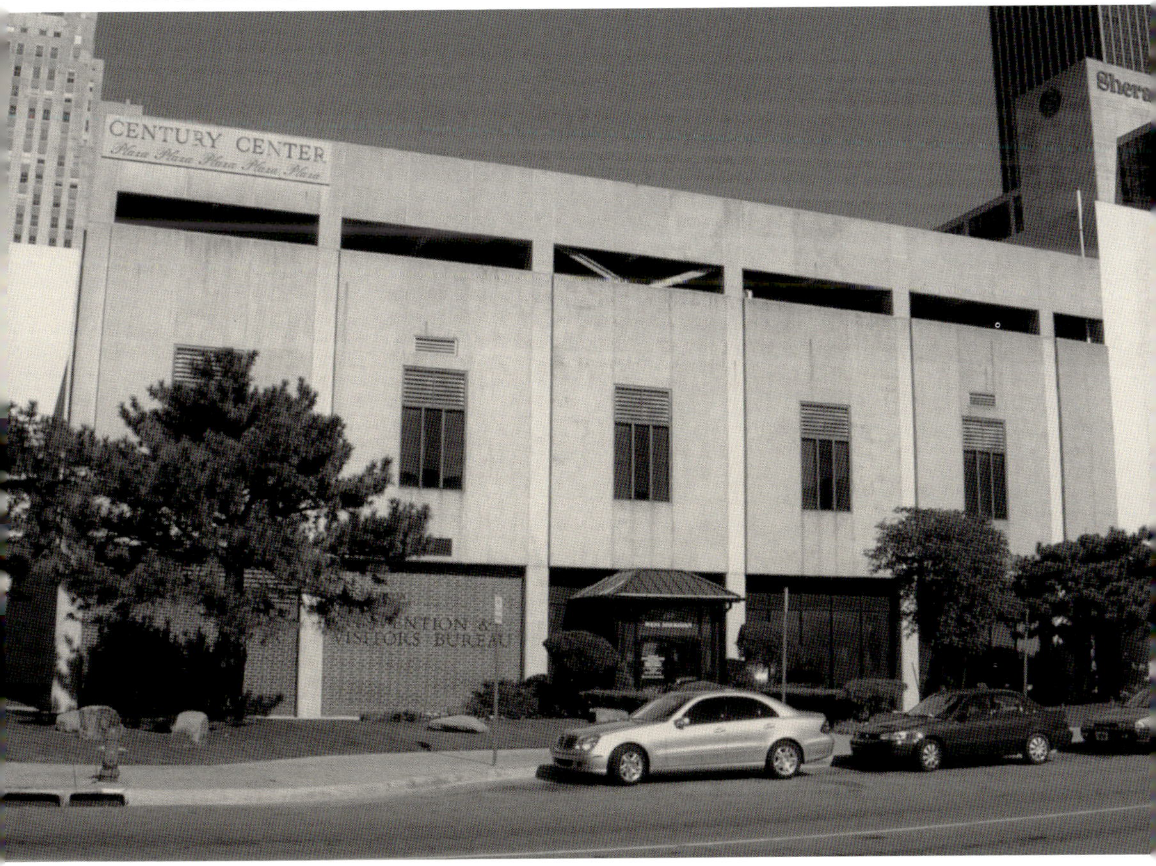

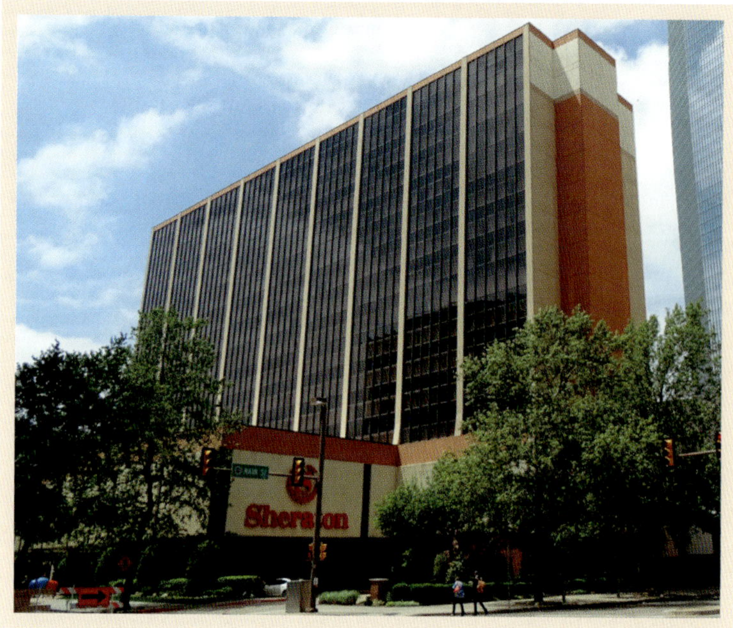

The Sheraton Century Center was the one and only hotel opened as part of the 1970s-era Urban Renewal effort to rebuild downtown Oklahoma City. The 410-room hotel opened in 1977 after several years of delays and was adjoined to a small shopping mall and garage. The hotel was the only one to be connected to downtown's pedestrian tunnels. (Past, courtesy of Oklahoma Historical Society.)

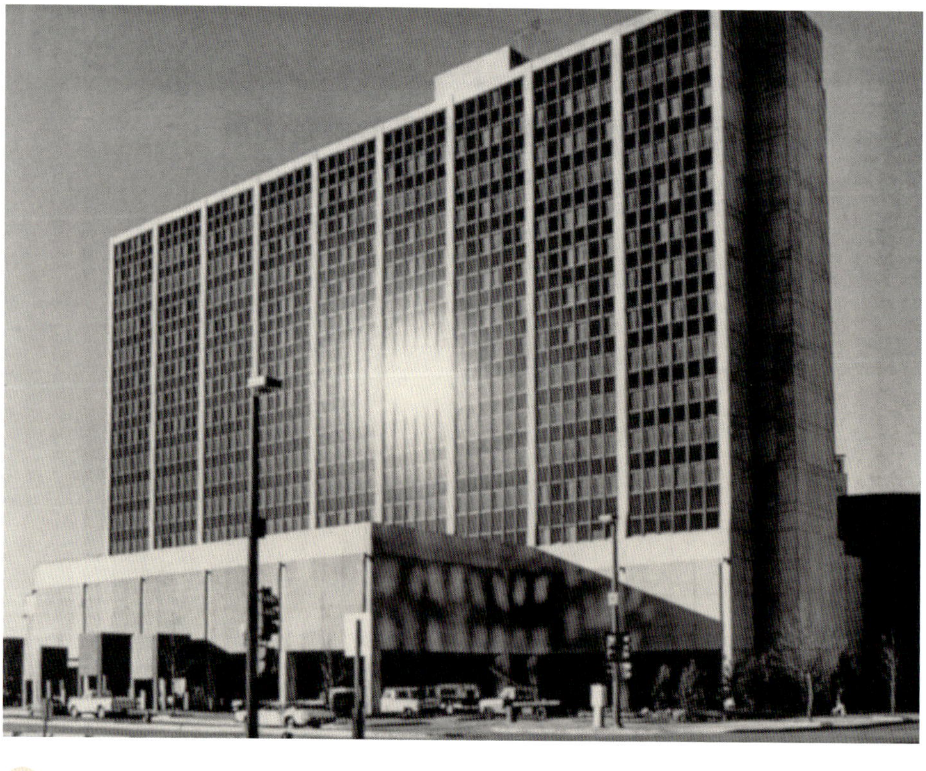

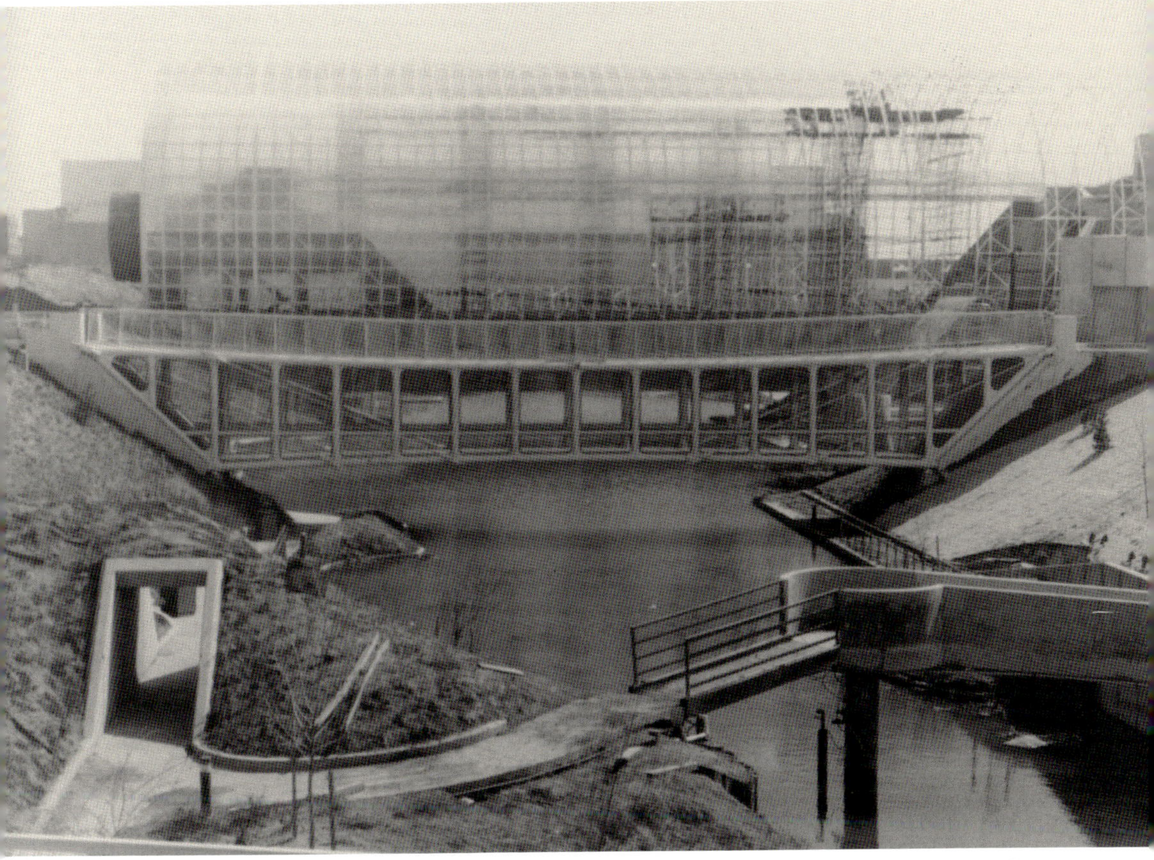

The Myriad Gardens was envisioned as the jewel of an urban renewal transformation of downtown. Championed by oilman Dean A. McGee, the gardens were inspired by the Tivoli Gardens in Copenhagen. Design and construction went through several stops and starts between 1971 and when it finally opened in 1988. The gardens underwent an extensive remodel as it approached its 25th anniversary. (Past, courtesy of Bill Welge.)

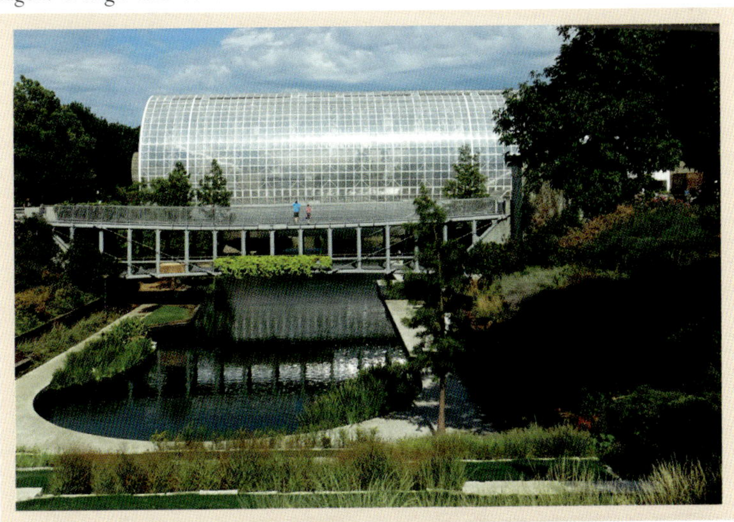

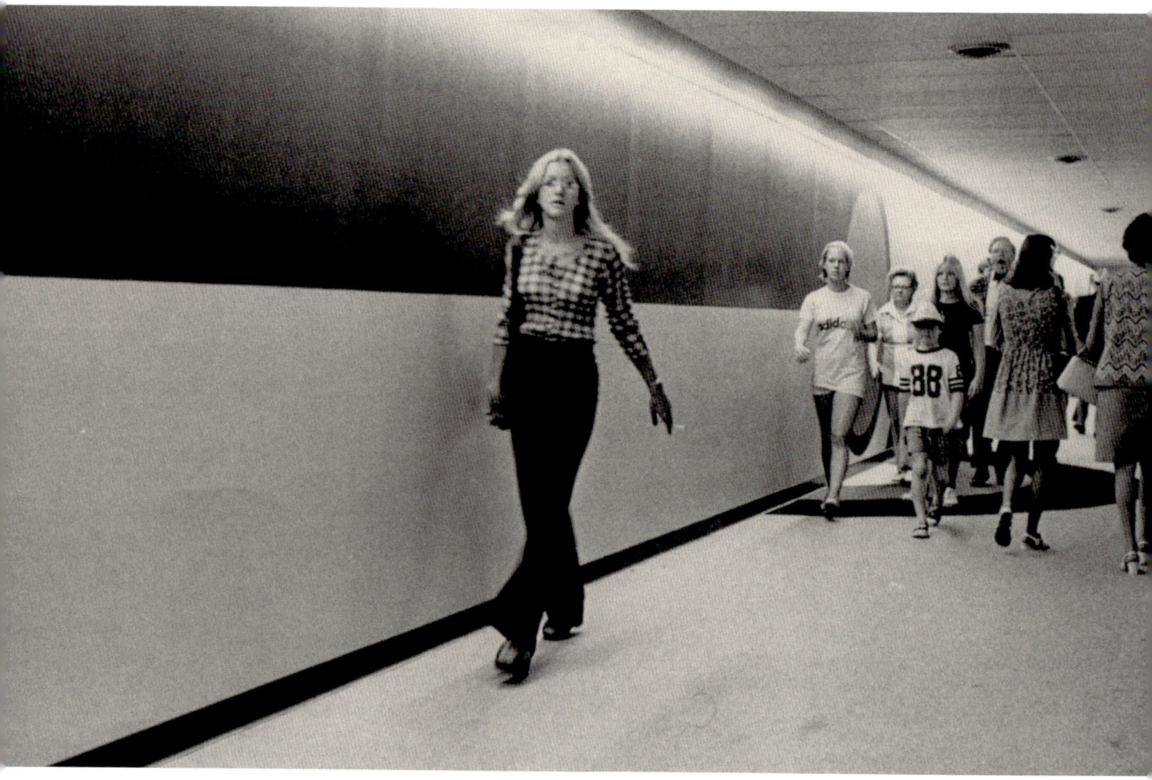

What is now known as the "Underground" began as a tunnel built in the 1930s between the Skirvin Hotel and Skirvin Tower and, eventually, evolved to connect 16 blocks and over a dozen buildings throughout downtown. In the 1970s and 1980s, developer Jack Conn expanded the system and named it the "Conncourse." In 2006, it was renamed the "Underground" and renovated by Elliott and Associates; it features color-coded tunnels and themes from Oklahoma City's history. (Past, courtesy of the *Oklahoman*.)

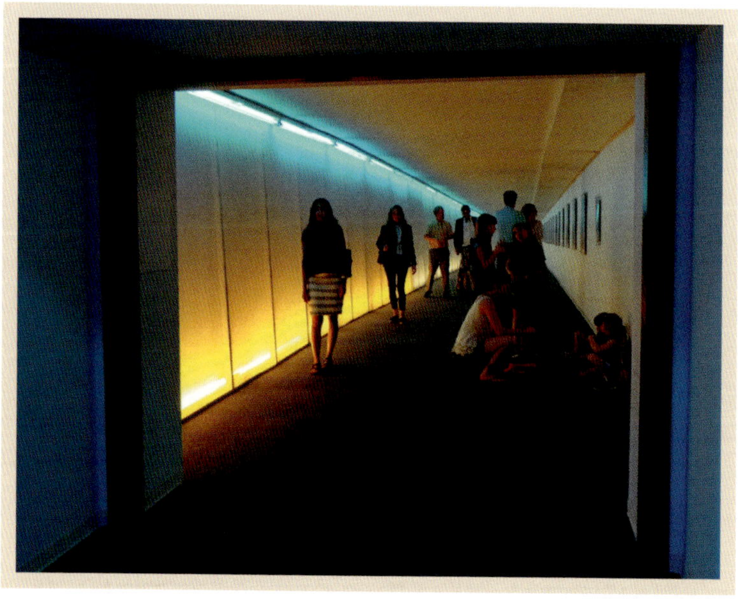

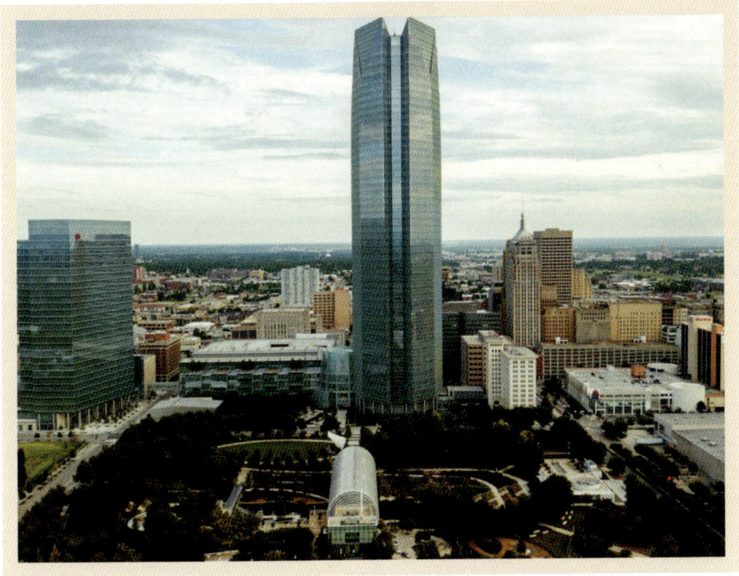

A large parking deck built for a Galleria mall that was never built left a huge hole in the downtown skyline when this photograph was taken in 1981. Devon Energy built a 50-story headquarters on the block in 2009. Other skyline changes include the 27-story BOK Park Plaza Tower (left) and a Century Center mall (right) transformed into a modern office building. (Past, courtesy of the Oklahoma Historical Society; present, courtesy of the *Oklahoman*.)

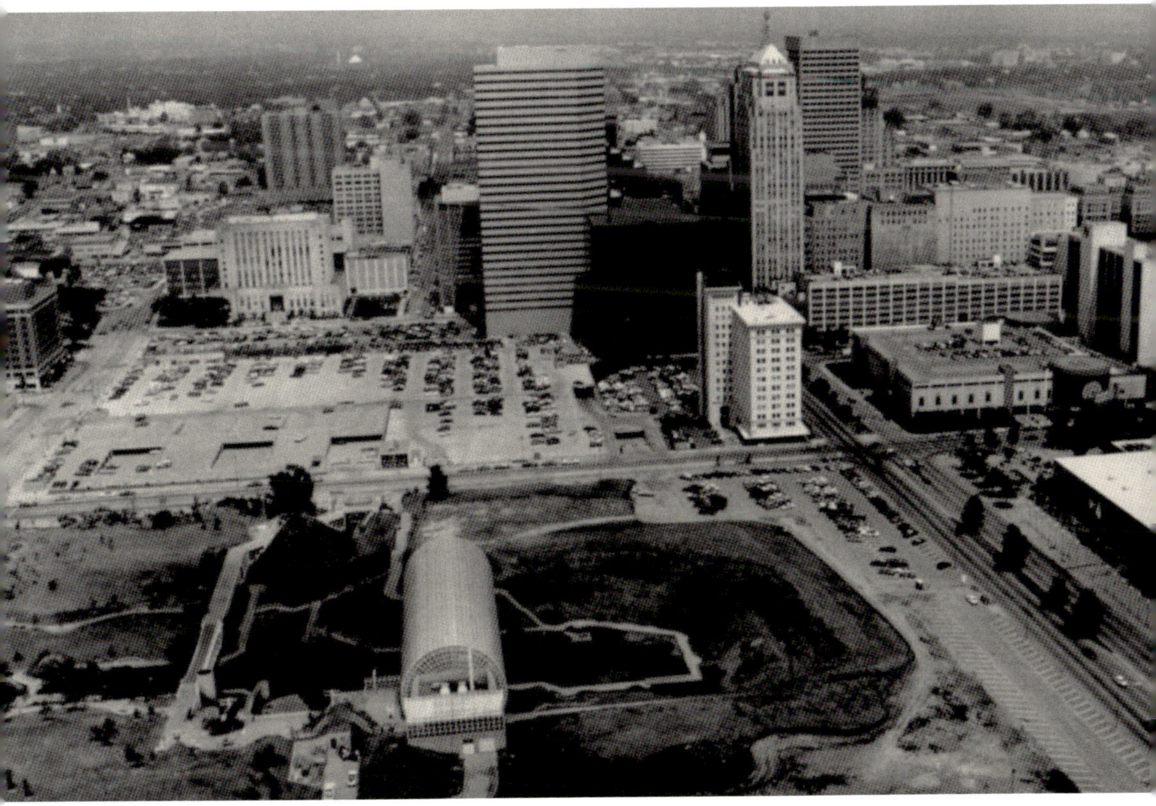